Turn Your
Struggles Into
Stepping
Stones

Daily Readings for Dynamic Living

Turn Your Struggles Into Stepping Stones

Lloyd Ogilvie

WORD PUBLISHING

Dallas·London·Vancouver·Melbourne

Unless indicated otherwise, all Scripture quotations are taken from The New King James Version (NKJV), copyright © 1979, 1980, 1982, Thomas Nelson, Inc., Publisher. Those marked TLB are from The Living Bible, copyright © 1971 by Tyndale House Publishers, Wheaton, Ill, and are used by permission. Those marked TEV are from The Good News Bible, Today's English Version, copyright © 1966, 1971, 1976 by the American Bible Society, and are used by permission.

Library of Congress Cataloging-in-Publication Data is available

ISBN 0–8499–3530–X
    0–8499–3578–4 (Special Ministry Edition)

3 4 5 6   LB   9 8 7 6 5 4 3 2 1

Printed in the United States of America.

Let God love you—
Turn your struggles into
steppingstones
Let Him Handle all of Life's
unknowns, my friend.
There's hope! Let God love you. . . .

Introduction

I had waded across the river at dawn. The water reached to the top of my wading boots. I wanted to get to the other side so I could fly-fish in a pond where I was sure there was a big salmon waiting to rise to my carefully cast fly. I fished all day in the rain. By evening the river had risen to the point that it was too high for me to recross. As it became darker I searched for a place in the river shallow enough for a safe crossing. Late at night I finally found a path that led to a point where there were rocks protruding above the fast-moving currents.

Cautiously I stepped from stone to stone. I paused on each stone to gain my balance to jump to the next one. Falling into the ice cold river would have been perilous. Finally I reached the other side. Exhausted, but thankful that I had made it across, I sat in the dark and reflected on the parable I had experienced.

The path leading to the crossing place had been beaten down by others before me. They had discovered that when the river rises this was the only place to cross safely. I was astounded as I thought about how perfectly placed were each of those steppingstones.

How like life, I said to myself. In the raging river of life's struggles, the Lord provides us with steppingstones. His words recorded in the Bible, along with His interventions to help us, provide safe stones to stand on before we move on to the next in some new challenge that is a further step toward His destination for us.

Each Monday as I begin a new work week, I feel like I did that night crossing the river. Challenges, opportunities, and problems confront me. Over the years I've discovered that each struggle can be a steppingstone for growth in becoming the person I was meant to be. Each one helps me, not only to make it through a day, but to make a great week without becoming weak!

The promises of Christ and the powerful truths about Him in Acts and the Epistles give me the steppingstones I need when life causes me to struggle. Christ is a solid rock on which I can stand regardless of the raging currents of problems swirling around me. Regardless of the struggle, I know that if I trust Christ He can make the very struggle itself into a steppingstone so that I can stand until I regain my stability and am ready to move on.

Introduction

I have collected the verses from the New Testament that have been steppingstones for me. The purpose of this book is to share them with you. My explanation of them is to give you a thought for each weekday.

During the past twenty years I have expressed some of these steppingstone thoughts in chapters of books that have been published by Word Publishing. I have drawn on some of these in this book and am thankful for the assistance of Patty Crowley and Mary Hollingsworth. They were very helpful in the collating and editing of this material. In addition I wrote many new daily thoughts on the central theme.

I have arranged these daily steppingstones so that they would deal with the struggles we all face. Years of listening to people share their struggles, and being honest about my own, guided the selection of verses from the New Testament that really give stability and strength.

My prayer is that each day Christ will help you turn whatever struggles you experience into steppingstones of strength and courage.

Lloyd Ogilvie

If we are to love others as He has loved us, the brokenhearted are the focus of our concern. As He has been with us, so we are to be with people who are hurting— not sympathetically aloof, but empathically involved. Loving as Christ loved means to identify, listen, understand, and comfort.

Most assuredly, I say to you, before Abraham was, I AM.

John 8:58

Struggles are the stuff of life for most of us. What are yours? I have mine. Few of us consistently feel good about ourselves; we all have times of insecurity and self-doubt, times when we lack self-esteem. Anxiety is a stranger to none of us. Fears and frustrations track us like angry dogs. We've all had periods of discouragement, disappointment, and feeling depressed. Every one of us has memories that haunt and unfulfilled dreams that hurt.

Who hasn't felt the loneliness that has little to do with the absence of people? We need love and yet persist in doing unlovable things. Broken relationships, misunderstandings with people, and distorted communication trouble all of us. Worry raps at the door of every heart and is entertained as an unwelcome tenant for what seems to be an endless visit.

Not all our struggles are internal. We all face difficult situations at work or in society. Progress is slow; conflict seems inevitable. Everyone has his or her share of impossible people. We listen to the news or read the daily paper, and our nerves are jangled by what's happening in the asphalt jungle around us. What could we do about things if we tried? A feeling of impotence engulfs us. We wring our hands in powerless frustration.

Listen to Christ as He speaks about who He is and what He can do to help us with our struggles. Twenty-two times in the Gospel of John we hear Jesus declare His divine authority over our sin, sickness, and suffering. In His bold "I Am" assertions, He claims to be none other than Yahweh, the "I Am" of Moses' burning bush, now present in Immanuel, God with us. Each one of Jesus' "I Am" statements—I am the bread of life; I am the light of the world; I am the way, the truth, and the life—is His answer to our aching needs. Christ is the reigning Lord. He comes to you and me to save us from our sins and to free us from our burdens so that we can live the abundant life.

That is what we need to know in our struggles. The Lord, the "I Am—" who defeated the demons of despair that deplete us and who vanquished death and all its power—is alive! Here and now. With you and me at this moment. He has the power to help us turn our struggles into steppingstones!

Lo, I am with you always.

Matthew 28:20

I have known Christ for forty-five years. In those years I have never faced a struggle in which Christ and His promises were not the answer. My problem has not been trusting Him with a specific struggle and finding Him inadequate or unresponsive, but rather not trusting Him soon enough. I have spent thirty-seven years listening to people and to their struggles. There has never been a need, a sin, a broken relationship, a problem, or an emotional ailment that Christ could not heal or solve.

Allow me to share four basic questions. How we answer them makes all the difference in how we handle life's struggles.

Do you believe that Jesus is who He says He is? Is He truly God with you and therefore Lord over all of life's circumstances, able to marshal all power in heaven and earth to meet your needs? Do you really believe that Jesus performed miracles in the physical, emotional, and spiritual struggles of people? Do you dare to believe that He can and will perform these same miracles today in your life? Can He who is creator, sustainer, and innovator of all that happens make things happen in your life? Are you willing to ask Him to be the triumphant "I Am" in your specific struggles?

I find that most people can say yes to the first two but become uncertain and reluctant about the last two, and I'm convinced the reason is that our idea of what Christ can do today is debilitated by layers of distorted thinking. One layer is formed by the idea that we should be able to handle life ourselves without asking for help. The next layer comes from thinking of our Lord more as a judge of our failures than as an enabler who loves us in spite of what we've done or been. A deeper layer is formed by self-depreciation; we think, How can the Lord care about me when there are millions of people with greater needs? But by far the thickest and most resistant layer results from thinking of the Lord in impersonal, historical terms. We live in two worlds—the world of bold beliefs about what He said and did and the world of bland agnosticism about what He can and will do today. We can start turning our struggles into steppingstones by claiming His promise to be with us. Christ gives His word, "I will never leave you nor forsake you."

But He said to them, "It is I; do not be afraid."

John 6:20

*U*nder all the layers we talked about yesterday is the person we really are, the real you and me, often feeling alone, troubled by life, constantly battling for security and peace. Christ wants to penetrate through those layers to find us right now. He wants to know us as we are and have us love Him as He is: present, powerful, promising new possibilities. The Lord who makes things happen wants to move us out of immobility, out of the cycle of strain, stress, and struggle.

Here's how to let Him do it.

First, identify the struggle that represents your deepest need right now. Press deeper to the real cause of the problem. Why are you struggling? What do you do to cause the struggle? What are the basic assumptions on which the struggle is based? What ideas or feelings cause your reactions to what's happening to you?

Second, imagine how Christ would have dealt with someone with this struggle during His earthly ministry. What would He have said? Now hear Him say, "I am the Lord who makes things happen." If you were that person, what would you tell Him about your need and what would you ask Him to do?

Third, affirm the fact that He knows, cares, and has come to you right now. Tell Him all about the struggle. Leave nothing out or hidden. Tell Him that, more than a solution to the struggle, you need Him. Turn the struggle over to Him completely. Leave the results to Him.

Fourth, expectantly anticipate the way He will make the struggle a steppingstone. Instead of asking, How can I get out of this? ask What can I get out of this?—to grow, to become stronger, to be more sensitive to others who struggle.

Fifth, praise Him that He can unleash resources, people, and unanticipated potentials which you could never have imagined possible to help you. That's the excitement of the adventure of the Christian life. When we least expect it, Christ breaks through with blessings—perfectly timed, magnificently suited to our needs.

But that you may know that the Son of Man has power on earth to forgive sins.

Mark 2:10

*A*ll through Jesus' ministry, the basic issue was the acceptance of His authority. When He healed the paralytic, He first forgave the man's sins. The leaders of Israel constantly asked, "By what authority are You doing these things? And who gave You this authority to do these things?" (Mark 11:28). He had told them; they were not listening. He had said again and again "I am!" His authority, then and now, is because He is the divine Son of God who existed with the Father God since time began.

Christ's authority is that of the creative Logos, the Word of God. He is the "author of life" (Heb. 12:2), the uncreated Creator, the verb of God who makes things happen. "For in Him dwells all the fullness of the Godhead bodily; and you are complete in Him, who is the head of all principality and power" (Col. 2:9–10). The fullness Paul affirmed is meant for us in the frustration of our struggles, but only if we accept the Lord's authority to call the shots.

One of the major causes of emotional sickness is the inability to accept and live with authority. We either acquiesce or rebel. Or, what's worse, we give lip service to Christ's authority and still insist on running our own lives. At this very moment, while I write this and you read it, we are all struggling with the central issue of life: Will we yield to our Lord's will and way? Who's going to be in charge? Who is the ultimate Lord of our lives?

Let's be very specific. Focus on the particular struggle that is frustrating you today. Then look beneath the circumstances to your inner condition. Can you commit the deeper struggle to our Lord? That's the inner secret of turning our struggles into steppingstones. The Lord knows all about what we're going through and knows what is best for us. He will bring grace and growth out of the pain. The author of life knows what He's doing. Trust Him!

Everyone who sees the Son and believes in Him may have everlasting life; and I will raise him up at the last day.

John 6:40

*M*any Christians have become habitual strugglers. We struggle with life's pressures, with difficult people, and with challenges. We want Jesus' strength for these minor struggles, but we resist His solution to our biggest struggle.

Committing our lives to Him as Lord is the secret of receiving His power for our daily problems and for our worry about death. All that He offers us for abundant living now and eternal life beyond the grave is available only when we surrender to His Lordship.

Without that unreserved surrender, we continue to live as spiritual paupers. It's as if we've been accustomed to not having adequate financial resources to meet our daily needs, but then we are told we've been given a limitless inheritance to spend. We are astounded, but our habit patterns of worrying over making ends meet keep us from drawing on the inheritance.

Hetty Green is a classic example. When she died she left an estate valued at over one hundred million dollars. She denied herself any pleasures. Beyond that, she did not use any of her wealth to help others. Her life was a constant struggle. She ate cold oatmeal to save on fuel. Her house was never warm, and her appearance was shabby. When her son needed medical attention for a growth on his leg, she delayed while trying to find a free clinic. In fact, she delayed so long that her son's leg finally had to be amputated. Hetty lived like a pauper when she was wealthy.

Many of us live like that spiritually. Our need is to realize the spiritual inheritance that is ours if we will only commit our lives to Jesus. He is the all-powerful, reigning Lord. Obedience to Him as Lord is the key to the filling of the hunger and thirst inside us that keeps us struggling.

Assuredly, I say to you, unless you are converted and become as little children, you will by no means enter the kingdom of heaven.

Matthew 18:3

$\mathcal{A}$ Scots pastor by the name of Ian Duncan never allows me to forget my need to keep alive the child in me as I grow in the Lord. We were fellow students at the University of Edinburgh years ago. When I'm in Scotland for my summer studies, I look him up and have a cup of tea with him. He's good for me.

Almost every year Ian asks, "Lloyd, are you movin' on with the Lord? Are you more excited about the Lord and sharing His love than you were a year ago?"

Ian believes that life in Christ should become more exciting year after year, and so do I. Each time he's asked, my response has been an enthusiastic yes!

Often it's in the struggles I face that I'm brought back to childlike dependence on the Lord and a desire to live spontaneously. Sometimes those struggles threaten to make me take myself too seriously and not take the Lord's promises seriously enough. For a time, I try to work things out on my own strength. It never works. Then, when the tension becomes unbearable, the Lord turns my attention from the struggle to Him and what He's done to help me in the past. My childlike trust is renewed, my basic conversion is rejuvenated, and I feel fresh courage to go on. I'm free to live confidently again. As a result, a new childlike enthusiasm for the Lord, life, and people around me is released. The delight of life and the desire for more life is strong again. My will is strengthened. I find I have a new will to turn to the Lord for His help.

When asked how she takes the immense problems of Calcutta, Mother Teresa responded, "I focus on the Lord and not the problems. Then I can deal with the problems holding the strong hand of Jesus."

[You] are kept by the power of God through faith for salvation ready to be revealed in the last time.

1 Peter 1:5

God's purposes are not thwarted by our problems. He is in charge and no problem is too big for Him. In fact, a careful study of history indicates that He works out His plan through the problems He allows in our lives. God is not the helpless victim of the problems we bring on ourselves, those caused by other people, or those that are the mischief of the force of evil in the world.

God gave us the awesome gift of freedom so that we could choose to love, glorify, and serve Him. The refusal to do that is the cause of many of the problems we bring on ourselves and is often the cause of those problems we face with others. Humankind's rebellion is often collusive in social evil, injustice, and suffering.

The bracing truth is that no problem can happen without God's permission. What He allows is always for a greater blessing than we could ever realize if we had no problems. He is our mighty, all-powerful Lord who wants us to grow in His nature, grace, and power. One of the ways He has elected to do that is through the problems we confront. Just as He created us in the beginning, so too He is the continuing creator who is at work in us and our world.

Actually, problems define the battle line of the Lord's transforming encounter with ignorance, pride, selfishness, laziness, and resistance to growth in all of us. Problems often motivate us to reach out to Him for help in dealing with our insensitivity, greed, and injustice in our relationships and in society.

We can be certain that when God allows a problem, it is because He wants us to grow as persons. When the problem is with another person, we can know there is something He is seeking to accomplish in that relationship. Of this we can be sure—God never gives us more than we can take. With each problem He seeks a new step for us to take in becoming truly dynamic people.

Yet in all these things we are more than conquerors through Him who loved us.

Romans 8:37

It is in each problem that we discover a perfectly matched promise from God of what He will do to help us. Recently I made a list of the thousands of problems people sent me in response to a survey. Then I went through the Bible and underlined the direct quotes of promises from God in the Old Testament and those made through Christ in the New Testament. I could not find one problem for which there was not a promise uniquely suited to help us face and conquer it.

We can take encouragement in the fact that times of problems give us the opportunity to understand, claim, and experience these promises of God. John Keats was right: "Nothing becomes real till it is experienced—even a proverb is no proverb to you till your life has illustrated it. . . . Call the world if you please, 'The vale of soul-making.'" The truth of God's promises is discovered and realized in our personal growth in the "vale of soul-making" forced upon us by our problems. The promises of God give us courage to receive the full potential for growth in all of our problems.

While there is much in life we can't be sure of, God's Word trumpets a truth we can count on—irrespective of the intensity of our problems, the Lord of all creation is with us. In fact, our problems are proof of the presence of the recreating Lord, not His absence. The bigger the problem, the more of His abiding presence we will receive. The more complex the problem, the more advanced will be the wisdom He offers. Equal to the strain of the problem will be the strength that is released. It is an evidence of the Lord's presence with us when He allows problems to focus the next step of what He wants to accomplish in our personal lives or through us in the lives of others, in the church, or in our society.

In everything give thanks; for this is the will of God in Christ Jesus for you.

1 Thessalonians 5:18

*P*raising the Lord in a problem is our ultimate level of surrender. It opens us up to the flow of the Lord's Spirit in us and in the problem. It isn't that the problem is good in and of itself, but that it is the occasion for deeper trust and for progress.

Recently a friend said to me, "How can I thank God for this problem? It's difficult, painful, and distressing." My response was, "Naturally, you aren't going to feel that the problem by itself is particularly beneficial. But you can be thankful that the Lord will use it to work out needed changes in your own life." In working toward the solution my friend was given wisdom beyond his understanding about how to handle the problem, and he finally overcame it. In the process, he grew immensely as a person and became the Lord's agent of reconciliation in what had seemed to be an insolvable problem.

Another friend of mine accepted the challenge to experiment with a thirty-day discipline of thanksgiving. The experiment broke the bonds of negative thinking. She concentrated on the positive potential of her problems. From morning until night, she centered her thinking on being thankful for whatever happened.

When a difficulty painted her into a corner of frustration, she thanked the Lord, knowing that He would show her the way out. As the days passed, she felt a new closeness with the Lord, a oneness with Him. Life became one endless prayer of thanksgiving. This is what she says: "What began as a thirty-day experiment now has become the strategy of my life for facing and solving problems. Problems upset me only when I take my eyes off the Lord and forget to thank Him for counting me worthy to be a person He can use to tackle and work through problems and one who can trust Him for answers. If I had never had problems, think of what I would have missed!"

But when the kindness and the love of God our Savior toward man appeared, not by works of righteousness which we have done, but according to His mercy He saved us, through the washing of regeneration and renewing of the Holy Spirit.

Titus 3:4–5

*L*ife is made up of a constant succession of new beginnings when Christ reigns in our hearts. We are never totally defeated. He has a way through and out of the problems and on to the next phase of our adventure with Him. He gives us guidance of how to begin again. He never gives up on us, and He gives us the courage and strength never to give up on life.

Now we can cut the losses of our past failures and move on. Having made a fresh start we have the strength to forgive ourselves and others. When people have caused our broken heart, He shows us how to express forgiveness. We are freed from having to be right or win every argument. All that's important to us is a new beginning. In response to other people's pain and distress, we feel deeply with the Lord's love pulsating through our hearts for them. But we are never immobilized by their problems. We know from our own experience that the Lord will use the problems to break open their hearts to Him and to the future He has prepared. Finally, in our own grief over the loss of loved ones or cherished projects, the Lord is the indwelling healer. We can express our grief, let it out without blaming Him, and experience the miraculous shifting of our feelings from the loss to what the Lord has ahead for us.

Now, in the light of that, how's your heart? Has life hardened it? Have you allowed experience to make it dry, crisp, and hard?

When problems break our hearts we are in a strategic place spiritually. We have the blessed opportunity of allowing the Lord to take charge of our hearts, break into the core of our self-determination, and set us free to receive His heart in us. The result will be a vibrant resiliency for the new beginning He has planned for us.

He who finds his life will lose it, and he who loses his life for My sake will find it.

Matthew 10:39

*A*ll our problems have built into them an opportunity for a deeper experience of the self-sacrificing heart of the Lord. As we confront our problems, we must choose between being self-serving or self-sacrificing. We are on the way to a right choice when we can ask in the midst of a problem, "What does love command? How can I forget about my own selfish desires and think about what this troublesome person or that complex situation needs?" Remember, we are not in the abundant life to conserve ourselves, but to give ourselves away. The more self-giving we are, the more we grow. Our character becomes more like Christ's.

For example, problems with people give us a splendid opportunity to reveal Christ's Spirit working through us as we show patience and are gracious and forgiving. At other times, His tenderness is coupled with toughness as we are called to take our stand for what He has shown us is right. Most people who become a problem to us are the way they are because they either need to meet the Savior or, if they have met Him, need to grow in Him. And His power is given to us for His program: to serve. A servant acts, speaks, gives to communicate healing love and to help people find a life worth giving away.

The frustrating, disturbing things people do are because they are involved in their own rendition of trying to save rather than lose their lives. Like us, they need to loosen their grip on life. And the secret of helping them let go is to communicate that they have a life of value to give. Problems with certain people are gifts from the Lord! It is because He has called, chosen, and cherished them that He allows them to become our problem. He wants to use us to expose what it means to find life and lose it for a new life filled with His Spirit.

So Jesus said to them, "Because of your unbelief; for assuredly, I say to you, if you have faith as a mustard seed, you will say to this mountain, 'Move from here to there,' and it will move; and nothing will be impossible for you."

Matthew 17:20

*A*ll of us have very real frustrations that become like mountains in our way. But we are not stopped. We have a "donated faith," a gift from the Lord to trust Him to show us how to conquer those mountains. He helps us understand His plans and goals for us. His mountain-removing power is available for that, not just for removing the little irritations of life. When some frustrating person or situation stands in the way of our being obedient to Him, He gives us the power to believe that the problem can be moved.

Notice that the power we are given is to say to our mountains, "Move from here to there." The promise is that the mountain will be moved out of the way of our progress. The Lord did not say that through faith we would always be able to get rid of mountains. What He did promise is that He will help us move them out of the way.

But that moving of the mountain begins inside us. Often our attitude toward the mountain is more debilitating than the mountain itself. We become defensive, allowing the people or problems that are our mountains to make us think they are controlling our destiny.

I am convinced that Jesus is talking about our discipleship in this metaphor of the mountain. When we commit our lives to Him, following Him obediently becomes the issue. Along the way, frustrating mountains do loom before us. But that's when He gives us the faith to say, "Be removed from here to there. I'm going to obey my Lord and press on to His goals for me!"

Assuredly, I say to you, if you have faith and do not doubt, you will not only do what was done to the fig tree, but also if you say to this mountain, "Be removed and be cast into the sea," it will be done.

Matthew 21:21

*P*robably nothing is more frustrating in our Christian pilgrimage than people, but even they do not need to keep us from our commitment to the Lord. In fact, only the Lord can help us cope with them. We do not need to be victims of difficult people! We choose to be victimized. It is our lack of strength in the Lord that often leaves us vulnerable to being manipulated. The Lord wants us to be free from any bondage to frustrating and troublesome people. Then, as free people, we can lovingly, but firmly, share what I like to call the "irreducible maximum" of our values, direction, and desires for our lives as Christians. And, in an atmosphere of love and caring, we can talk out the things that frustrate us in the difficult people of our lives.

Once the mountain is out of the way in our minds and we are in the flow of the Lord's grace, we can share what is distressing us. That attitude on our part often helps the other person to unload the reason he or she has been acting in a frustrating way. At the same time we may learn that we've been frustrating that person too!

Of course, there are times we have to "shake the dust off our feet" and move on in following the Master. Not all relationships with frustrating people can be solved. We must remember that people have the free will not to change. But they should not keep us from the ones who can and will change.

The most important thing for our relationship with the Lord and for peace of mind is that we commit to Him whatever or whomever is the "mountain" we perceive standing in our way. Remember He can change us and our attitude. After the removal of that high-reaching mountain—whatever it is—nothing that He wills is impossible. We can be free of frustration!

frustration

But seek the kingdom of God, and all these things shall be added to you.
Luke 12:31

The first step to overcoming anxious thinking is to make an unreserved commitment of our minds to the Lord, asking Him to guide and direct our thinking so that our thoughts can be conformed to His will for us. Paul encouraged the Philippians, "Let this mind be in you which was also in Christ Jesus" (Phil. 2:5). So often we think of the ministry of the indwelling Christ in us only as a source of strength and courage, but He offers us so much more. He captures our thinking and guides the development of our hopes.

From within our minds, the Lord expands our thinking to include possibilities our self-generated wishing would never have dared envision. He gives us a picture of what He will do in and around us. No need to be anxious about the accomplishment of these hopes. They are backed up by the promises and power of the Lord Himself.

The second step is a basic formula to use in the development of our hopes. It is contained in the admonition and assurance Jesus gives after telling us not to have an anxious mind and giving us the promise that God knows. "But seek the kingdom of God, and all these things shall be added to you. Do not fear, little flock, for it is your Father's good pleasure to give you the kingdom" (Luke 12:31–32). Note the close connection between "Seek the kingdom of God" and "it is your Father's good pleasure to give you the kingdom."

The kingdom of God is His rule and reign in us, in our relationships, and in all the affairs of life. When the Lord's will is our dominate desire, He will use many different ways to make it abundantly clear. The Bible, prayer, meditation, circumstances, insights from trusted fellow Christians will all be utilized to guide us. Our part is to commit our minds to kingdom thinking and hoping rather than meteoric wishing and yearning.

And of His fullness we have all received, and grace for grace.

John 1:16

*P*raying that Christ in His fullness will be formed in us relieves us of three of the most troublesome struggles of life. The first is our struggle with our human nature. That struggle includes our thoughts, inner feelings, and selfishness. It's a wearying, grim battle to try to change ourselves. Resolutions, improvement programs, and self-discipline efforts yield little change in our basic nature. But when we honestly confess our defeat in trying to get better and we ask for the fullness of Christ, He enters in and performs a continuing miracle of making us like Himself.

Second, we are freed from the struggle to be adequate. I know I am insufficient for the demands of life, but I also know Christ is all-sufficient. I can't imagine any problem He can't solve, any person He could not love, or any challenge He would not be able to tackle. And so, from within me as well as around me, Christ is at work giving me what I could never produce without Him.

And third, we don't have to struggle with worries over what the future holds. We can be assured that what the Lord allows to happen will be used for greater growth of His fullness in us. We can relax. Whatever we face will be an opportunity for new dimensions of His character to be formed in us.

All this is based on a reverent conviction. Just as in the incarnation the Spirit of God was blended in perfect harmony with Jesus' human nature, so too, in a powerful way, His Spirit dwells in our humanness and He is formed in us. The more we yield our lives to Him, the more He forms us into His image. It is a lifelong process, and He's never finished with us.

Every time we are caught in a bind of worry is a new occasion for an exchange with our Lord. We accept His promise to be with us and we give Him our wearying worry. Consider the immensity of His promise: "I will never leave you or forsake you." Think of both aspects of that. How could the Lord ever fail us? It would be by leaving us friendless and alone in a dangerous situation. And He promises He never will!

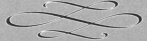

What man of you, having a hundred sheep, if he loses one of them, does not leave the ninety-nine in the wilderness and go after the one which is lost until he finds it?

Luke 15:4

*T*he parable of the lost sheep in Luke 15:4–7 reminds us that the Father cares about individuals. In Christ, the Good Shepherd, He watches over His beloved flock as a whole, but when one wanders away, He sets out in a relentless search.

The lost sheep nibbled its way from the flock and the shepherd. Its total concentration was on self-satisfaction. One green pasture led to another. The drift was not deliberate. Having taken its eyes off the shepherd, the sheep did not know how far away it had gone. Eventually it was in danger.

Don't forget that the sheep still belongs to the shepherd. We too belong to the Lord regardless of how far we wander from Him. We wander away in so many different ways. We get busy with our own concerns and pressures. We think a lot about ourselves and what we want. The lust for success entices us. At no point do we renounce our faith; it simply has less meaning for us. Then some difficulty or crisis hits us. We realize we can't face life without the Lord. The loneliness we feel without the Good Shepherd is our own inner experience of His search for us.

When the Lord finds us in our need, we are amazed at His individual care for us. In our impersonal, computerized society, where we often feel like one of billions of numbers rather than persons, we need to know not only that He understands and cares about us, but that He both motivates our plea for help and answers it. In that moment of reclamation, we feel that we are the total focus of His concern. It's then that Jesus' picture of His ministry as the Good Shepherd has personal impact. We have the awesome sense of being the one lost sheep and that He has put aside all other concerns to go out and find us. It happens often, and each time He refinds us, there is joy in heaven.

Then Jesus said to them again, "Most assuredly, I say to you, I am the door of the sheep."

John 10:7

$\mathcal{R}$ecently, I became anxious in a time of tremendous pressure. There was no way I could meet all the demands that had hit with hurricane force on my life. I added hours to my schedule, trying to catch up. Sleep and exercise were put off. The old feelings of inadequacy stalked around in my emotions.

When I realized what was happening, I dropped everything for a prolonged walk on the beach and a time of prayer. As I walked and talked with the Lord, He helped me analyze what had happened to me. The work had piled up. A period of insecurity had prompted me to take on responsibilities that, I realized now, had not been guided by the Lord and were not a maximum part of His strategy for me. In the flood of work, time for myself, my wife, my family, and my friends was being denied me. Feelings of anger were focused with a fierce blast on myself.

"Lord, what's wrong?" I asked. Then I listened intently. After a time of silence, corrective and clarifying thoughts came flooding into my mind. Forgiveness for running my own life was given and received. I experienced new love for myself as loved by the Lord. Creative energy began to surge.

Decisiveness followed. First things were put first. A plan and the power to work the plan were given. I was set free from being my own worst enemy to being my own best friend. Then I returned to do what portion of the work the Lord had given priority. I was free of the anxiety that had been draining off all the energy.

Jesus stands at the door, calling us to come home to Him. When we have entered into that union once again, we feel His love surging into our fears, frustrations, angers, and hostilities. We begin to feel delight in being who we are—His sheep. Now we can rest and expect that He can handle our tomorrows. While we are relaxing in safety and security, He stands by the door as our protector, gurading us against the danger from others—and ourselves.

Which of you by worrying can add one cubit to his stature?
                                                    Matthew 6:27

*S*alvation means wholeness, healing, and health. Christ, our Good Shepherd, promises that we shall "go in and out and find pasture." This is our assurance that all our psychological and physical needs will be met in companionship with Him as He shepherds us. The adventure of the Christian life is not only the assurance of eternal security but the experience of daily security now. Our Shepherd knows us and calls us.

When Jesus calls us by name to belong to Him, fear of death is past. We are reconciled forever. Nothing can change our elected status. But that's only the beginning. He couples reconciliation with regeneration. The process of growing in His love means that He will penetrate our conscious and subconscious natures. Anything that could debilitate us will be exposed and exorcised. Mental health is the Lord's gift to His loved ones. He loves us just as we are, but He never leaves us that way.

Our Lord really knows us. He understands how anxious we become over having adequate resources for our daily lives. He knows about unpaid bills and low bank balances. He is aware of how we worry about appearance, success, and security. He empathizes with our concern about deadlines and pressure. He sees into our hearts and knows all about our distress over people we love. Life is not easy. Often it is an endless succession of impossible challenges that press us from one crisis to another. We become insecure, wondering if we have what it takes to pull it off.

The only cure for this kind of objective anxiety, focused in real troubles in a very real world, is found in the Lord's admonition: "But seek first the kingdom of God and His righteousness, and all these things shall be added to you. Therefore do not worry about tomorrow, for tomorrow will worry about its own things. Sufficient for the day is its own trouble" (Matt. 6:33–34).

I am the Good Shepherd. The good shepherd gives His life for the sheep.
John 10:11

A good shepherd counts no cost too high to protect his sheep. At no time, regardless of what happens, will he leave the flock. He even will lay down his own life to protect them. He stands immovably between the sheep and the ravaging wolves.

Catch the impact of that. Picture it in your mind. Jesus stands between us and whatever causes us to worry—physical danger, people who would use or misuse us, a hostile fate that would disturb or destroy us, powers of evil. When the going is tough, Jesus will be there! Imagine each of your worries as separate wolves lurking about, ready to attack. Are they too much for the Good Shepherd to handle? Jesus is God with us. He has all power. His providence is our peace. We will never be alone or bereft again.

In that context I want to share a prescription for worry. Like some prescriptions it has two parts: something we are to take and something we are to do. It is a companion Scripture to Jesus' "I am" promise about being the Good Shepherd. If I could give you a gift, it would be the freedom to receive and respond to Hebrews 13:5–6: "For He Himself has said, 'I will never leave you nor forsake you.' So we may boldly say: 'The LORD is my helper; I will not fear. What can man do to me?'"

Every time we are caught in the bind of worry is a new occasion for an exchange with our Lord. We accept His promise to be with us and we give Him our wearying worry. Consider the immensity of His promise: "I will never fail you nor forsake you." Think about both aspects of that. How could the Lord ever fail us? It would be by leaving us friendless and alone in a dangerous situation. And He claims He never will!

Let your conduct be without covetousness; be content with such things as you have. For He Himself has said, "I will never leave you nor forsake you."

Hebrews 13:5

A time of worry over money is often dispelled by a courageous, daring faith gift. I have found that when I get into a bind, either personally or professionally in some venture of my ministry, that is the crisis moment to take a significant portion of what I have and give it to the Lord. That faith gift breaks the cycle of worry. It also says to the Lord that I am seriously committed and involved in what I am asking Him to bless.

This happened recently when I was concerned about the financial needs for my radio and television ministry. I made a faith promise of money I did not have. It was then that the Lord began to release financial resources from others for the ministry. And He has provided extra funds I could not have anticipated for me to pay my own faith pledge.

If you are in financial need right now, make a daring faith gift from whatever you have to the Lord's work somewhere. It's the antidote to worry over money.

Oswald Chambers has a way of sending straight arrows of truth into my heart. He usually presses me on in the adventure beyond where I ever thought I would dare to go. I hope His penetrating word about worry gives you the jab it gave me: "Are you looking unto Jesus now, in the immediate matter that is pressing, and receiving from His peace? If so, He will be a gracious benediction of peace in and through you. But if you try to worry it out, you obliterate Him and deserve all you get." Ouch!

We come back to the Good Shepherd. He owns, protects, sacrifices for the sheep. We can have a carefree contentment rather than the soul-twisting, nerve-stretching rack of worry.

Join me in a commitment not to worry for three days this next week: yesterday, tomorrow, and today; that makes a worry-free week!

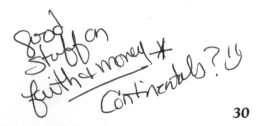

But we have the mind of Christ.

1 Corinthians 2:16

Someone said that the shortest duration of time is between the moment a traffic light changes from red to green and the guy behind you blows his horn. So many of us are racing toward uncertain destinations at breakneck speed. The Lord's warning is: Slow down or break down. Some people pride themselves in saying, "I may wear out but I will never rust out." Neither is a good alternative. There's always enough time to do what the Lord wants us to do.

Also, Christ's indwelling presence produces a profound peace. Isaiah was right: "You will keep him in perfect peace, Whose mind is stayed on You, Because he trusts in You" (Isa. 26:3).

Paul encourages us to have the mind of Christ (Phil. 2:5). The word *mind* can also mean disposition or attitude. We can have more than the Lord's guidance; we can have His disposition when He lives in us as the equalizer of pressure. Viktor Frankl wisely said, "Everything can be taken from a man but one thing: the last of the human freedoms—to choose one's attitude in any given circumstance." How true! Yet acquiring the Lord's attitude requires listening to His inner voice. We need a quiet time at the beginning of each day and then frequently during the day to see things from the Lord's perspective. Then we can ask Him to take charge of things and show us how to act and react.

All of this is sound biblical advice. If we follow it, we will be on the way to peace in pressure. But there will also be times when we will fall back into an old pressure pattern. But we can know it and realize that we were never intended to live that way, confess what caused the pressure, and amend what we did to others and ourselves. The moment we admit that we are under pressure, the Lord is there ready to help us. Our struggle will become a steppingstone!

struggles &
Lord is our
stepping stone,
just Ask.

31

Nevertheless I have this against you, that you have left your first love.
Revelation 2:4

*T*hink back to the first time you felt the love of Christ for you person-ally. It may have been when you became a Christian or in some experi-ence when He broke through all your barriers and gave you a profound assurance of His loving care for you. It may have been a time when you faced an impossible situation and Christ gave you strength and courage, not only to survive, but to be victorious. Or it might have been a time of illness when, as the Great Physician, He touched you with healing love.

Whatever the circumstances, you knew you were loved, and in re-sponse you knew that you loved Christ more than anything or anyone else. That knowledge was more profound than romantic love and was more exhilarating than any human affection. You fell in love with Christ.

For some that happened when they became Christians. For others, whose first commitment to Christ was more an acceptance of truth and less a gripping experience, falling in love with Christ came later. For still others it's never happened, and it is their greatest need. But for all of us—whether it has happened, needs to be renewed, or needs to happen—the intensity and inspiration of a first-love *ecstasy* is offered each day.

Ecstasy? Isn't that word a bit strong to describe our daily relationship with Christ? I don't think so. Ecstasy means to be moved deeply by an overpowering emotion or mental exaltation. Both happen when we meet Christ and He abides in us. We feel love that is greater than any we've ever felt in any human relationship. It's more powerful than romantic infatuation, yet it has some of the same carefree delight. It is more last-ing than the best of human love because it is rooted in Christ's faithful-ness and undying love.

Now may the Lord of peace Himself give you peace always in every way. The Lord be with you all.

2 Thessalonians 3:16

I talked to a man who was on the edge of experiencing the gift of a heart truly open to God. He had lost his twenty-five-year-old son. "I'm really angry at God for doing this!" he said. "How could he take this boy from me? He was a fine young man, believed in God, and had a great future. Now he's gone."

The man had three problems: the loss of his beloved son and the grief that was causing, the anger he was feeling that was blocking him from receiving the only source of comfort, and he was belaboring false assumptions that this life is the best of all lives and that his son was being denied a long life. Most of all, the man was aching over the denial of his enjoyment of his son. Very human reactions. But beneath all the grief was a hardened, self-determining will that had been threatened. Though the man claimed to be a Christian, he had never yielded the core of his heart to the Lord.

The bright side of the story is that the Lord did not leave the man to muddle in his grief forever. I did all that I could to help him clarify his thinking about death and eternal life. One day I felt led to say, "My friend, the Lord is going to give you a burning desire to open your heart to Him. He knows your grief. He gave His own Son to deal with the problem of death and to open heaven to us. I promise you that before long you will realize you can't make it without Him. That will open you to receive what He has been longing to give you. You are angry with God because you think He canceled your plans."

Some days later the man suddenly felt differently inside. He was gripped by an undeniable desire to surrender his grief and to confess how tenaciously he had held his own life and those he loved in his control. The Lord broke open the citadel of the man's heart and flooded it with His peace.

For you are the temple of the living God. As God has said: "I will dwell in them and walk among them. I will be their God, and they shall be My people."

2 Corinthians 6:16

*T*he Lord sees us with trifocal lenses. He sees with magnified clarity all that has happened to us to twist our self-images. Then He sees what we are going through now that tears the scabs off old wounds to our self-esteem. But then He focuses on the persons we can be in His image. In intimate communication He can take us back into those experiences that distorted our self-acceptance. Feeling His love, we can dare to see the negative influences of childhood and adolescence that gave us the wrong picture of our potential. Then He asks, "Will you dare to forgive as I have forgiven you? Will you let go of the hurts?"

He wants to reform our thinking about ourselves. He can confront our debilitating comparisons. "Don't take your measurements from what others do or accomplish. There's no one else in the world exactly like you. You have a unique destiny to fulfill. Trust Me to show you your special place to stand." How shall we respond? Are we willing to give up the security of self-negation and replace it with the Lord's affirmation?

But He is not finished. We can feel the touch of His presence on our bodies. So much of our insecurity is caused by negative feelings about our physical selves. We are all uniquely wrapped. We can change proportions, but basically we must all live with what we have been given. Our dislike of ourselves is manifested in the way we mistreat our bodies. The Lord speaks tenderly: "This is My temple. I love you as you are. I have used the tall and the short, the fat and the thin, the handsome and the ugly to do My work through the ages. My Spirit living in you can make you the radiant person you long to be. Get in touch with your body. Rediscover the joy of breathing, touching, tasting, seeing, hearing. What a wonder you are!"

Let us draw near with a true heart in full assurance of faith, having our hearts sprinkled from an evil conscience and our bodies washed with pure water.

Hebrews 10:22

Conversion is a gift. It is a total redirection, a complete change of mind, a transformation of our personalities, and the reorientation of our wills. Conversion is a miracle of the Lord's grace. It begins with His choice of us. He singles us out to be the recipients of His love and forgiveness and then works through the circumstances of our lives to bring us to a realization that the life we are living is a grim substitute for the full-orbed joy He wants us to have. Graciously, He convicts us of the sin of our independence from Him and all we have done to cripple ourselves and hurt others.

A longing desire to know and love Him begins to grow in us as a direct result of His persistent movements in our minds. This brings us to repentance of our emptiness, our failure to live to the fullest, and our own inability to change ourselves. That's when we are given the magnificent endowment of faith to claim Christ's forgiveness through the atonement of the cross and the power of His resurrection as the assurance of His presence with us and of our participation in eternal life. Then the same Lord who has brought us through the process of turning us around from self-centered ambition to complete trust in Him actually comes to live in us as the new people He's enabled us to be. Dwelling within us He continues His transformation of making us like Himself!

The other day a man asked me when I was converted. My response was, "In May of 1949, repeatedly through the years, and most recently, yesterday." I went on to explain my initial turning to Christ as a college freshman and my frequent need to turn anew whenever I have drifted from my love for, and obedience to, the Lord. In each of those times, He drew me back and created a fresh desire to live more fully in Him.

Fear not, for I am with you; Be not dismayed, for I am your God. I will strengthen you, Yes, I will help you, I will uphold you with My righteous right hand.

Isaiah 41:10

*F*ear has reached epidemic proportions in America. It is contagious. We become infected by it and pass it on to others. Like a disease, fear saps our energy and robs us of joy in life.

Far from being the exclusive problem of the neurotic, fear cripples most Christians and often pervades our families, even our churches.

Fear is loneliness for God. We were created to receive His love and love Him. He has chosen and called us to live in an intimate relationship with Him. He is initiator of that relationship, constantly seeking us, pursuing us with relentless love.

Many of us have heard and read about God's grace all our lives, and yet we still battle with fear. Why is it so difficult for us to really believe in God's love. The Lord's constant word to us is "Fear not!" There are 366 "Fear not!" verses in the Bible—one for every day of the year and an extra one for leap year! Most of the admonitions are followed by a firm assurance of the Lord's presence or a stirring reminder of an aspect of His nature—like His faithfulness, goodness, loving-kindness, or intervening power in times of need.

The Lord takes hold of our right hand with His righteous, grace-filled right hand. That puts us eye to eye with Him. It's exactly what God intends. He has something He wants to say to us that He wants to hear with the ears of our soul. He wants to get through to that deep inner place in us where our fears fester.

"You don't need to be afraid," He says. "I am in charge of your life. I will never leave or forsake you. Trust me. Take this first step to living without fear. I am Jehovah-Shammah, the Lord is there. And wherever you are, be more sure of this than you are of your next breath—I will be there."

For you did not receive the spirit of bondage again to fear, but you received the Spirit of adoption by whom we cry out, "Abba, Father."

Romans 8:15

I will overcome my crippling fears with a creative fear of God expressed with awe and wonder, adoration and faithful obedience. He is the only Person I have to please.

Healthy fear of the Lord has very positive results. That's the promise the psalmist gives in one of my favorite verses about the fear of the Lord. "The secret of the LORD is with those who fear Him, And He will show them His covenant" (Ps. 25:14).

The Hebrew word for "secret" really means "friendship." Charles Spurgeon said it implies "confidential intimacy and select fellowship."

What does God do when we come to Him with reverent fear? He welcomes us as friends and shows us His covenant. A covenant is a promise that establishes a relationship of mutual trust. The psalmist is speaking, of course, of the covenant the Lord made with Abraham and later confirmed to the nation of Israel, "I shall be your God and you shall be My people."

But we become the Lord's people under a new and better covenant. God comes to us in Christ, Immanuel, "God with us." He comes first in judgment and then in grace. He confronts us with what we are and then with what He has destined us to be. Again we respond with awe and wonder. He knows all about us!

The depth of God's love is revealed in this covenant. He reconciles us to Himself through Christ's death on the cross. When we experience the Father's wondrous love for us, we are filled with even greater awe than before. No longer do we dread God but call Him by the most intimate of names. We rejoice with sheer astonishment over His glory and His reconciling love.

There is no fear in love; but perfect love casts out fear, because fear involves torment. But he who fears has not been made perfect in love.
1 John 4:18

I will face my fears, retrace them to their source in my heart, displace them by making my heart Christ's home, and erase them with His perfect love.

Face your fears; don't submerge them.

There are two sure things about our fears. They are real to us, and they won't go away simply by wishing them away. So we ask, "What is it in my life that causes me to fear?" Whatever it is, step up to it and look it squarely in the eye.

Next, retrace your fears—refocus on your mind's eye the source of your present fears. Remember, if we don't deal with our past, we will compulsively repeat it.

In retracing our fears it is important for us to remember that what we think we fear is usually not what we fear. Most of our external fears are rooted in our deeper guilt-motivated fear that is the result of alienation from God. We have gnawing feelings of guilt not just because of things we've done, but because we skillfully avoid intimacy with the Lord.

After facing and retracing our fears, the next step is to ask Christ to move in and live in our hearts. This opens the way for Him to have His way in our hearts.

We can't evict fear on our own—only Christ can do that. The secret is to focus on Him and not on our fears. In doing that we will deliberately refuse to spend time rehearsing our fears.

Only Christ can erase our fears. It's His miracle. Our part is to pray, "Lord, I don't want this fear anymore. I don't want to hang on to it as a false security any longer. I ask you to erase it and clean it off the blackboard of my memory."

Remember that Jesus Christ, of the seed of David, was raised from the dead according to my gospel.

2 Timothy 2:8

I will let go of my hurting memories of the past. I will not anticipate the repetition of past pain; I will accept forgiveness from the Lord and will forgive everything and everyone in the past—including myself.

Keeping short accounts with the Lord is so crucial because we become what we remember. Unresolved guilt, unconfessed failures, and unforgiven injuries make us fearful and cautious. Our obsession with negative memories short-circuits positive memories and causes us to forget God's goodness in the past—how He enables us to face and overcome previous difficulties.

In the Gospel account Jesus told His disciples—and us—"Do this in remembrance of Me." We're prone to limit this to the celebration of the Lord's Supper. But I believe Jesus' words go beyond that to include remembering what He has done for us in His death and resurrection. We are to act in remembrance of Jesus in all of life.

"Remember Jesus Christ!" were Paul's watchwords. Because he did, his memories of past sins and failures were wiped out and his expectation of continued blessing was energized. The apostle could face his problems because he remembered Jesus Christ, and with confidence he could say, "according to my gospel."

Each of us has a gospel—the Good News of Christ according to our experience. It's the account of what His cross means to us and a record of what He has done in our own personal lives. The objective truth of the biblical Gospels becomes our own gospel, gives us the courage to be honest about what still needs to be healed in our memories. Knowing that Christ has forgiven us must be coupled with our forgiveness of ourselves and others. Does your gospel include how the Lord has healed and continues to heal your memory through the power of forgiveness?

But by the grace of God I am what I am, and His grace toward me was not in vain; but I labored more abundantly than they all, yet not I, but the grace of God which was with me.

1 Corinthians 15:10

*F*ear is estrangement from myself. What I fear in others I first fear in myself. Therefore, in response to God's unqualified acceptance, I will embrace myself as worthy of my own affirmation and encouragement.

In 1 Corinthians 15:10, Paul allows us to get inside his mind as he embraces himself as a man in Christ. That personal parenthesis comes in the midst of Paul's soaring rhetoric about Christ's death for our forgiveness, His resurrection for our victory over death, His appearances to Peter, James, the other apostles, and last of all, to Paul himself. The appearance of the risen Christ was very important to Paul because it was his badge of apostleship.

But not everyone in the early church accepted that. Some questioned Paul's authority. Others differed sharply with his policy of accepting Gentile converts into the church.

I am convinced that Paul's healthy, fearless self-acceptance in the context of the Lord's love for him explains why he was one of the most loving, forgiving, adventuresome, courageous human beings who ever lived.

Paul's embrace of himself as a new creation in Christ not only enabled honest confession and humble praise, but also led him to the step of embracing himself. He became involved in heroic service. That's always the sure test of the "I am what I am by grace" embrace of self-acceptance.

None of Paul's critics, not even the other apostles, accomplished what the Lord did through Paul's missionary journeys in the centers of human religions, commerce, philosophy, and power. All felt the impact of a transformed Pharisee who knew Christ's embrace, embraced himself, and was free to embrace others from the least to the mighty.

God has not promised skies always blue,
Flower-strewn pathways all our lives through;
God has not promised sun without rain,
Joy without sorrow, peace without pain.

God has not promised smooth roads and wide
swift easy travel heeding no guide
God has not promised that we shall not bear
many a burden, many a care.

But God has promised strength for the day,
rest for the labor, light for the way
Grace for the trials, help from above
unfailing sympathy, undying love.

Annie Johnson Flint

For God has not given us a spirit of fear, but of power and of love and of a sound mind.

2 Timothy 1:7

I admit I am inadequate to meet life's opportunities, but I will conquer my fear by becoming a riverbed for the flow of God's guidance, love, and power.

The first gift of the Spirit's activity in us to make us adequate is a "sound mind." The Greek word Paul uses here is descriptive of a Spirit-anointed, disciplined mind, one totally under the control of the Spirit of Christ. It is a mind able to think His thoughts and see the potential of people and situations the way He does. In a sound mind the powers of imagination are whole and healthy. With a sound mind the Christian focuses on the Lord's vision for the specific opportunities of life.

A "sound mind" overcomes fears of inadequacy by a Spirit-produced thinking or attitude about those things we are to do and the resources we need and will be given to accomplish them. A Christ-inspired, "sound mind" provides reliable guidance and a clear vision. It lifts our focus beyond what we can do in our own strength to what the Lord wants to do through us.

Let's face it. We need the Lord's help in every relationship, situation, and problem where life dishes out challenges beyond us. Whenever we feel inadequate—in marriage, with our families, on the job, and in the impossible tasks the Lord has given us to do—we need to confess, "Lord, I can't make it on my own; this is beyond me. I just don't have what it takes!"

To such a prayer, I believe His response would be, "Good—you were never meant to be adequate on your own. Now, relax and allow Me to think through your mind, and I'll reveal My strategy and show you how you will accomplish it with My strength." We don't have to thrash about with uncertainty. The Lord will guide and provide.

Rejoice with those who rejoice, and weep with those who weep.
                                        Romans 12:15

Be an affirmer. It is the power to bless. If we are to speak well of those people on the fringes of our lives who make things difficult for us, we certainly should be careful to motivate those close to us with love and not manipulate them with fear.

What we say to or about a person has the power to bless or curse. And a lack of blessing is in itself a curse. It locks a person into his or her own present stage of growth. We all need affirmation of our worth as persons and our potential to be more than we are now. Affirmation provides self-esteem and hope for our future. It is not dishonest, fulsome flattery, but a communication that we are *for* people and not against them.

An affirmer is one who has experienced the ultimate affirmation of Christ. In spite of all that we've done and been, He loves us. He came to live and die for us that we might know that we are loved and forgiven. Now, as reigning Lord, God with us, He constantly reassures us that we belong to Him. He will never let us go.

When we know that, we can become affirmers of others even when they frustrate us. What they do cannot keep us from believing in what they can become by Christ's transforming power. Our trust is in what He will do; our only responsibility is to affirm that we love them.

A vital expression of our affirmation is to be involved with people in their times of delight and times of suffering. Life is a bittersweet blend of success and failure, joy and sorrow. As genuine affirmers of other people, we are to be willing to share not only their mountain-peak experiences but their darkest valleys as well.

Love your enemies, bless those who curse you.

Matthew 5:44

Secure in God's love, I will not surrender my self-worth to the opinions and judgments of others. When I am rejected, I will not retaliate; when I am hurt, I will allow God to heal me. Knowing the pain of rejection, I will seek to love those who suffer from its anguish.

When we look back over the years, we realize how the Lord strategically placed people in our lives who believed in us and spurred us on. We've actually seen the goodness of the Lord in these people. When we were discouraged, they believed in our potential; when we were tempted to give up on ourselves, they communicated hope.

I've come to believe that the Lord balances the scales: When we are rejected by someone, He sends someone else to encourage us. In fact, when I am downhearted I actually anticipate with expectancy the person He will use to mediate His uplifting love. I pray, "Well, Lord, who will it be this time?" I've never been disappointed.

People express their needs in their tone of voice, the expression on their faces, and in their body language. Life is difficult for most people. A ministry of encouragement leaves us little time to nurse our own feelings of rejection.

Recently the board of elders and the pastors of our church had a discussion concerning the people in our lives who had made the greatest impact on us, and we considered what we remember most about them. A large number of us had been introduced to Christ by the encourager He put in our lives. The discussion pushed us to ask ourselves, "How many of us are encouragers?"

The Lord delights in surprising us in the way He sends people to us when we need help and in the opportunities He gives us to help others. That makes life an exhilarating adventure.

Not everyone who says to Me, "Lord, Lord," shall enter the kingdom of heaven, but he who does the will of My Father in heaven.

Matthew 7:21

Today I will turn over the control of my life to the Lord. I will trust His control over what I was never meant to control. With His guidance I will take responsibility for what He has given me to do for His glory and by His power.

Here are six ways to accept Christ's control.

1. Admit that the need to be in charge of your life has resulted in a fear of losing control. Acknowledge that this is rooted in pride and that you need to receive more of the Lord's grace in your life.

2. Humbly tell the Lord about your panic over losing control. Accept His healing love and forgiveness for the limits you've placed on yourself and other people by always wanting to be in charge.

3. Make today the first day of a new beginning. Commit your life to the Lord's authority.

4. Experiment with trust and experience the results. Move quickly to the problems and needs you face right now. Give them over to Christ's control.

5. Keep a logbook in which you record what you have committed to Christ and what happens. Write a few paragraphs daily about the results of living under Christ's control. Discover how He works and note what is happening to heal your fears.

6. Ask the Lord to assign you challenges with people and situations needing His love and power. Trust Him!

I firmly believe that anyone who follows these six suggestions for thirty days will experience an exhilarating release and will never again be tempted to control everything and everybody again.

*Inasmuch then as the children have partaken of flesh and blood, He
Himself likewise shared in the same, that through death He might destroy
him who had the power of death, that is, the devil, and release those who
through fear of death were all their lifetime subject to bondage.*

Hebrews 2:14–15

I will face my eventual physical death and claim that I am alive eter-
nally. Therefore, I can live abundantly without panic for the rest of my
time on earth.

In the interval between Christ's resurrection and His return, physical illness and death will confront us. But through the miracle of our own
personal, spiritual resurrection now and our regeneration into new
people in Christ, we can know with assurance that our physical dying
will be only a transition in the onward flow of our eternal life.

The conquest of the fear of death begins with Christ's death and resurrection. That's not just "Easter talk." It is the central fact that sparks
faith and provides the solid reason for assurance. The preexistent Christ,
the One through whom all things were made, the Author of life, the creating power of God, lived among us as Life in all its fullness. He who said,
"I have come that they may have life, and that they may have it more
abundantly" (John 10:10) and "I am the way, the truth, and the life"
(John 14:6), is the same Lord who suffered on the cross for our forgiveness and rose from the dead as victor over the power of death.

Christ reigns as Lord to love us, to give us the gift of faith in Him,
and to enable us to claim His triumphant defeat of death by rising from
the dead. His resurrection is our personal assurance that death holds no
power over us. It's more than an idea we accept; it's an experience that
can transform us.

For that, we need a firsthand experience of the presence of the resurrected, living Lord and a personal realization that because He lives we
also shall live now and forever.

Jesus said to her, "I am the resurrection and the life. He who believes in Me, though he may die, he shall live."

John 11:25

*P*reparation for death begins now. It's so much more than claiming Christ's victory over the grave. That's only the beginning. The greatest miracle of the living Lord is our resurrection, not just at the time of our physical death, but now. Without that, we are unprepared to die and unable to live triumphantly without fear.

Christ said, "I am the resurrection and the life. He who believes in Me, though he may die, he shall live. And whoever lives and believes in Me shall never die" (John 11:25–26).

Well, do you believe it? Yes, we say, but often in a vague way that does little to overcome our own panic about death. It is true that we claim Christ's promise when a loved one dies or when we are seriously ill. But often we are doing little more than clutching for immortality and wishing that in some mysterious way our physical death won't be the end. But even with that, we loathe the eventuality of death. Why?

The idea that we will live forever does little to overcome our fear of death because, if that is all we have, we are haunted with a deeper fear— where and how we will spend our forever. That's why repeated affirmation that death is not an ending really makes us more fearful. It's what might happen after death that makes dying so frightening. That's why to many the idea of immortality is meaningless. Life after death? Who wants to live forever?

Only those people for whom heaven has begun now want to live forever. For the Christian, eternal life is now, through the life, death, and resurrection of Jesus. His promise wasn't just to "live forever." Instead, He gave us life with both quality and quantity.

Though now you do not see Him, yet believing, you rejoice with joy inexpressible and full of glory, receiving the end of your faith—the salvation of your souls.

1 Peter 1:8–9

Christ invades our lives with the power of His grace. In countless ways, He shows us that the life we are living is no life at all in comparison with abundant life in Him. He helps us admit that we are sinners, separated from God. Persistently and tenderly, Christ creates in us a profound sense of our emptiness and loneliness. Lovingly, He forces us to see what we are doing to hurt ourselves and others. He faces us with the disturbing truth that our arrogant efforts to run our own lives are failing. Not even our good works and achievements qualify us for status with God or assurance of eternal life.

It's usually some crisis that breaks our pride, some challenge that convinces us we don't have what it takes, or some opportunity that's beyond us, that forces us to admit our need for Christ. For some people, the need for Christ is realized at a time of failure. For others the need surfaces in response to the needs of people and the cultural plight of the world. For still others, the need for Christ is realized by the witness of Christians who are attempting honestly to live out their faith each day. The Lord will use whatever is necessary to break through our defenses and open us up to the reality of His love for us.

It is then that we begin to experience the joy in losing our lives by being disciples of Jesus. As His followers, we submit ourselves to His leadership in every decision because we want Him to be the absolute Lord of our lives.

The great good news of all times is that when we respond, accepting Him as our Savior *and* committing our lives to Him as Lord, we are resurrected out of an old life into a new life in Him. It's then that heaven begins, and with it comes the exciting process of regeneration.

Be kindly affectionate to one another with brotherly love, in honor giving preference to one another.

Romans 12:10

*T*oday, I commit myself to motivating people with love rather than motivating them with fear.

Our love must be expressed in unfailing friendship. Being an understanding and caring friend may well be our most Christ-like act.

Friendship has become a lightweight word in our time. Not so in the Scriptures. It was the highest affirmation of Abraham that he was called a friend of God. Jesus ushered His disciples into a sublime level of intimacy. To be Christ's friend means befriending others.

Paul lists very specific ways to express that friendship. We are to be kind in communicating real affection for the people we want to help. That means telling people how important they are to us, how much we value them, and how fervently we believe in them and their potential.

We are to treat them as brothers or sisters who long for the Lord's best in their lives. Time with them is given high priority. Listening and caring about their needs honors them as persons.

We are to be available, quick to respond to their call for help without hesitation. Night or day we are to be on call as truly reliable friends of those we are seeking to help and inspire.

Is this too much to ask? Not if we think of the people we're trying to help in the context of serving the Lord.

The thought that Christ may come to us in the very people who sometimes frustrate us the most—in the people we want to change—fills us with awe. How we respond to them is really our response to Christ. But the liberating assurance is that He will give us the love for people that's required to motivate them.

Be kindly affectionate to one another with brotherly love, . . . rejoicing in hope, patient in tribulation, continuing steadfastly in prayer.

Romans 12:10, 12

*P*ray for the people you want to motivate. We need to spend more time talking to the Lord about a person we want to help than we spend talking to him or her!

Steadfast, consistent, prolonged prayer gives us both hope and patience. Praying for people helps us focus on what the Lord wants for them rather than on our ideas of what they should be or do. Intercessory prayer is not for the purpose of getting the Lord to accomplish our vision for people. Rather, we are to allow Him to show us what He wants to do in their lives.

So often my frustration over people has driven me to prayer for them. I usually begin by telling the Lord my agenda for them. Not surprisingly, that never works. But when I commit the people to Him and ask for His vision, what I begin to see is so much greater than my wishes. Then my prayers shift into high gear. I know that what I'm asking for is what the Lord is ready to give. I can rejoice in the hope that in His timing and way, it shall be so.

But not only does prayer clarify our hopes for people, it also gives us patience in the process of trying to help them. We need not be precipitous and resort to using fear tactics. Instead we can know that the Lord is at work in the people for whom we pray.

With infinite wisdom He's influencing people's thoughts, creating a desire to change. As He works out His purpose in circumstances, He is arranging opportunities and preparing the way for our efforts to encourage people. Christ will be with us to love through us, to inspire the right words, and to give us strength when we get discouraged.

Be renewed in the spirit of your mind.

Ephesians 4:23

The central challenge of the Christian motivator is to help people envision what their lives would be like if committed to Christ, filled with His Spirit, and guided by His priorities and goals for them. Our task is not to bend them to our will or our ideas of what might be best for them. Instead, we are to ask penetrating questions that press them to evaluate where they are going in their lives, the kind of persons they want to be, and the quality of relationships they want to have. Our challenge is to help put people in touch with the Master.

Too few Christians have discovered the gift of the indwelling mind of Christ. That's why our thinking about life is often so confused, our values and priorities are so inconsistent with His, and our personalities are so far from being like Him. Any effort to motivate people to change or grow that skims over the deepest need we all have—to receive more of the mind of Christ—is surface meddling that brings no lasting results.

Often, problems and crises provide opportunities to talk with people about the direction and goals of their lives. The presence of conflict in our relationships should awaken us to be sensitive to the kinds of things we may be doing that would turn people off and stand in the way of their response to the Lord.

Any confrontation must always be preceded by caring and companionship. Only then can we share with people how Christ is working in our lives to deal with problems or challenges similar to theirs. It's then that they will feel free to ask themselves hard questions about their lives, and it's only when they have come to their own conclusions about their needs that we can lovingly share our hope and vision for them.

Be of the same mind toward one another. Do not set your mind on high things, but associate with the humble. Do not be wise in your own opinion.

Romans 12:16

*I*n the dynamic process of motivating people, vulnerability about our own needs and discoveries is essential. Only a person who is changing can help others to change. No one has it all together. Anyone who tries to pretend that he has is disqualified as a motivator. In fact, we can reproduce in others only what we are constantly rediscovering in our own lives. Since the things that usually disturb us in others are the very things that either have been or are trouble spots in our own lives, we can readily recognize them and respond creatively.

Vulnerability makes us approachable. When we are free to share what the Lord is doing with the raw material of our imperfect personalities, people are drawn to us and feel free to share their lives with us. Since the Lord is never finished with us, there's always a next step of growth we need to take.

With all my mind and heart, I believe that motivating people with love is the only alternative to manipulating them with fear.

Usually, my impatience is caused by inner impatience with myself. That's when I must take an extra measure of time in my own prayers to receive fresh grace. The Lord is faithful: He reminds me of how patient He has had to be with me over the years. In these times of prayer I am refreshed and renewed to be a loving and vulnerable motivator of people.

Believe me, the Lord has a way of knocking down our arrogant perfectionism by showing us what we really are. At such moments we become well aware that the kind of growth we are trying to inspire in others is also needed in our own lives.

And we know that all things work together for good to those who love
God, to those who are the called according to His purpose.

Romans 8:28

I will give up the vague idea that given time, things work out. I will
boldly face the future unafraid with the sure confidence that God will
work all things together for my ultimate good and His glory.

The crucial truth the Lord, our Interpreter, wants to make plain is
that He will use everything that happens to us for the accomplishment
of His awesome purpose.

We can't face the future without fear until we are absolutely sure of
that truth. Of course, we still make mistakes, bring problems on ourselves, and resist the Lord's best for our lives. But there is just no way one
can face the future with confidence without the firm hope that the Lord
will make the best of our efforts and help us to grow through our failures.

At the same time it is important we understand that not all of our
problems are of our own making. Often we are victims of other people's
ineptness or confused motives. Our future is peopled with the full spec-
trum of proud, selfish, competitive, greedy humankind. Our tomorrows
will be invaded by conflict and broken relationships. But we can endure
the people problems if only we know for sure that the Lord will help us
and that He will use even the difficulties to deepen our relationship with
Him.

Our assurance that He will use all things for our growth and His glory
must also extend to the realities of pain, sickness, and death. In it all, we
will need to know that He is both our healer and our strength to endure.
We will know His miraculous interventions and His patience when we
need to wait. Mysteriously, He will use our times of physical weakness to
teach us to depend on Him. When we walk through the valley of the
shadow of death, He will be there to lead us all the way to heaven.

Therefore do not worry about tomorrow, for tomorrow will worry about its own things. Sufficient for the day is its own trouble.

                                                    Matthew 6:34

*B*elieving that God works all things together for good does not exempt us from the difficulties of life, but it does assure us of exceptional power in handling them. It helps to remember that God does not send trouble to force us to grow. There's already an abundance of trouble in this fallen, rebellious world that refuses to accept His sovereignty. And yet, in spite of humankind's rejection of Him, He rules and overrules to protect, guide, and care for "those who are the called according to His purpose."

The way the Lord "works things together for good" is to block us from getting into some troubles, strengthen us in others, and turn still others into stepping stones. Nothing escapes His loving providence. He is constantly working to increase our joys and strengthen us in our difficulties.

The Greek verb for "works together" also means "to work with." The Lord not only works things together with perfect timing for our good, but He works with us in helping us understand what He is doing in and through us. We discover that often it is in life's tight places, troublesome problems, and painful experiences that we have made the longest strides in our growth as people.

That's the confidence that cures our fears of the future. We are promised neither a trouble-free future nor one in which things will eventually work out. What we are promised is that God will work all things together with creative continuity for our ultimate good. Tomorrow is under His control. We don't have to try to hold back the dawn or flinch at the problems it may bring.

We can rest comfortably with the assurance that God knows what He's doing! He's with us in Christ!

> *But as it is written: "Eye has not seen, nor ear heard, Nor have entered into the heart of man the things which God has prepared for those who love Him."*
>
> *1 Corinthians 2:9*

I confess my fearful imagination and I ask the Lord through His Spirit to make my imagination a channel of His vision and not a breeding place of fear.

We've heard, "It's all in your imagination," all through our lives. That saying has been used to convince us that our fears were hallucinations or self-deceptions. Our fears were dismissed as absurd and exaggerated.

I want to say "It's all in your imagination" with a different meaning—stressing the importance of the imagination rather than ridiculing it.

All thought is processed by imagination. That's why a Christ-anointed imagination is so vital. Without that liberating gift our worst ideas of frightening possibilities will be aggravated and intensified.

The circuit between our imagination and our emotions and body systems will be activated. Powerful feelings of fear will pump adrenaline into our bloodstream. Inordinate stress will result.

The only way to reverse the process is, indeed, all in our imaginations. And Christ can do it. When we surrender our imaginations to His control, He actually blocks some fears from even entering them. Others He reorients by showing us how He will be bringing good out of troublesome situations. Most of all, He keeps our imaginations so busy picturing what He wants us to be and do that there's little time left to look for new things to worry about.

The Lord wants to set us free to focus on His strategy for our lives, families, and churches. We can't serve Him effectively if we are crippled with a fearful imagination. And yet He waits for us to ask for the transforming miracle of His anointing of our imaginations.

For this reason we also, since the day we heard it, do not cease to pray for you, and to ask that you may be . . . strengthened with all might, according to His glorious power, for all patience and longsuffering with joy.

Colossians 1:9, 11

Our confidence is not that things work out, but that God works out things!

With that assurance we can retake the twelve steps to living without fear we've been considering the past few days. I've never outgrown my need to review them daily and claim the Lord's power for each bold step. As I do, the Lord reminds me of His fear-conquering presence.

Fear not, I am with you. I will never leave or forsake you. You are Mine for eternity.

Seek to please only Me, and you'll have nothing and no one to fear.

Face your fears, retrace them to their root in your soul, displace them with My indwelling presence, and erase them with an assurance of My forgiving love.

Love yourself as I love you. I have healed your frightening memories. My love casts out fear.

You don't have to worry about being inadequate ever again. I am your strength, wisdom, and courage.

When others reject you, be sure of My unqualified love for you.

Let go of your own control and humbly trust Me to guide you each step of the way.

You have the gift of imagination to picture and live My best for your life.

Don't spend your life worrying about sickness and death—live your life to the fullest now.

You don't need fear to manipulate people anymore. You are free to motivate them with love.

Be sure of this—the "good work" I have begun in you will be completed. You have nothing to fear. I love you!

*The Beatitudes are the Master's
Magna Carta
of a truly happy life.
The happiness He offers is rooted in grace
nurtured in profound joy,
and expressed in our daily life
and relationships.
Happiness is the outer expression of the
inner experience of grace-oriented joy.
It is knowing we are loved unreservedly
and forgiven unconditionally.
The Beatitudes help us grasp the
reality of that assurance.
They tell us what we can be and do
to experience
a profound intimacy with God
that will give us a
happiness the world or
the people of our lives
can neither give nor take away.*

Therefore you shall be perfect, just as your Father in heaven is perfect.
Matthew 5:48

One of the most moving times of renewal in my life took place on the Mount of Beatitudes above the Sea of Galilee. There, on the site where Jesus delivered the Sermon on the Mount, I would read a few verses of His message and then try to picture in my mind's eye the Master delivering the words. What had been blunted with familiarity in my mind came alive with fresh intensity and meaning.

I'll never forget the experience of imagining what it must have been like when the disciples and the crowd first heard the bracing promise, "You must be perfect, just as your Father in heaven is perfect." I pictured the astonishment on the faces of the people and their amazed exchanges with each other. I too was startled, as if really hearing the promise for the first time. The rest of the day was spent thinking and praying about what Jesus meant. I was gripped by the realization that the promise is really the secret of continuous, authentic renewal.

I think Jesus promised that we shall accomplish our purpose or goal even as the Father accomplishes His. But what is the Father's purpose? To help us fulfill our purpose. His goal is to enable us to live at full potential, living life as He planned it to be lived. We shall be all that He has meant us to be because it is the Father's "good pleasure" to accomplish it.

So the promise of the Father through Christ is not a challenge to human perfectionism but an assurance that there is unlimited power available for us to be His daughters and sons, expressing our family likeness by emulating His giving, forgiving, unstintingly generous heart. The early church father Irenaeus was on target: "The glory of God is a person fully alive." The triumph of the purpose of God is to reproduce that glory and majesty in us. Awesome? Yes!

Each of the eight Beatitudes we will consider in the following days reveals a secret of how to experience the glory of being fully alive.

Blessed are the poor in spirit, For theirs is the kingdom of heaven.
Matthew 5:3

*W*e are shocked when we consider the secret of true happiness. The poor in spirit? How can poverty of spirit bring the blessedness of true happiness?

What Jesus meant was that happiness is rooted in humbleness in a person's deep, inner self; his or her spirit.

The first step to happiness is to cry honestly, "God help me!" The humble-spirited have three sublime qualities: awe, which issues in wonder and praise; realization of need; and receptivity to what God wants to give more than we dare to ask. J. B. Phillips was on the mark when he translated the Beatitude, "How happy are the humble-minded, for the kingdom of heaven is theirs!"

Jesus is congratulating those in whom He found the maturity of true humility. For me, the essence of the first Beatitude is, "O how very happy are those of you who know your need for God. Ask Him to help you and be willing to receive His blessings." Unhappiness is always caused by self-sufficiency that arrogantly demands our making it on our own strength.

The opposite of humility is pride. Charles H. Spurgeon warned us not to be proud of race, face, or place. The reason is that none of these can make us happy. Pride keeps us from the joy of receiving what God wants to give: Himself. Forgiveness and love. Intimate companionship.

Pride is the result of the deepest kind of inferiority. It is the sure sign of profound insecurity. Phillips Brooks said, "The true way to be humble is not to stoop until you are smaller than yourself, but to stand at your real height against some higher nature that will show you what the real smallness of your greatness is." Only Jesus Christ can do that for us!

Blessed are those who mourn, For they shall be comforted.

Matthew 5:4

The Greek word for "comfort" in the second Beatitude is inexhaustible in the richness of its meaning. Basic and most important, it is the word that describes the companionship of the Lord with us. He is the Comforter who comes to us in our time of need. He is waiting, longing to invade us with forgiveness and love.

But the Comforter does more than accept and assure us. The same Greek word also means a helper who stands by our side—a witness, a counselor. He becomes our ally in life's battles.

The Holy Spirit, the Lord with us—presence and power—is the Comforter. All that He is ready to do in us and through us comes as a result of His anointing and infilling. Lasting happiness is not only knowing the Lord but being filled with His Spirit. That's the secret Jesus does not want us to miss in this Beatitude: We will be comforted—but only as we allow ourselves to mourn. Mourning in the profound sense Jesus intended is the kind that brings us to confession of our sins. It also gives us a deep empathy for the failures, hurts, and sufferings of others. And as we mourn over the troubled world in which we live, we feel with God His pain over the brokenness, rebellion, and pride of humankind. And then, at whatever point we find ourselves with God, ourselves, others, or society, we can say the appropriate three words that open us to receive the comfort of His presence.

Well, there we have them, the words that spell happiness. There is no lasting happiness until we experience and express forgiveness in the basic relationships of life. With God, we say, "Father, forgive me!" To ourselves we say, "I forgive myself!" With others, our prayer "Father, forgive them!" becomes "I forgive you!" and then we stand with the suffering of our world and say, "Father, forgive us!" That's what it means to mourn creatively. Happy are those who express the need for forgiveness, for they will know the power of the Comforter!

"Blessed are the meek, For they shall inherit the earth."
                                                                Matthew 5:5

The door to true happiness is double locked. It takes two keys to open. Jesus gives us both keys in His third Beatitude. The two keys are in the two words *gentle* and *inherit*. One key is relinquishment and the other is receptivity: surrender and expectation, trust and hope.

Meekness is not weakness. The Hebrew word for meek or gentle is *anaw*. Jesus' Beatitude has its roots in Psalm 37:11. "But the meek shall possess the land, and delight themselves in abundant prosperity." The work "meek" is used to describe a person, who, out of love and obedience, openly accepts the providence and guidance of God. He or she lives with the certainty of God's power and presence in all of life. The Greek word *praus* was used for an animal that had been tamed and had learned to follow the commands of its master. So meek really means receptive and leadable. Happiness depends on trusting the Lord and willingness to be led by Him.

The second key, inherit the earth for Jesus meant more than territory on the earth, but a quality of life to be lived on earth. He envisioned all that He would accomplish through His life, death, resurrection, and presence when He would reign as Lord of all. Today we know what is our inheritance. We are "joint heirs with Christ." Nothing that we either want or need is left out. Claiming the inheritance of our forgiveness, redemption, and Christ-filled lives frees us to live expectantly. Our inheritance is residual. Its resources are applied to life's challenges and opportunities. We can relax knowing that the Lord will act today at the right time and in the ultimately creative way.

So make today a day to live in the happiness of being under the reins of the reign of Christ and claim your inheritance as a loved and forgiven, cherished and chosen person.

Blessed are the meek, For they shall inherit the earth.

Matthew 5:5

*T*he gentle can wait for each new payment of their inheritance. They have been called to reign with Christ! He told those who trusted in Him that they would inherit the kingdom prepared for them (Matt. 25:34) and the gift of eternal life (Matt. 19:29) in quality now and forever. What more do we need? The kingdom of God is His reign, and eternal life is the intimate relationship with God that begins now and which death cannot end.

Paul speaks of the "riches of the glory of His inheritance in the saints" (Eph. 1:18), and Peter reminds us that in Christ we have "an inheritance incorruptible and undefiled and that does not fade away, reserved in heaven for you." But note that Peter goes on to tell us that daily payments of that inheritance are given to the gentle, "who are kept by the power of God" (1 Pet. 1:4–5).

The power of God, the Holy Spirit, is our inheritance to be received in life's tensions. The legacy of the Lord was, "You shall receive power when the Holy Spirit has come upon you" (Acts 1:8). That's the inexhaustible inheritance we can depend on. We will never be left alone. Sufficient power will be given for each demanding tension. The gifts of the Spirit are ours—wisdom, knowledge, discernment, insight, and faith. We will have all that we need for each situation. Life is unpredictable, but the Lord's presence will be predictable.

What the Holy Spirit will give in us will be coupled with what He will do around us to surprise us. Expectancy and true happiness are inseparable.

The Lord's question to us is, "Would you like to see My happiness room?" Our inheritance is there waiting. But the door is double-locked. Here are the keys: the surrender of meekness and the expectation of our legacy. And our response is to take the keys and open the door.

Blessed are those who hunger and thirst for righteousness, For they shall be filled.

Matthew 5:6

I had a dream. I was standing in front of thousands of people. The Lord drew near and stood beside me. "What's the greatest need in these people?" He asked. "And, what's the one thing you want to ask Me to give them?"

"Salvation . . . so they can live forever."

"No, Lloyd," He said. "They already have that. I completed that two thousand years ago. It's theirs!"

"Tell me, Lord!" I pleaded.

"I want My people to want Me!" He said winsomely and tenderly. "I long for My people to long for Me as much as I long for them."

"But, Lord," I protested, "I thought that the desire to know You was our gift to You, not Your gift to us. Isn't that what we do to claim what You've done for us?"

"That's where you have missed it! You want to take credit in choosing Me. You think it's some kind of human accomplishment when you think through truth and decide you can believe. Or when you give up the human struggle with problems and decide to trust Me. Or when you make a mess of things and need My forgiveness. These are not your gift or achievement, but My grace.

"Allow me to sear into your mind a basic, liberating truth: *What I desire, I inspire.* The longing to know Me and have a relationship with Me is My primary gift to My people whom I have chosen to belong to Me. The hunger and thirst of a consuming passion for Me is not a human choice but My blessing. I have made you right with Me through the cross. You *are* forgiven. I have given you the gift of faith to accept your righteousness in Me. And the desire to live righteously is inspired by Me. I have blessed you with the hunger and thirst for knowing Me and doing My will. Happiness is being a willing receiver and being filled!"

Blessed are you who hunger now, For you shall be filled. Blessed are you who weep now, For you shall laugh.

Luke 6:21

$\mathcal{I}$ remember calling on a woman in the hospital whose sickness had diminished her appetite and thirst. I'll never forget the happiness she expressed when she was taken off intravenous feeding and began to feel thirst and hunger pangs again. "I never knew what a blessing it was to be hungry," she said.

The same is true for spiritual hunger and thirst. It's a miracle of the LORD when He breaks through our diminished appetite that has been sated by distracting satisfactions that have left us undernourished and dehydrated spiritually.

A man said to me recently, "I'm really very dissatisfied with my life."

"Congratulations!" I exclaimed.

"What do you mean by that? My life is a mess. I'm not happy at all about the way things are going."

My second exclamation didn't please him any more than my first. "You are very fortunate!" I said.

I went on to explain. "Thank the LORD for your dissatisfaction. He's got something much better in store for you. The discontent you feel is a sign that you are a special, chosen person. The Lord is invading your life!"

As we talked, the man became very excited about what the Lord might be saying to him. But more than any change in his life, the real longing was for an intimate companionship with Him.

So often the things we find wrong in ourselves, other people, or our situations are manifestations of our yearning for God. He wants us to experience His love for us. Then we can see what's wrong in a different perspective and how they might be made right by His guidance and power.

Blessed are the merciful, For they shall obtain mercy.

Matthew 5:7

*I*f you had to choose one word to describe the nature of God, what word would you choose? All-powerful? All-knowing? Forgiving? Gracious?

My word would be *merciful*. Whatever other words I might use are all part of this magnificent quality of mercy. I'm not alone in my choice. In the Old Testament the word is used nearly two hundred times to describe the nature of God. The Hebrew word *chesedh* means both identification and empathy, involvement and intense feeling. It describes the feeling of getting inside a person's skin and feeling what he or she is feeling, hoping, or aching. God knows and cares about what's going on inside us. Mercy is our pain in His heart!

We need to savor that. God is not up there or out there, aloof from our needs. The mercy of God, from my experience and the biblical witness, is His favor, forgiveness, forbearance, and fortuitous intervention. Our pain in His heart results in outgoing, ingoing, and ongoing love for each of us. The psalmist summarized all the aspects of mercy when he exclaimed, "Bless the LORD, O my soul; And all that is within me, bless His holy name! Bless the LORD, O my soul, And forget not all His benefits: Who forgives all your iniquities, Who heals all your diseases, Who redeems your life from destruction, Who crowns you with lovingkindness and tender mercies, Who satisfies your mouth with good things, So that your youth is renewed like the eagle's" (Ps. 103:1–5).

That's our theme song! Everything within us wants to bless the Lord because He can feel our pain in His heart and respond with unmerited favor for us, forgiving us even before we ask, forbearing our rebellion and sin, surprising us with fortuitous, on-time blessings when we expect them or deserve them the least. The experience of the mercy of God is the basis of trust and confidence, strength and courage, hope and joy.

[You] pay attention to the one wearing the fine clothes and say to him, "You sit here in a good place," and say to the poor man, "You stand there," or, "Sit here at my footstool."

James 2:3

*W*hy is it so few feel the happiness of the mercy of God? The psalmist tells us: "But the mercy of the LORD is from everlasting to everlasting on those who fear Him, and His righteousness to children's children, to such as keep His covenant, and to those who remember His commandments to do them" (Ps. 103:17–18). Ah, there it is. A true experience of mercy results in awe, never taking God for granted. Those who receive mercy keep the covenant and do the commandments. The two great commandments were to love God(Deut. 6:5) and one's neighbor as oneself (Lev. 19:18). God's people were to be distinguished by having His nature imputed. The recipients of mercy were to be merciful. But were they? The sad account of the people of God is that they were not—neither to each other nor to other nations. The Old Testament closes with the pleas of the prophets for the people to do justice, have mercy, and walk humbly with their God. But not even their refusal took their pain out of God's heart; it only intensified it. That's why He came, mercy incarnate, in Jesus Christ. Favor indeed. Forgiveness unreserved. Forbearance unlimited. Fortification while we were helpless. A manger. A vivid personification of mercy. A cross. The resurrection. Merciful comfort in the Holy Spirit.

When Mercy Himself revealed the heart of God, He put it clearly so we could not miss it. "Blessed are the merciful For they shall obtain mercy." A congratulatory challenge. "Bravo to the merciful!" He said. "You can experience more of the mercy of God!"

But God, who is rich in mercy, because of His great love with which He loved us.

Ephesians 2:4

*P*aul reminded the Ephesians that God is rich in mercy. And yet for his own relationships he had to rediscover again and again what being merciful meant. The account of his relationship with Mark is a good example that even a spiritual giant like Paul had trouble being merciful to a young missionary failure who had defected in Pamphylia. The apostle refused to take Mark along on a subsequent missionary journey at the cost of contention with Barnabas and, in fact, their parting. But near the end of Paul's life he wrote to the Colossians, commending Mark as one who was with him in prison and affirmed him with love. Fresh mercy had been received and expressed. I wonder about the Marks in my life—and yours. Who needs mercy from us?

Take a sheet of paper. On the top, write, "Relationships in which I want to communicate mercy." On one side of the sheet, list the persons and situations specifically. Then on the other side, put down which aspects of mercy that most need to be mediated through your words, attitudes, and actions. Describe what you will say, how you will look and act, as you express mercy.

Two things will happen. You will be amazed again that God has your pain in His heart. Suddenly, you will feel the pain of others in yours. No longer will there be negative judgment or aloof, uninvolved sympathy. Your heart will beat with the Lord's. And at the deepest levels of your soul, you'll hear Him say, "Congratulations, blessed one! You now know the true happiness of feeling what others are feeling. The mercy you have received from Me will now flow from you to them. You and I are one in the ministry of mercy!"

Having then gifts differing according to the grace that is given to us, let us use them: . . . he who exhorts, in exhortation; he who gives, with liberality; he who leads, with diligence; he who shows mercy, with cheerfulness.

Romans 12:6, 8

The other day a man told me he could not forgive what his wife had done to him. "Then I hope you never fail!" I said. The man was alarmed. Then I pressed him to tell me of the times in his life when he had felt the mercy of God. He found that difficult. No wonder he was so hard on his wife's failure. I tried to tell him about his pain in God's heart, the forgiveness that had been given before he asked, the continuing relationship as if he had never failed, acceptance in countless new beginnings. When I went back over Calvary and the immensity of God's mercy, the man's hard shell of judgmentalism was finally cracked. With a fresh realization of mercy, he was able to make a commitment to be merciful to his wife as God has been to him.

Some time after that visit, I talked to his wife. She was grateful for the breakthrough her husband had made. She said, "I'm so thankful for our new relationship. The last few years have been very difficult. I kept feeling I had to do something to measure up because of my mistake. It's been hard to live with a merciless pout."

A merciless pout! So often we say we forgive or try to express in spite of love but hold another person at arm's length with our hurt and bruised feelings. We create a purgatory for people to wait in until we decide they are worthy of our acceptance.

Many of us think of ourselves as magnanimous people who express forbearance and forgiveness. But the favor is lacking. Our body language shouts our lack of mercy in a bland tolerance or a sticky sweetness that hides our real feelings.

Paul challenges us to show mercy with cheerfulness. Mercy with cheerful laughter and joy! There's an antidote for a merciless, purgatorial pout!

Blessed are the pure in heart, For they shall see God.

                                                            Matthew 5:8

*T*hink of the many different ways we use the words *I see*. We say, "I see," when we focus something with the vision of our eyes. What a magnificent gift seeing is! We can behold the wonder of God's signature in the natural world.

But we use the same words for intellectual comprehension. We say, "Oh, now I see!" when truth has been registered in our brain with understanding. After the gift of insight into some complicated thought problem, we say, "I never saw that before." A scientist in his laboratory, upon making a great discovery, will say, "Now I see what I've been searching for!"

In the same way, in the realm of spiritual growth, we say, "I now see myself as I am and see God in His love and forgiveness." Spiritual perception is seeing. We exclaim, "I was blind and now I see!" when we receive the gift of faith.

Also, in interpersonal relationships when our intuitive capacity is exercised with empathy, we express our identification with another person in mixed metaphor, "I see how you feel." With the gift of our hearts, we "see" with x-ray penetration into the emotional condition around us. We are able to see what is happening to us and others. We see with the gift of wisdom.

The reason for the multiple uses of the words *I see* is that we have eyes in our hearts as well as in our heads. In the sixth Beatitude, Jesus congratulates those who have twenty-twenty heart-eyes. "Happy are you! Congratulations to you! You are blessed, you who are single-hearted, for with your heart-eyes you shall see God." The Beatitude offers a potential and a promise and, in between, a qualification. It is an affirmation and an assurance and holds the danger of an affliction. We all have eyes in our hearts, but not everyone sees. Seeing requires purity of heart. A pure heart is one that is cleansed of divided loyalties. Sören Kierkegaard said that purity of heart is to will one thing: to glorify and serve God.

The eyes of your understanding being enlightened.

Ephesians 1:18

A man who had just had a cataract operation was amazed at what he could see again. He said something we all may need to say. "Now that I have had the cataracts of my eyes removed, I need your help to remove the cataracts of my soul. I feel a murky, cloudy, fuzzy veil over my heart." We talked at length about his longing to see with his heart. Though he was a church member, he had never committed his life to Christ nor invited Him to take up residence in him. He had no ultimate priority. His life had drifted among a multiplicity of loyalties and responsibilities. I explained Jesus' promise in the sixth Beatitude and asked him if he wanted a pure, single heart in which Christ reigned supreme. He did and we prayed together.

That day in the hospital was the turning point. Some months later he came to see me. "I'm amazed at what I can see of God in my own life and the world around me. My eyes in both my head and heart have been opened!" Paul would have been pleased. What he prayed for the Ephesians had happened to this man. I shared the verse and it is now his life verse. " [I] do not cease to give thanks for you, making mention of you in my prayers: that the God of our Lord Jesus Christ, the Father of glory, may give to you the spirit of wisdom and revelation in the knowledge of Him, the eyes of your understanding being enlightened; that you may know what is the hope of His calling, what are the riches of the glory of His inheritance in the saints" (Eph. 1:16–18). The same gift is offered to all of us. All we need is the desire of a Bartimaeus. When Jesus asked what he wanted Him to do for him, his response was clear, decisive, insistent: "Lord, I want to see!" The same petition is the prelude to the healing of the spiritual eyes of our hearts. And Jesus' word is, "You receive not because you ask not."

Draw near to God and He will draw near to you. Cleanse your hands, you sinners; and purify your hearts, you double-minded.

James 4:8

$\mathcal{R}$ecently, I met a man who told me that he earned his living as an "attention getter." That caught my interest. "What do you mean?" I asked. His reply was fascinating. "My job is to get the attention of the American people. I am an advertising executive. It is my task to use everything I can—media, print, billboards—to impress the people with the absolute necessity of buying the products I promote."

That same week I met with a group of businessmen who talked about the one thing in their lives that made it difficult to be faithful and obedient to Christ. The last man to share cut to the core of our inability to see with our hearts. "I have too many commitments competing with my ultimate commitment. I'm going in a hundred directions. I think about the Lord only in a crisis." A distracted attention—the man's heart was not pure, single, focused. All he could see were the confusing demands.

A woman confessed the same problem in a different way. "What do you do with a wandering attention? When I pray, I can't keep my mind on God for more than a few minutes. I drift off into all sorts of worries, fears, and fantasies."

All these encounters occurred while I was thinking about our heart-eyes and why so few Christians see. James gives us more of an answer than we want. What is in our heart determines what the eyes of our heart see. It is what's inside that counts. The old saying is wrong: "What you see is what you get." In the light of this Scripture it should be, "What you've got is what you see." When we focus our attention on the Lord and open our hearts to Him, He comes within us to dilate our spiritual vision.

The lamp of the body is the eye. If therefore your eye is good, your whole body will be full of light.

Matthew 6:22

$\mathcal{A}$ woman exclaimed wistfully, "How I wish my husband could see me. The real me! He looks at me, but somehow he looks right past me. I try to tell him about me, but he doesn't *see* what I'm saying." The tragedy is that her husband is a Christian who has never had Christ's healing touch on the scales over his heart-eyes. His wife and his friends all long for him to be healed. He is missing the wonder of intimacy in which the essential *I* meets the real *you*.

A personal word. I had been a Christian and a pastor for several years before I had an experience that healed my heart-eyes. It was when I discovered the promise of the indwelling Christ that I began to see. A new discernment came as a result. I began to see beneath the surface of people and events. The indwelling Lord refracted my spiritual vision and gave me x-ray intuition. I saw the meaning of the Scriptures as never before. An understanding of how to communicate Christ's strength for people's struggles was imputed as a gift. Sensitivity in situations multiplied my analytical capacity. Most of all, I began to "see" my family and friends. I could say with Elizabeth Barrett Browning: "Earth's crammed with heaven, and every common bush afire with God." The secret was in saying yes to the Lord's offer to live in me and be my heart-eyes. Christ Himself is the eye of the heart.

Happiness is having eyes in your heart. Congratulations to the single-hearted, for you will know intimate communion with the Lord and see with His eyes!

We need the peace of Christ
especially in times of failure.
In every human failure there are
three elements: what happened,
how we react to what happened,
and what we allow Christ
to give us to change our
reaction to what happened.

Blessed are the peacemakers, For they shall be called sons of God.
                                                                    Matthew 5:9

*T*here is a delightful New Year's Eve custom in Scotland called "first-footing it." The idea is to be the first person to step across a friend's threshold to wish him "Happy New Year!" and toast his health and happiness.

I want to build on that tradition in establishing what might be "The Holy Order of First-Steppers." Or it could be called "The Happy Fellowship of Initiative Reconcilers."

The only qualification necessary is that we be willing to take the first step. We all want to be first in something. This is our chance! We can be first-stepping peacemakers.

Our motto could be Jesus' challenging seventh Beatitude: "Blessed are the peacemakers, For they shall be called sons of God." The various translations of the Beatitude shed penetrating light on the meaning. The New English Bible has it, "How blest are the peacemakers; God shall call them his sons." J. B. Phillips renders it, "Happy are those who make peace, for they will be known as the sons of God!" William Barclay's incisive translation is, "Blessed are those who produce right relationships in every sphere of life, for they are doing a God-like work." My own study has resulted in something like this: "Happy are the initiating enablers of peace with God, themselves, and others, for they are the kin of God in the healing of the wounds of the world." However you put it, the impact of the Beatitude is the same. We are called to receive the peace of Christ and to take the initiative in sharing it in life's relationships and responsibilities.

Let the peace of God rule in your hearts.

Colossians 3:15

A vital credential of a peacemaker is freedom from gossip. Nothing dis-qualifies us in being reconcilers more than talking *about* people rather than talking *to* them. The old Spanish proverb is on target: "Whoever gossips to you will gossip of you."

Relationships are strained and guarded when we are not absolutely trustable. When we gossip to others, always the question can linger of what we will say about them.

A peacemaker never says anything about another person that he has not first said to that person directly. After that, why tell anyone else?

The reward of a peacemaker is to be called a son of God. There is no greater joy for parents than to have their children want to be like them. God has made us sons and daughters to reproduce His character in us.

The last part of this verse gives us the secret source of our strength to be peacemakers. God is an initiator. He came in Christ. He loves us before we respond, forgives us before we ask to be forgiven, blesses us even when we are undeserving. And when we accept our status as His cherished, beloved children, we begin to grow in His likeness. We shall be like Him in spreading peace.

Paul shared this same secret with the Corinthians. "Become com-plete. Be of good comfort, be of one mind, live in peace; and the God of love and peace will be with you" (2 Cor. 13:11). In other words, if we want to know God, we must join Him in what He is doing.

Therefore let us pursue the things which make for peace and the things by which one may edify another.

Romans 14:19

A woman said to me recently, "Why should I go to her? She hurt me! Let her take the first step." She missed the joy of being a first-stepper. A man confessed, "I'm filled with resentment and I'm depressed. I resent people, my job, and what life has dealt me." I tried to share that his inverted anger was causing the depression. We talked about the people he resented. "Why not go to them and talk out how you feel? Find out the causes of the broken relationships. Seek forgiveness where you're wrong and give forgiveness where you've been wronged." His response excluded him from being a first-stepper. "Why should I do that? I'm the one they should come to." I asked, "Would you forgive them and make peace if they did?" He was not ready for that question or the cost of the answer.

None of us finds it easy to be an initiator in making peace. It is a demanding, soul-stretching responsibility our Lord has given us. We cannot do it without Him. Peace is a key word of Jesus' life and ministry. He came to establish it, His message explained it, His death purchased it, and His resurrected presence enables it. The messianic predictions were that He would be the Prince of Peace (Isa. 9:6). The angels who announced His birth sang, "On earth, peace, goodwill toward men!" (Luke 2:14). His persistent word of absolution to sinners was, "Go in peace!" Just before He was crucified, the Lord's last will and testament was, "Peace I leave with you, My peace I give to you; not as the world gives do I give to you" (John 14:27). When the Lord returned after the resurrection, His first word to the disciples was "Shalom." Peace. The life of Jesus was saturated with His mission to bring the peace of God and to initiate the healing relationships of peace with God and with one another.

He Himself is our peace.

Ephesians 2:14

Peace is a sure sign that Christ has taken up residence in us. From within, He assures us that nothing can make Him stop loving us. He has settled our destiny on the cross. Paul knew that and wrote, "For it pleased the Father that in Him all the fullness should dwell, and by Him to reconcile all things to Himself, by Him, whether things on earth or things in heaven, having made peace through the blood of His cross" (Col. 1:19–20).

When we share that bold conviction, we can allow the peace of God to rule in our hearts (Col. 3:15). The word for "rule" in Greek is *umpire*. He calls the shots and keeps us from anything that would rob us of the peace He died to give us. He guards our hearts with His peace. "Be anxious for nothing, but in everything by prayer and supplication, with thanksgiving, let your requests be made known to God; and the peace of God, which surpasses all understanding, will guard your hearts and minds through Christ Jesus" (Phil. 4:6–7). Peace will be our protector and guide. It will settle our jangled nerves, and in the midst of conflict and confusion give us the assurance that God will work all together for good because He is in charge.

But we can give only what is real to us. Peacemaking begins with an experience of peace in our own hearts. When we have received the gift of peace, we know an ordered and harmonious functioning unity, wholeness, a being knit together. That is what happens when the character implant of Christ in us takes place. The fruit of the Spirit is ours. "The fruit of the Spirit . . . is peace" (Gal. 5:22).

I have been crucified with Christ; it is no longer I who live, but Christ lives in me; and the life which I now live in the flesh I live by faith in the Son of God, who loved me and gave Himself for me.

Galatians 2:20

*W*e need the peace of Christ especially in times of failure. In every human failure there are three elements: what happened, how we react to what happened, and what we allow Christ to give us to change our reaction to what happened. Usually we brood over the failure in our own strength. That almost always leads to remorse and to justifying ourselves by explaining it away or by blaming someone else or some other circumstances. On the other hand, the peace Christ offers is radically different. It is the peace that floods our hearts when we honestly acknowledge whatever part we've had in the failure. When we experience Christ's forgiveness, we can forgive ourselves. Out of that comes the freedom to forgive the people who may have caused the failure. Being a Christian doesn't mean we always have to take the blame, but it does mean that we must forgive. The sooner the better.

Failures bring us back to the death and the resurrection experience of profound peace. When we fail or must forgive someone whose failure has caused us pain, eventually we have to admit we can't handle it ourselves. That shatters our false pride. In a mysterious way that willful person inside us has to die so that the new person Christ wants to make us can live. I think that's a vital part of what it means to take up our cross. Our pride is crucified, we die to our own pride, and out of the ashes of whatever the failure was, we are raised up to a new beginning to live with the calm confidence of Christ's peace and the fear-dispelling strength of His courage. Then we can say with Paul, "I have been crucified with Christ; it is no longer I who live, but Christ lives in me; and the life which I now live in the flesh I live by faith in the Son of God, who loved me and gave Himself for me" (Gal. 2:20).

Therefore let us pursue the things which make for peace and the things by which one may edify another.

Romans 14:19

Our first step as peacemaker is toward ourselves. Most of us find it difficult to initiate peace with others because we are not at peace with the person who lives in our own skin. We need to meet that unique person inside. Often we are harder on that person than anyone else.

We find it difficult to forgive ourselves, even after we've heard and accepted the forgiveness of the cross. But it is blasphemy to contradict the Lord, and He has loved us unreservedly. We need to ask Him to help us love ourselves as much as He does. That alone will free us of self-condemnation, negation, and lambasting.

A test of our acceptance of ourselves as Christ-loved and forgiven persons will be abiding peace. A profound center of calm is the result of creative delight and enjoyment of ourselves. Happy are the peacemakers—with themselves.

The natural overflow of that inner peace will be a transformed attitude toward the people around us. Then we can become initiating peacemakers with others. That ministry has three parts: making peace between us and others; between people we know who are separated from one another because of misunderstanding, hurt, and hatred; and between groups in our society.

Paul gives us marching orders for all three: "Therefore let us pursue the things which make for peace" (Rom. 14:19).

Blessed are those who are persecuted for righteousness' sake, For theirs is the kingdom of heaven.

Matthew 5:10

*T*he church has never been without persecution, brash or subtle. The bold preaching of Christ and the adventuresome living of His message in all of life have consistently brought stern resistance and cruel rejection. From Pentecost to the present, the martyrs and heroes of the faith have suffered for what they believed. But never alone. The unseen Friend was there.

The Book of Acts is really the biography of that Friend at work through His friends. No prison could exclude Him, no stoning elude Him, no angry mob evict Him, no hatred expunge Him. He was with Peter before the Sanhedrin to give him boldness and with him on a tanner's roof in Joppa pressing him beyond the Judaic to the Gentile world. He was the Lord of Paul's Damascus road and the Lord of the Troas road and a call to evangelize Europe. Persecution in Philippi and Thessalonia was sustained in the knowledge that it was better to be in difficulty with the Lord than anywhere else without Him. Resurrection resiliency and the Lord's indwelling power never left Paul. He was constantly in trouble and never without Christ. The Lord's night visits and daily companionship brought courage. "Do not be afraid, but speak, and do not keep silent; for I am with you" (Acts 18:9–10).

What more do any of us need to know? Paul's question can be answered with assurance. "If God is for us, who can be against us?" (Rom. 8:31). Karle Wilson Baker was right: "Courage is fear that has said its prayers." And prayer is the cumulative expression of friendship with our Lord.

You are the salt of the earth; but if the salt loses its flavor, how shall it be seasoned?

Matthew 5:13

𝒫eople and their needs are our agenda. Our faith, expressed in the eight happy dimensions of the Beatitudes, is for our influence on others. When we settle that, life becomes blessed indeed! We were meant to have impact, influence, and inspiration in the lives of the people we touch.

When Jesus called the disciples the salt of the earth, He was giving them an affirming image of value, vitality, and viability. All three are implied, as a study of salt at that time reveals. Salt was used to pack fish, as the fishermen among the disciples knew. All the disciples knew that salt was very valuable. In fact, the word *salary* comes from the wages of a sack of salt paid to Roman soldiers: *sal*—salt; *salarus*—salary. Salt was also used beneath the tiles of an oven. But the main use of the precious commodity was to season and preserve food. Jesus' implied message is that our influence is to pervade, permeate, purify, and preserve. We are to be combatants against blandness and dullness. It is quite a revolution of images to think of ourselves as the zest and flavor of the world. But like salt, our influence is to be inadvertent. We are to bring out the essential qualities of others. No one can at the same time draw attention to himself and make others great.

Christ is the salt of our lives so that we can be the salt of the earth. All that we are to be to others, He first is to us. Each of the qualities of the Beatitudes is part of Christ's portrait. All are part of the seasoning of our influence. The Lord has called us to be a distinctly different, new breed of humanity. We are to be a model for the world, and He is the source of renewal and refurbishment for us. You and I are the salt of the earth. When Christ lives in us we will not lose our savor. Today, think of your life as zest for others!

Let your speech always be with grace, seasoned with salt.

Colossians 4:6

I will never forget when I first heard the four most powerful words a person can say to another. They changed my life. I can remember the occasion as if it happened yesterday.

I was a frightened seventeen-year-old speech student waiting in the wings of an auditorium to compete in the finals of a national oratorical contest. My future education and development hung on the results. I shook inside with anxiety. Pacing back and forth, I rehearsed in my mind the lines of my carefully prepared oration.

Then suddenly there was someone standing beside me. It was John Davies, my coach and inspiring teacher who had helped me find courage and confidence so often in my high school years. He turned me around, put his hands on my shoulders, looked me in the eye, and said the four esteem-building words, "I believe in you!" With that ringing in my heart, I went out to win the contest and an opportunity to go to college.

Through the years, these four words have been spoken when I needed them most. In times of challenge, of self-doubt, of opportunity, the Lord has given me friends who have dared to say, "I believe in you!" The words have turned fear into hope, uncertainty into courage, and anxiety into confidence.

It's one thing to have a friend say that, but it's all the more liberating to hear the Lord tell us that He believes in us. When the Savior of the world looks us in the eye and says, "I believe in you!" we know that anything is possible.

Salt is good, but if the salt loses its flavor, how will you season it? Have salt in yourselves, and have peace with one another.

Mark 9:50

*T*he other day, a man called me with a very generous offer. "I want to put you in touch with some very influential people." "Isn't everyone?" I asked. "No, I mean I want you to meet some really important people," he said persistently. "Isn't everyone?" I asked. "You don't understand," he said impatiently. "These people can open doors for you!" Again my response was, "Can't everyone?"

I appreciated the man's desire to help me, and I am thankful for what people in positions of power have done to encourage me through the years, but the man was missing the significance of his own and everyone's influence.

And yet the more I reflected on the man's offer, the more I realized that he had given me the three dimensions of influence entrusted to every Christian. We are all important as salt and light; we all have influence to help people find life as it was meant to be; and we all can be door-openers to help others step over the threshold to eternal life.

You are an influential person! Do you believe in your awesome power? Christ does. Every day, in hundreds of ways, you and I are influencing people about what it means (or does not mean!) to live the abundant life in Christ. If the people of our lives had to write a definition of Christianity from what they see and hear from us, what would they write? Our influence is either positive or negative. People are reading the signals all the time. What kind of salt and light have we been?

Let your light so shine before men, that they may see your good works and glorify your Father in heaven.

Matthew 5:16

*W*hat stands in the way of people seeing Christ's light burning in us? For some, it's our personalities, which need Christ's transformation; for others, it's privatism, which keeps us from sharing our faith; for still others, it is simply the lack of loving concern.

A woman who had been healed of a dreaded disease through a new method of treatment gave me an unsettling illustration. After she talked about her healing, she said, "What if I were at a party with you and someone suffering from the disease from which I've just been cured asked me to share the treatment that saved me? Wouldn't it be the height of ingratitude if I told him I never talked about it because it was too personal? In the same way many Christians hide their lights under a bushel."

We have been given the secret of true happiness. The Lord has come to us down the corridor of our crises when we've cried out, "Help me!" He has comforted us with forgiveness when we've prayed the words that spell happiness. Out of love, He has given us the two keys to unlock the abundant life. The consuming passion for righteousness He has desired from us He has inspired in us. Mercifully, He has felt our pain in His heart so that we could become the merciful people who empathize and communicate identifying love. He has healed our heart-eyes so that we can see our abject need and His adequacy and then *dilated* our vision to see the wonder of life, people, and the world. The original, initiating Peacemaker died on the cross to give us peace and make us first-steppers. And He's been our friend in all of life's struggles—all so that we could join Him in the ministry of reconciliation.

Listen to Him in the depth of your soul: "I believe in you. You are the light of the world!"

But now having been set free from sin, and having become slaves of God,
you have your fruit to holiness, and the end, everlasting life.

Romans 6:22

A woman said to me, "I really wish we'd stick to the simple gospel rather than all this talk about commitment and our ministry as members!" I could hardly believe what I had heard. I felt led to reply with a question couched in a bit of humor. "Which pages of the Bible do you want to tear out?" She didn't catch the humor, nor the challenge. Her idea of the church was a place of comfort and reassurance. Beneath that was a conception of a cultural brand of Christianity that calls for little personal involvement or consecration. She had heard little of what I was saying in expositions from the Scripture about surrendering our wills, inviting Christ to live in us, and becoming obedient disciples in sharing our faith and working for justice. There was a grid over her carefully protected, strong-willed ego. This woman had only part of the gospel, and she was stuck on dead-center spiritually.

There was nothing to do but put her on the top of my prayer list. She was using her brand of religion to oppose God. It took a crisis in her personal life with her son to force her to realize that she was not able to communicate the "simple gospel" she had cherished so long. When pious phrases and simplistic, guilt-producing admonitions didn't help her son, the Lord began to crack the hard shell around her mind. The difficulties finally led to her own commitment and a new life of both abiding in Christ and allowing Him to abide in her. Then she was given a whole new set of priorities conditioned by the kingdom and not her cultural religion.

The experience taught me again to take no one for granted and to realize that inside heads nodding in approval or displaying signs of comprehension there may be steel-trapped brains with the doors tightly closed. The encouraging thing is that the Spirit can and does open those doors!

But seek first the kingdom of God and His righteousness, and all these things shall be added to you.

Matthew 6:33

*I*f I live until I am eighty, I will have spent twenty thousand hours worrying about money.

I pay my bills twice a month. It takes me about five hours to go through them all and write all the checks. Stress often mounts when I get nearer the bottom of the stack and wonder if I'll have enough left to pay all I owe. I groan inside over the high cost of living and question my own or my wife's expenditures. When some company's computer has overcharged me, I feel like a victimized number rather than a person who seeks to be financially responsible. And when I talk over bills with my family I've been known to be less than saintly! In fact, my wife used to know which days I'd paid bills by the way I looked and acted when I came home. Though the Lord has always met our needs and been gracious to pull us out of difficulties in times of financial crisis, I tend to forget that and become anxious.

Is the Lord concerned about our daily choices when it comes to money? Yes! If the majority of our worries come from it and diminish our effectiveness, we can be sure He is ready and willing to help us. The key to financial management is Christ's own instruction to seek first God's kingdom and righteousness, and all things we *need* will be added to us.

That's more than just good advice. When we ask to receive the mind of Christ to control our thoughts, He does more than remind us of His admonition; He actually gives us the thoughts, discernment, and will to implement it. He lives out His own challenge within us. We don't do it for Him; He engenders the insight we need to respond. Our minds become the realm of the kingdom—His reign and rule.

So let each one give as he purposes in his heart, not grudgingly or of necessity; for God loves a cheerful giver.

2 Corinthians 9:7

*O*ften the Lord allows financial problems to surface to bring us to the place of losing our grip on our money and material things. The first step to the solution of financial worries is to begin to tithe. That may seem absurd to those who are facing excruciating anxiety about financial pressures and shortages.

Recently a woman shared with me her panic over her family's financial problems. She and her husband had gone through a painful period of not being able to make ends meet. The husband's loss of a job for a long period and the illness of their son had drained all their resources.

Now, though her husband was back at work, they were struggling back to some measure of financial security. In spite of my emphasis on the importance of tithing, they had decided to wait to begin tithing until they were back in shape financially. But their money problems persisted.

In desperation they both felt moved to begin tithing even though they were still hard pressed. It was the turning point. It wasn't long before the husband got a promotion and a raise in salary. Certain people who owed them money for a long time paid up. They started to pull out of their financial tailspin.

A success story? Yes, but only one of thousands I could tell. Sadly, there are an equal number of accounts of Christians who are financially secure whose spiritual life is locked on dead-center because they have missed the secret that the joy of living is the delight of giving. Their reluctance to give their money is only a sign of their resistance to give their whole lives to Christ.

Stinginess in giving our money will not keep us out of heaven, but it will shrink and distort the quality of soul we take with us to heaven.

Who has known the mind of the LORD that he may instruct Him?
1 Corinthians 2:16

The Lord is not finished with us. He knows that insecurity is also caused by a feeling of inadequate resources to meet life's challenges. In the quiet of our oneness with Him, He reminds us of the power available through His indwelling Spirit. We *are* inadequate; we were created that way so that we would depend on Him for what we need to do His work. He can show us the kind of persons we could be if filled with His Spirit. The gifts and fruit of the Holy Spirit are given one after the other; we can see ourselves filled with wisdom, knowledge, faith, discernment, healing power, and praise. Love, joy, peace, patience, kindness, goodness, faithfulness, gentleness, and self-control are manifested in the amazing picture He can give us of our new selves. "Why do you live in spiritual poverty when all of this is available to you? No wonder you feel insecure!" He says with incisive challenge.

We are given the opportunity to dream. The future is going to be more exciting than anything in the past, the Lord tells us. "What would you do and be if you did not worry about your self-imposed limitations? If you dared discard your reservations, what would you dare to attempt!" The moment is electric. Now we must ask Him for guidance before we answer. "Lord, I want Your dreams for me to be the focus of my vision. What do You have planned for me?" We are surprised and amazed by His response: "Don't fall back into that imagined separation between you and Me. We are one. I prayed for that and went to the cross to make it possible. You belong to Me now. I possess the thoughts of your brain. Your imagination is My gift to you. Dare to believe that your dreams are My inspirations!"

Make me a captive, Lord
And then I shall be free;
Force me to render up my sword,
And I shall conqueror be.
I sink in life's alarms
When by myself I stand;
Imprison me within Thine arms
And strong will be my hand.

My heart is weak and poor
Until its master find;
It has no spring of action sure -
It varies in the wind
It cannot freely move
'Til Thou has wrought its chain;
Enslave it with thy matchless love,
And deathless it shall reign.

My will is not my own
'Til Thou hast made it Thine;
If it would reach a monarch's throne
It must its crown resign;
It only stands unbent
Amid the clashing strife
When on Thy bosom it has leant
And found in Thee its life.

George Matheson

And he showed me a pure river of water of life, clear as crystal, proceeding from the throne of God and of the Lamb.

Revelation 22:1

I remember the seasoned instruction of a Canadian guide who told me how to keep my directions clear and not get lost while canoeing in the wilds. "Stay in the main river. Let it carry you south. Don't get off into side streams that only appear to be the way to go, or you'll never make it!" Sound advice for life in the Spirit!

I must confess that I don't enjoy ambiguity. There are times I wish the Lord would write out the instructions and send them by some angelic messenger so that I would know what I am to do and say for every moment of the rest of my life. But the Lord knows me too well to do that! He knows that I would put my trust in the instructions and not in daily, momentary communication with Him. He gives me the long-range goals, to be sure. I am not in doubt about the central purpose of my life to proclaim the gospel, communicate love to individuals, and be part of the adventure of the church. But for the daily decisions about priorities and programs, He gives only as much as I need to know in order to do His will in each situation. The risk is in daring to believe that He will be faithful to give me all I need to know, say, and do in the momentary challenge or opportunity. That way I can learn from both the failures and successes. When I offer the Holy Spirit a ready and eager mind, an alert and aware sensitivity, and live in consistent communication, He does give me discernment.

Along the path, there will be surprises we never anticipated. Our assurance is that God knows what He is doing, He can get through to us with His plan, our willingness makes possible His wonders, and He will use our obedience as occasions of productivity we never imagined possible.

I beseech you therefore, brethren, by the mercies of God, that you present your bodies a living sacrifice, holy, acceptable to God, which is your reasonable service.

Romans 12:1

*W*hat is God's perfect will for my life? To know Him as He has revealed Himself in Jesus Christ! He is with us in the power of the Holy Spirit. The perfect will of God is Christ: meeting Him, knowing Him, being filled with His Spirit, and allowing our character to be transformed to be like Him. Now we can savor what Paul meant. We can present our total life as a living sacrifice. It is our reasoned choice controlling the surrender of our wills. We can be extricated from the world's floundering in God's permissive will of what He allows. Our minds can be engendered with clear guidance of the implications of God's perfect will of what He intends for each day's choices and decisions.

There's a humorous but pointed story about Robert Redford, the actor and director. One day he was walking through a hotel lobby. A woman saw him and followed him to the elevator. "Are you the real Robert Redford?" she questioned with star-struck excitement. As the doors of the elevator closed he replied, "Only when I'm alone."

It's who we are when we are alone with ourselves that reveals whether we are in God's perfect will or living with the second best of His permissive will.

Our concerns about God's will usually arises at a time of crisis or choices: whom we shall marry, what job we should take, how we should decide at a crossroads impasse. Times like these force us to get back to basics. Often God will withhold clarity about secondary choices until we meet Paul's delineation of knowing God's will:

1. The surrender of our total life to God.

2. The experience of this indwelling Spirit.

3. The commitment of our wills to do God's will.

If anyone wills to do His will, he shall know concerning the doctrine,
whether it is from God or whether I speak on My own authority.

John 7:17

*W*hen some of the recruits for the Crusades were enlisted, baptism
was required for the warriors in the cause. Some of them, however, kept
their sword hand out of the water, reserving for their own will how they
would wield their weapon.

For some of us, our wills were left out of the water of our commitment
to Christ. Or perhaps it was our presuppositions or our prejudices or our
determined course for life, career, or future.

We are like the young man who was confused about the direction of
his life. He went into a church sanctuary alone to find God's perfect will
for his life. He knelt down, took a piece of paper, wrote down all the
promises that he was going to do for God, and signed it. He sat back then
and waited for God to tell him His perfect will, but no response came.
Then after hours of waiting, the Lord spoke in his inner heart. "You are
going about it all wrong. I don't want a consecration like that. Tear up
what you've written." The young man reluctantly followed the instructions. Then the voice of the Lord whispered, "Son, I want you to take a
blank piece of paper, sign your name at the bottom, and let Me fill it in."
Years later, after years of missionary service, the man confessed, "It was
just a secret between God and me as I signed the page. God has been filling it in for the past twenty-six years."

This moving account makes us wonder what we have written on our
page, expecting God to bless it. We will not know the joy of God's un-
folding, perfect will until we sign the blank sheet, leaving the results up
to Him. The signature is itself God's perfect will that we should depend
totally on Him.

Once we have expressed our ultimate purpose of knowing and following Christ, He never leaves us in a quandary. He helps us to think
with Him, feel what is maximum, and will what He wants.

If we confess our sins, He is faithful and just to forgive us our sins and to cleanse us from all unrighteousness.

1 John 1:9

We all can look back on what time has proven to be a bad decision that had more rebellion than relinquishment in it. We acted out of self-ishness, pride, or prejudice. God could not bless what we were doing; His permissive will allowed it. But that did not end the matter. We must live with the mess we've made. And yet the moment we confess it and ask for God's help, He weaves it into His ultimate plan for us. God uses what He has allowed to work for what He intended.

Now we must press on to consider the things that happen to us because of others who are stretching out the long rope of God's permissive will. What do we say about the tragedy or misery caused by those who are not in God's perfect will? What about the circumstances we did nothing to cause?

Leslie Weatherhead worked out a helpful delineation. He talks about God's intentional, circumstantial, and ultimate wills. For those who have experienced the assurance of being in God's perfect will, all three are crucial. We can trust what God intends, believe that He will use whatever happens, and know that His ultimate will cannot be dissuaded. What a profound assurance!

From within the context of God's perfect will we can dare to live with confidence. He will never guide anything that will destroy that relationship with Him for which we were born, now and for eternity.

We often use the expression "It's all downhill from here." In a way, that's the motto of a person who has experienced the purpose of being in God's perfect will. All our choices and decisions are easy after the ultimate choice to be His person. And now not even our wrong choices can separate us from Him.

Peace I leave with you, My peace I give to you; not as the world gives do I give to you. Let not your heart be troubled, neither let it be afraid.

John 14:27

Some time ago I was on an island during a hurricane. The winds blew with ferocious force from one direction. Then, suddenly, they ceased and there was a welcome calm. I remarked to a friend who lived there, "Well, I'm glad that's over!" In response he cautioned, "Not so! We're now in the calm of the eye of the hurricane. In a few minutes the winds will come back with the same force from the other direction." He was right. My confidence that the storm was over was ill-founded. It was only half-over.

Life is like that. Perhaps you are enjoying one of those times of calm right now. You can't imagine you'd ever fail the Master again. But the winds will blow another day. Times will come when we'll fall back on our own strength to try to stand against the winds, or pick ourselves up and try to keep going by our grit. But the Lord offers us something much more powerful to brace us for the storm. He gives us the calm of the eye of the hurricane to be our inner confidence when the winds beat on us again. It is then we will hear Him say what He said to the disciples during a storm on the Sea of Galilee, "Take courage, it is I." In the storm and in the calm we'll glorify Him for His peace.

With that assurance from the Lord we can face all the unresolved, hurting memories of the past and all the present unhealed brokenness inside and claim Christ's victorious power. Then we won't have to pretend outwardly that we're living the victorious Christian life while feeling defeated inside. We won't have to prove we're victorious. Christ alone will be our victory.

And He said to me [Paul], "My grace is sufficient for you, for My strength is made perfect in weakness."

2 Corinthians 12:9

The purpose of prayer is to persist until we have made a dynamic contact with the Lord of all life. Christ will not quickly answer if in the answer we are not drawn closer to Him.

Prayer is profoundly personal. It is meant to penetrate into the deepest levels of our inner hearts. We come to Christ with our requests; He begins a renovation of our total life. When I go to my physician with one ailment, he usually wants to give me a total checkup. He is concerned about my total health and well-being. He is not quick to give nifty nostrums that merely bandage what might be a deeper problem. Since I often use busyness as an excuse for neglecting regular examinations, he usually responds to my request for a prescription with, "Why don't you come to my office and let me take a good look at you?"

Our Lord is no less thorough when we come to Him asking for a speedy answer to some need. He wants to talk to us about who we are, really, and where we are going with the precious gift of life. No prayer is unanswered if as a result of lingering in His presence we can say, "He said to me . . ."

And what does He say? What He said to Paul: "My grace is sufficient for you." Pause to savor that! Grace is His unmerited, unchanging, unqualified love. With that we have everything; without it, whatever else we might receive is empty. We need fresh grace each day. Prayer is the dynamic dialogue in which we spread out our needs and receive healing love and liberating forgiveness. Conversation with the Lord enlarges our hearts until we are able to receive His Spirit.

He alone is sufficient. Christ knows our deepest needs. There are times He answers our prayers by not granting our requests. But also, a delay in answering our prayers brings us to the realization that our greatest longing is for the Lord Himself. Any quick provision that makes us less dependent on consistent fellowship with the Provider is no answer at all!

If you ask anything in My name, I will do it.

John 14:14

When we finally believe that all prayers are answered, though sometimes differently than we expected and often involving us in the answer, we are freed from using prayer as a time of bartering for blessings. Often I hear people say that they will give up some habit or act differently in their relationships if the Lord will only hear and answer their prayers. This is a subtle kind of works-oriented self-justification. We treat Him like a friend who always wants something from us in return for a favor.

The Lord of answered prayer is so much more than these. He wants to liberate us from this tendency to anthropopathy—projecting on Him the reactions of our humanness and expecting Him to react as we would.

If, as we pray, we are convicted about something we've done or are doing that makes us uncomfortable in the Lord's presence, that also may be part of answered prayer. Acting on that guidance will make us more receptive to the answers He has waiting for us. But promising to change in order to get Him to act is evidence that we have not accepted His unconditional love.

The greatest answer to prayer is the Lord Himself. His will for us is an intimate relationship of profound trust. He has a plan for our lives. Consistent times in prayer enable us to know Him and what He wants us to do. But when we complain of unanswered prayer, we are really confessing that we haven't truly prayed. For when we want Him more than the answers we demand, we'll have the ultimate answer from which all lesser answers flow.

So the so-called problem of answered prayer is not really a problem after all. An answer to prayer, though it is challenging and demanding, is given to open the way, not block it. Even when the answer is a closed door, we can know the Lord has another door open, waiting. When we must wait for direction to that door, we know that the Lord's timing is perfect.

If you abide in Me, and My words abide in you, you will ask what you desire, and it shall be done for you.

John 15:7

I am convinced that Christ knows what is best for me. I have been brought back to that assurance repeatedly! There is no peace until I surrender my circumstances knowing that He will grant me only what will be ultimately good for me. There's so much that I can't see and don't know. Unanswered prayer is really an answer. What I ask for may not have been sufficiently perfected through prolonged abiding. Either the time is not right, or what I've asked for may not be maximum in His plans for me.

I have learned a great deal during the waiting periods. Most important of all, I have found that Christ, not just His answers, is sufficient. Waiting prepares me for what He has prepared and guides me to ask wisely. What is delayed is developed. My prayers are perfected. Relaxing in His presence refines the requests. John Baillie said, "If I thought that God were going to grant me all my prayers simply for the asking, without even passing them under His own gracious review, without even bringing to bear upon them His own greater wisdom, I think there would be very few prayers that I would dare to pray."

I am thankful that the Lord has not answered many of my prayers! As I look back over the years and contemplate what might have happened if some of them had been answered when and the way I wanted, I am alarmed. I agree with Henry Longfellow: "What discord should we bring into the universe if our prayers were all answered! Then we should govern the world and not God. And do we think we should govern it better? . . . Thanksgiving with a full heart—and the rest silence and submission to the divine will!"

But the manifestation of the Spirit is given to each one for the profit of all: for to one is given the word of wisdom through the Spirit . . . to another faith by the same Spirit, to another gifts of healings by the same Spirit.
                                                        1 Corinthians 12:7–9

*I*n every situation and relationship, problem or perplexity, the person who has the gift of faith asks, "What does God want?" and has the courage to believe that it will be done. The majority of Christians do not have the lively expectancy that comes from the faith of a gifted life. They had enough faith to accept what Christ did for them on Calvary, but not enough to believe what He can do for and through them today.

For years after my conversion, I tried to live out my commitment. But it was all self-effort. I read my Bible, prayed, tithed my income, and shared with others as much as I knew of the Lord. There was no question I was in Christ, and if I had died then, I would have known the blessings of eternal salvation. And yet, for daily life, there was the flat striving of my own strength. I could imagine as possible only what I could do in my own wisdom and energy, resources and ability.

You guessed it—the Lord had much more in mind for me than what I could do for Him. He wanted me to move on to the faith that would picture what He could do in my life and problems—and dare to trust Him for nothing less. Through a series of crises that brought me to the end of my tether, I cried out for help. Challenged by the evident power I saw in others who seemed to be able to envision possibilities and see them fulfilled, I cried out for more faith. It was then that I experienced the power that had been offered at the time of my conversion but had not been appropriated. The Lord in whom I had believed filled my being with His own Spirit. The most remarkable result was a ready-for-anything, nothing-is-impossible, I'll-attempt-anything-God-guides kind of vision coupled with intrepid faith.

Most assuredly, I say to you, he who believes in Me, the works that I do he will do also; and greater works than these he will do, because I go to My Father.

John 14:12

*T*he sure test that we have received the gift of audacious faith is that we can thank God in advance for what He has guided us to ask. George Müller of Bristol, England, had that quality of faith a generation ago. Over a period of sixty years he cared for more than ten thousand orphans. He started with two shillings in his pocket and received more than five million dollars through the years. (That would be more than ten million now.) There are hundreds of stories about his faith ministry. One stirs us particularly. One day when he had no food to feed hundreds of hungry children seated expectantly at the breakfast table, he prayed, "Father, we thank Thee for the food Thou art going to give us." After a pause, a knock came at the door. It was a baker who said that he had been awakened at 2:00 A.M. and was compelled to bake bread for the children. Shortly after, a milkman knocked at the door. He said, "My milk wagon just broke down in front of your place. I must get rid of these cans of milk before I can take the wagon in for repairs. Can you use the milk?"

Müller writes that thousands of times they were without food or funds and their needs were met. He never made appeals. He believed that if God knew the need, He was perfectly capable of making that need known to the people who had resources to help.

Stories like that quicken our faith. They also disturb us. It's difficult for most of us to be that dependent. Or to reach out beyond our own capabilities or resources. And so our lives are built around what we can do for God rather than what He can do for us.

But Simon Peter answered Him, "Lord, to whom shall we go? You have the words of eternal life."

John 6:68

$\mathcal{A}$ mind alive to new truth results in a heart ablaze with new excitement for the Lord. A consistent, daily study of the Scriptures is one of the most powerful ways the Lord talks to us. He focuses our need and then answers through the passages we study. When we come to the Bible with an open mind, sincerely asking for the Lord's truth to meet whatever we are facing, He speaks to us. Then we are ready for receptive prayer.

Prayer is listening to the Lord. When we are silent, patiently waiting, He talks to us. He floods our minds with insight and wisdom, guidance and discernment. So often people ask me, "What do you mean—the Lord talks to you?" There is only one answer: When I become quiet and really want to hear what He has to say about my life and ministry, He speaks. I do not hear voices. I don't need to. The thoughts He places within my mind are like spoken words, and yet they are more powerful than an articulated sound.

I have never been disappointed. Alone and in my solitude, He speaks to me. X-ray vision and insight into people and situations are given. Mistakes and failures in my life come because I acted or spoke precipitously without waiting on the Lord. But even in the failures, when I return to Him seeking forgiveness and a new chance, He shows the way. When there seems to be no immediate answer in some situation I've surrendered to Him, this is a sure sign that I'm to wait.

My heart burns within me both when He clearly speaks and when His silence cautions me to wait. In times of heartache as well as thanksgiving, intimacy with the Lord brings healing and hope. There can be no lasting antidote to dullness that does not consistently include prolonged listening.

*I am not ashamed, for I know whom I have believed and am persuaded
that He is able to keep what I have committed to Him until that Day.*
                                                                2 Timothy 1:12

*I*n the Greek, the word translated above as "committed" literally means
a deposit committed to another person, or a trust for safekeeping. The
word translated as "keep" means to guard against robbery or loss and
implies an investment with a high return.

No venture is accomplished without commitment of our inherent
talents and Christ's imputed gifts. When we feel led to dare to attempt
something, it requires clearly established goals, tireless effort, and complete dependence on the Lord's power to pull it off.

No athlete sets a new record without constant practice and preparation. There are no great, long-term marriages that have not required the
commitment of both husband and wife. Marriage requires the hard work
of mutual adjustment, forgiveness, and effort to discern and do what love
requires. The significant accomplishments in scientific research are the
result of endless hours of committed investigation. Battles are won,
movements begun and sustained, programs for human welfare launched
and accomplished because of the commitment of an individual or group
who believe that what needs to be done can be done.

I am convinced that the Lord offers each of us a challenge that we
must be committed to do. Often it changes as we and the circumstances
around us change. What is it for you—right now? What seemingly impossible task is before you? If you are sure it has been given to you to do,
have you committed yourself to do it by the talents you already have and
the spiritual power the Lord will give you? It will be accomplished. Don't
give up! The final stages of success are always preceded by disappointment and discouragement. Press on—victory is near. Our task is to be
faithful to the vision the Lord has entrusted to us—the final result is up
to Him. If we have "deposited" the goal, it is being multiplied by the investment of "interest" from the Lord. We were created to be co-investors
with Him. Dare to risk the commitment of all you have.

Therefore I say to you, whatever things you ask when you pray, believe that you receive them, and you will have them.

Mark 11:24

$\mathcal{A}$ woman came to see me about her inability to pray for her sick husband. They had been married for a few years. She had lost a previous husband through cancer. She prayed for him and he died. She felt panicked not only by the danger of further loss, but by the "failure" of her prayers for her first husband. What she could not trust was God's sovereignty—that He is all-powerful to deal with each situation according to a greater plan than often we can fathom. The significant difference between the two men was that her first husband was a Christian; her ailing second was not. Then I asked her what she would pray if she did not limit God by what she accused Him of not doing when she asked before. Her reply was very revealing. "I've thought a lot about that," she said. "I'd ask that the Lord bring him to a relationship with Him, and I'd ask that nothing happen to him until he was sure of that."

I told her that all that thinking about what to pray had been a prayer in itself. The Lord was getting her ready to ask. Her prayer was answered. He became a Christian and is alive today.

Expectation is a crucial part of dynamic prayer. But it must be built on the insight and guidance of prolonged prayer to know how to pray. Building our prayers on unguided, negative expectations is disastrous. We expect far too little, we ask for it, and then are disappointed that the Lord didn't do better for us.

The formula for creative intercessory prayer is: Listen carefully, ask boldly, trust completely, and know that the answer is part of the tapestry of God's greater plan. He uses everything for His glory and our growth if we allow Him.

Then Jesus, looking at him, loved him, and said to him, "One thing you lack: Go your way, sell whatever you have and give to the poor, and you will have treasure in heaven; and come, take up the cross, and follow Me."

Mark 10:21

I've often wondered if the promise of treasure in heaven Jesus offered to the rich young ruler was something much more than life in heaven after death. The more I reflect on it, the more I'm convinced that Jesus was offering him the awesome opportunity right then, here on earth, of being a treasure chest of God in whom would be deposited the spiritual wealth of abundant living now as well as eternal life forever. There is no material treasure to be compared with that! When we realize that our lust for material things will rob us of that, we become alarmed. We begin to wonder what has filled the treasure chest of our own hearts. Are we adopting our culture's preoccupation with the accumulation of things and letting it stuff our hearts?

We see now that the rich young ruler was forced to make a decision. Mark describes his heartbreaking response. "He was sad at this word, and went away sorrowful, for he had great possessions" (Mark 10:22). For the young man, his possessions were inseparable from the person he had become. He could not imagine life without them. They were more than his security; they were his life.

The rich young ruler was not the only one who felt grief that day. Even greater was the grief that Jesus felt as the young man walked away downcast. I imagine that the Master stood watching him, aching for him, as he disappeared from sight. It is very significant that Jesus didn't run after the young man and offer to change the terms of discipleship. That too is part of the character of Jesus. His love is unqualified and His offer of new life is unreserved, but He will not accommodate our secondary loyalties by changing His demand for our absolute commitment. We have a choice. And that's awesome . . . frightening!

It is easier for a camel to go through the eye of a needle than for a rich man to enter the kingdom of God.

Mark 10:25

The kingdom of God refers to His reign and rule over everything—our relationships, our responsibilities, and all of life, including our possessions. All that we have and are belongs to the Lord. Like the rich young ruler, what we have received as a gift can keep us from meeting, knowing, and enjoying the Giver. Or, what's worse, we can try to manipulate the Lord to keep a steady flow, not only of the necessities of life, but of the luxuries we want.

The issue of entering the kingdom involves accepting Christ not only as our Savior, but also as our Lord. That's the disturbing difficulty of most Christians today. We want Christ's love and forgiveness and assurance of life beyond the grave, but we find trusting Him in *all* of life is much more demanding.

Jesus insists on being Lord of all. If we draw our security and sense of significance from our possessions, we have filled the "Lordship void" in all of us with things and not with Christ, and we are still caught in the eye of the needle. Not only does that rob us of the joy of discipleship now, but it would make us very uncomfortable in heaven. When the things we can't take with us become more important than the one thing we will take—our souls—then our eternal life is in jeopardy.

We count on our belief in Christ as Savior to assure us of heaven while we run our own lives now. But Christ calls us to make Him our Savior and our Lord, and making Him absolute Lord of our lives is the only way to make it through the eye of the needle.

The antithesis of boredom is joy.
It is constant regardless of where we are
or what we have.
Joy is unassailable, undiminishable
by circumstances.
It's the special gift of union with
Christ, the Life.
With His joy we can face difficulties,
deal with impossible situations,
and endure the most drab,
uninspiring, mundane
circumstances of life.
Joy is the identifiable outward sign of
the inner experience of grace.
A joyless Christian is a
contradiction of terms!

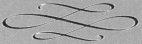

But without faith it is impossible to please Him, for he who comes to God must believe that He is, and that He is a rewarder of those who diligently seek Him.

Hebrews 11:6

*I*n 1754 Horace Walpole read a Persian fairy tale that brought spring-time joy into his life. In a letter he told about the "thrilling approach to life" the folk tale had given him and how it had helped him recapture an expectant excitement about his daily work.

The tale was about three princes of Ceylon who had set out in search of great treasures. Though they did not find the treasure, they were constantly surprised by more magnificent treasures they had not anticipated.

The ancient name of the island of Ceylon is Serendip, which accounts for the title of the fascinating story of unanticipated discoveries— "The Three Princes of Serendip." From this, Walpole coined the word *serendipity*. It explained a reality that he had known through his studies and work: His most significant and valued experiences had happened to him while he was least expecting them, and the serendipity was always more precious than the thing sought for.

Serendipity. It is the breakthrough of the Holy Spirit into our usual circumstances, the surprise that occurs to us when we are seeking to know and do God's will.

A serendipitous life is distinguished by surprisability. A ninth Beatitude might be, "Blessed are those who are surprisable, for the unexpected always happens." When we lose our capacity to be surprised we settle into life's rut of responsibilities and demands with the terrible conviction that we must do everything ourselves. We expect very little and are not disappointed; we aim at nothing and we hit it. One thing I know about God: He delights to surprise us with serendipities we never expected.

Therefore comfort each other and edify one another, just as you also are doing.

1 Thessalonians 5:11

Some years ago I had a wonderful visit in New York with my friend Norman Vincent Peale. He was eighty-two then. After we'd shared our faith and encouraged each other, we got down on our knees for a time of prayer. When we finished, I said, "That was great! Why don't we form a covenant to pray for each other every day wherever we are in the world?" "Wonderful," Norman replied with gusto. "Let's make it for twenty years!"

"But Norman," I said, "you'll be 102 years old then."

"That's right," he rejoined, "and I'll need your prayers then more than ever!"

Free of the past and filled with expectation for the future, Norman is a spontaneous person, open to live fully in the now.

Latter I was with the Peales at the Tabernacle in Ocean City, New Jersey. I preached in the morning and Norman in the evening. After the evening service where Dr. Peale preached Christ with great power, I escorted his wife Ruth to a room while Norman greeted some of the thronging crowd that had come to hear him. When we were alone, she turned to me and said with radiant enthusiasm, "Lloyd, isn't he wonderful? Imagine, preaching the gospel like that at eighty-two!"

I agreed and thought to myself, "Now I know part of the secret of Norman's success: his trust in the Lord *and* Ruth's unbounding freedom to be an affirmer." Later I thought about the people in my life who might need to know that I think they are wonderful. I made a list and the next day I phoned several and wrote others.

But how often we put off those spontaneous urgings. We stifle the childlike freedom in us and shrivel up inside and become unexpressive, dull people on the outside. The good news is that we don't have to stay that way.

I have come that they may have life, and that they may have it more abundantly.

John 10:10

*L*ife in Christ is the thrilling alternative to boredom. It must begin with an intimate companionship with the Lord Himself. We will be bored until that exciting friendship is begun. This should not be confused with religion or churchmanship, both of which can be boring without a personal relationship with Christ. I know too many bored church members and clergy to mislead you in believing that more theology, rituals, or church organizations will cure boredom. Something deeper is needed.

In Trinity Church, Boston, there is a remarkable statue of Phillips Brooks by Augustus Saint-Gaudens. The spiritual giant stands at a pulpit with an open Bible. Behind him stands Jesus with His hand on the preacher's shoulder. The reason for Brooks's greatness is preserved for posterity. In a letter to a friend he wrote, "All experience comes to be but more and more the pressure of Christ's life upon ours. I cannot tell you how personal this grows to me. He is here. He knows me and I know Him. It is no figure of speech; it is the realest thing in the world." No wonder that one of Brooks's biographers says, "He conversed with Christ as his most intimate friend. He loved his earthly friends and enjoyed their companionship, but for none of them had he such attachment as for Christ."

The experience of joy is the sure test that we have begun this new life. Jesus said, "These things I have spoken to you, that My joy may remain in you, and that your joy may be full" (John 15:11). The antithesis of boredom is joy. It is constant, regardless of where we are or what we have. Joy is unassailable, undiminishable by circumstances. It's the special gift of union with Christ, *the* Life. With His joy we can face difficulties, deal with impossible situations, and endure the most drab, uninspiring, mundane circumstances of life. A joyless Christian is a contradiction of terms!

Jesus said to him, "I am the way, the truth, and the life. No one comes to the Father except through Me."

                                                                    John 14:6

Sören Kierkegaard said, "What is anxiety? The next day!" And I say, what is boredom? It's the fear that the next day will be the same as today! We long to escape into some new experience that will cure our boredom. For many, life is lived in anticipation that some hoped-for change, event, person, or rearrangement of circumstances will suddenly release them from the prison of boredom. When the anticipated future turns out to have been oversold, there's nothing left but the ruts of routine.

It's startling to realize how few people are finding life today an exciting adventure. Boredom, more than being the condition of a few unadjusted people, is the spiritual sickness of millions of Americans—young and old, single and married, people in strategic jobs and people in unrewarding jobs that do little more than provide bread on the table, the famous people and people who are seldom noticed.

We will be bored until we find a purpose and passion in life that will be thrilling in spite of the drab surroundings, the dull people, and the deadly routine of life. Only Jesus Christ can make life thrilling in a consistent, lasting, and vibrant way.

Jesus summed up His whole ministry with the startling statement, "I am the way, the truth, and the life" (John 14:6). He called His followers into an exciting quality of life in fellowship with Him and gave them a commission that would banish boredom from their lives forever. Jesus Christ came to make life thrilling. The key word that describes the new life Jesus imparted is *joy*—joy that is independent of people, places, positions, or pleasantries. The joy of life in Christ and Christ in us is the only lasting antidote to boredom.

Abide in Me, and I in you. As the branch cannot bear fruit of itself, unless it abides in the vine, neither can you, unless you abide in Me. . . . These things I have spoken to you, that My joy may remain in you, and that your joy may be full.

John 15:4, 11

Christ Himself is the source of joy. The sap of the vine that surges into the branches is grace-unqualified love. The words *grace* and *joy* come from the same Greek root. Joy is the delight of being loved. Everything that Christ said and did and continues to do in our lives today tells us that we are cherished, valued, and loved. He died for us, rose from the dead for us, and is with us now and is ready to heal us with accepting and affirming love.

There is no authentic joy apart from being loved by Christ. His joy persists regardless of life's circumstances. On the other hand, happiness is conditioned by what's happening to and around us. The word *happiness* comes from *hap* ("chance"), and chances change. That's why there is such a great difference between happiness and joy. Life is undependable; human affection is often conditioned by our adequacy or performance, and situations we counted on remaining stable can fluctuate and scuttle our carefully laid plans.

Whenever our security is in people or possessions, we may know a measure of happiness for a time, but not joy. That precious spiritual gift is the result of experiencing a love that will never change, that not even our failures will diminish in the least degree and that will remain constant whatever people do or say to hurt us. Where do you find a love like that? Only in Christ. And from that gracious love joy flows.

That they may have My joy fulfilled in themselves.

John 17:13

*T*here's a delightful story told about Lloyd Douglas, author of *The Robe*. He enjoyed visiting a little old violin teacher in a shabby, small walk-up room he proudly called his studio.

Douglas liked to drop in on him because he had the kind of lovely wisdom about life that refreshed him. One morning he stopped by to see the old man. "Well, what's the good news today?" he asked. Putting down his violin, the old violin teacher stepped over to a tuning fork suspended from a silk cord. He struck it a smart blow with a padded mallet and said, "There's the good news for today. That, my friend, is A. It was A all day yesterday. It will be A all day tomorrow, next week, and for a thousand years."

That story tunes our minds to the A of true joy. Like Christ, who is its only source, joy is the same yesterday, today, and tomorrow. It is artesian, never changes, and is consistent irrespective of people or circumstances. At the same time, joy is not a quality we can find by searching or earn by effort. It comes from something—really Someone else.

Here are some basic thoughts to guide our thinking concerning true joy.

1. Joy resounds in the heart of God and is an outward expression of His love.

2. Joy is the ecstasy of heaven and the triumphant experience of those who have begun eternal life here and now.

3. Joy was revealed in Jesus Christ, the joyous heart of God with us.

4. Joy can be our constant experience by abiding in Christ's love and allowing Him to abide in us.

5. Joy is the identifiable mark of a Christian and a truly vital church.

6. Joy is not an option.

And you became followers of us and of the Lord, having received the word in much affliction, with joy of the Holy Spirit.

1 Thessalonians 1:6

I have a super friend who, after a good visit, shakes my hand, looks me squarely in the eye, and leaves me with this parting shot: "Whatever you do, don't miss the joy!"

Last year, I shared my friend's benedictory blessing with a group of people at a conference where I was speaking. They picked it up immediately, and it became the slogan of the conference. When people passed one another on the conference grounds, they would say, "Don't miss the joy!"

And yet many people miss the joy. There's a grimness that pervades life today. Everywhere we look we see grim, "white-knuckled" people who are desperately hanging on, enduring life rather than enjoying it.

There are those who miss the joy of life in a grim determination to be responsible. To them, life is a serious business; there is little time for joy in the pressure of meeting life's demands. Others are in such a frantic search for happiness that they miss the joy. Happiness is so much less than joy; it is dependent on circumstances, people, or success. Joy is deeper. It is a condition of the soul that is utterly unassailable by life's ups and downs.

Still others feel unworthy of joy and miss its delight. Many people think of joy as a reward for perfection, performance, pertinacity. And who ever measures up to one's own standards?

There's a great need for joy today. It should be the identifiable mark of the Christian and the impelling ingredient of his or her contagion. The church should be the fellowship of uncontainable joy. New Testament scholar William Barclay was right: "A gloomy Christian is a contradiction, and nothing in all religious history has done Christianity more harm than its connection with black clothes and long faces."

I am the true vine, and My Father is the vinedresser.

John 15:1

*I*t is a ceaseless source of joy to abide in Jesus' words and command-ments. He has a word for all seasons. When we attempt to obey His com-mandments to love God, ourselves, and others, the floodgates of the rivers of power are opened.

Prayer is intimate communication, Person to person. When we abide in God, listening receptively, we experience the ecstasy of joy. Let the word stand—*ecstasy*. It is the intense emotion that bursts within us when the Lord breaks through. Then we can say with Blaise Pascal, "Joy! Joy! Unspeakable joy!"

It was this spiritual ecstasy that Peter affirmed in the early church: "Whom having not seen you love. Though now you do not see Him [with eye perception], yet believing [heart and mind perception through prayer], you rejoice with joy inexpressible and full of glory" (1 Pet. 1:8).

In a much deeper way, we can express about Christ what Michel Fyquem de Montaigne said of a friend: "How is it that we were so much to one another, you and I? It was because you were you and I was I." Grim people like us need the joy only a Savior can give. Only the great "I am" can meet our needs. We can echo Charles Kingsley's simple assurance when asked how he took the pressure in his life. "I had a friend" was his only reply. Jesus, the vine, draws the joy from the reservoir of the eter-nal and sends it into our thirsty branches.

My friend's parting benedictory encouragement—mentioned yester-day—is now my deepest prayer for you. I pray it in the context of Jesus' triumphant "I am" promise: "I am the vine, you are the branches" (John 15:5). "Abide in me, and I in you. . . . that My joy may remain in you, and that your joy may be full" (John 15:4, 11).

Whatever you do, don't miss the joy!

But the fruit of the Spirit is love, joy, peace, longsuffering, kindness, goodness, faithfulness, gentleness, self-control. Against such there is no law.

Galatians 5:22–23

*W*e can look at life's hard places as either judgment, condemnation, fate, or opportunities for learning what the Lord longs to teach us. Life seldom works out as we had hoped or planned. When we are distressed physically, emotionally, or relationally (with people we love), the Lord can use the interruption in our happiness to give us joy. Joy is His special gift to people whose suffering has been submitted to Him for His intervention and inspiration. We are pruned back, but the subsequent growth is worth the pain.

I know this is true. Life's complexities present me with two alternatives—bitterness or blessing. I can be hardened or softened as supple clay for the Lord's creative molding. The deepest conviction of my heart is that each of the unresolved decisions or distressing disappointments with people and institutional Christianity, any of the worries that are the stuff of life, can be accepted as pruning and sources of fresh joy.

True joy, which is the fruit of the Lord's Spirit when we abide in Him and He abides in us, seldom comes when things are easy and tranquil. During difficult periods of our lives it blossoms with the realization that nothing can happen to us that the Lord cannot use for an experience of fresh grace and new growth. Also, in these times we become the special focus of the Lord's intervention. Joy leaps in us when we know that the Lord knows and cares about our concerns. We are delighted anew each time we feel the release of new dependence on Him and the warmth of His presence with us in the testing time. Then, when we receive an answer or a miraculous resolution of the problem that only He could have accomplished, we feel a fresh burst of joy.

Though now you do not see Him, yet believing, you rejoice with joy inexpressible and full of glory.

1 Peter 1:8

The joy of the Lord becomes our strength. God's Spirit is joy. Christ incarnated that joy and promised us nothing less than His own joy. A bad mood is a signal that we need His indwelling presence. Christ is joy. The fruit of His Spirit is ebullient, ever-flowing joy.

That leaves us with a choice and an awesome responsibility. We can decide to change our mood! When a mood seeks to dominate us, we can make a decision of the will to be different. If we follow the process of analyzing the cause, we can also follow the prescription for the cure. The Lord has entrusted us with the jurisdiction of our moods. Saul had a problem with himself for which he chose to blame David. So too we have a problem with ourselves; we blame others. Our bad moods simply do not work. They are ineffective and hurt ourselves and everyone around us. The question is, "Who needs it?"

Whenever I'm tempted to coddle a bad mood, I think of Annie Johnson Flint. She is one of my favorite poets. Her grand and glad thoughts came in the midst of suffering. If anyone had a right to bad and low moods, she did. She lost her parents early in life, had to work hard for her education, and was never free of financial worries. As a young woman she endured the encroachment of arthritis that worsened until she was completely crippled and physically helpless. And yet she gave to the world poems of joy. The secret was in her experience of God's grace. Look at the last verse of her most famous poem:

> His love has no limit, His grace has no measure,
> His power no boundary known unto men;
> For out of His infinite riches in Jesus
> He giveth and giveth and giveth again.

Now may the God of hope fill you with all joy and peace in believing, that you may abound in hope by the power of the Holy Spirit.

Romans 15:13

*A*s I have reflected on the thought that joy is Christ's strategy for reaching others through us, the question has arisen in my mind—Do I express that kind of joy in my words and actions? Is *joy* a word people would use to describe my attitude, especially in the problems and pressures of life?

These questions have then caused me to ask myself why at certain times do I communicate anything less than joy? Usually it's because I have taken my eyes off of Christ and fastened them on difficult circumstances. A lack of joy usually alerts me to the fact that I've cut off the flow of grace by trying too hard through self-effort. Most of all, times of joylessness have alarmed me with the realization that in a busy life I have not taken time to "abide in the vine" and allow Him to infuse His gracious Spirit and healing love into me as His branch.

Daily prayer and Bible study can become routine and ineffective unless they are "abiding times" of resting in Christ's presence, letting go of our tight grip of worry over problems, and allowing Him to love us. At moments like this, He will help us to visualize, actually see ourselves as joyous people able to cope with the problems ahead of us. The amazing thing to me is that the picture comes true!

Joy is not an option. It's what the Lord desires and what the world around us desperately needs. The joy of being loved is inseparable from the joy of living.

You are My friends if you do whatever I command you. No longer do I call you servants, for a servant does not know what his master is doing; but I have called you friends.

John 15:14–15

I want you to meet my best Friend. I've known him for forty-five years. He's been with me through trials and tragedies, pain and persecution, ups and downs, success and failure. He is the kind of friend who knows all about me and never goes away. He has a special way of helping me to see myself and do something about it. He accepts me the way I am, and yet that very acceptance makes me want to be all that I was meant to be in spite of all the difficulties around me. He laughs with me over my mistakes and weeps with me in my sorrows. He has been faithful all through life's battles. I have never been left alone when I suffered criticism, hostility, or resistance for doing what love demanded. He is with me when truth triumphs and is always there to absorb the anguish of defeat in a righteous cause.

We share a vision, a hope, a dream together . . . my Friend and I. As a matter of fact, He gives me the daring to be true to what I believe regardless of cost. He meets all the qualifications of a real friend: He loves without limit, He is loyal when others turn away, He listens to my hurts, and He liberates me to grasp life with gusto, regardless of the consequences.

I have only one hope: When I come to the end of this portion of heaven and pass on to the next, the one thing people will remember is that I was His Friend. My best Friend is Jesus Christ!

No longer do I call you servants, for a servant does not know what his master is doing; but I have called you friends, for all things that I heard from My Father I have made known to you.

John 15:15

*W*e cannot respond to the high cost of loving without the daily experience of what I like to call the enabling connection of the vine and the branch. Jesus says, "You are My friends if you do whatever I command you" (John 15:14). The source of the love we need to express is the sap of His spirit moving from Him, the Vine, into us, the branches. It is through this love-connection that we listen for the Lord's guidance for what He wants us to say and do. What a great promise! We will be given orders for what it will mean to be Christ's love to people. When we ask, He will make it plain. Be sure of that! But also be sure of something else: When we do today what He tells us to do in our problematical relationships, we will receive further clarity in the future. The Lord draws us into His confidence, helps us to picture what we are to express, and then promises to be with us to give us the strength to implement that guidance.

This is the cooperative partnership we are offered in Christ's promise that He is our friend and we are called to be His friends. And so He goes on to affirm, "No longer do I call you servants, for a servant does not know what his master is doing; but I have called you friends, for all things that I heard from My Father I have made known to you" (John 15:15).

We are profoundly moved by the trust our Friend places in us as His friends. No longer are we only servants with the mandate, "Ours is not to question why, but to do with no reply," but now we are friends with the motto, "Ours is to know the reason why and to do is our reply." We are given the mind of Christ to understand, the grace of Christ to express His love, and the power of the indwelling Christ to act in the most creative way and at the right time.

And whatever you ask in My name, that I will do, that the Father may be glorified in the Son.

John 14:13

Some of the most effective, reproductive, fruit-bearing Christians I know think of their efforts to win others to Christ as the awesome privilege of simply being friends. Their caring and concern for people is not expressed as religious zeal or manipulation.

As a friend of mine says, "I just make as many deep friendships with people as I can. Then when life percolates some big problem to the surface in their lives, I'm ready and available to stand with them. And somewhere along the way I get my chance to share what my Friend Christ can make out of the raw material of problems." Dozens of people have become alive in Christ and will live forever because of His friendship evangelism. His fruit remains . . . it lasts.

The idea of friendship evangelism can change our attitude toward problem people. Instead of being obstructions to our plans or happiness, they become opportunities.

This simply means that when this kind of person disturbs us it is time to ask, "Lord, what's Your plan and strategy? Change my attitude, give me Your love and patience. I surrender to You anything that is contributing to a negative picture of this person. Help me, Lord. I can't do it by myself, but You can do something wonderful in this person's life."

So often, though, we hesitate to befriend problem people because of the false notion that our gesture of friendship will in some way look like we are condoning their actions and patterns of behavior. Actually, just the opposite usually happens. It is in an environment of friendship—Christ-inspired and Christ-guided friendship—that people change. Blasting a person with advice never works. Blaming is not our business; providing the friendly relationships in which people can share and face their problems is our calling.

You did not choose Me, but I chose you and appointed you that you should go and bear fruit, and that your fruit should remain, that whatever you ask the Father in My name He may give you.

John 15:16

*T*here's a great freedom in knowing that we are chosen and appointed by Christ to be His friends and that we are to befriend others, even the most difficult people in our lives.

Our fruit-bearing ministry as friends of the Lord is His idea. He has called us to it. Here's a purpose big enough to make life exciting. Do we have to question our authority? He is the prime mover—always ahead of us and always anticipating our needs. He chose us, called us, and we can be sure that He goes before us to prepare the way for our efforts to befriend others.

When we become aware of a need in another person's life, it is never a question of what the Lord will do, but of what *we* are willing to allow Him to do through us.

When the Lord allows a big problem to surface, it is because He is ready to do a great work. We are called to be His agents of healing, His workers. As we work for Him, we will learn to look at the problems people are wrestling with as the opportunity for them to either meet their Friend, Jesus Christ, or be drawn into deeper, intimate relationship with Him.

Presenting Christ as Friend and the Christian life as friendship with Him is the most effective means of fruit-bearing evangelism. The test of our friendship with Christ is that we introduce others to Him as life's greatest Friend. All of His love, atoning death, resurrection power, and abiding presence can be summarized in this lovely word *friend*. Jesus is the Friend of sinners—the lonely, the insecure, the troubled. When we listen to them with empathy and sensitivity, we will have earned the right and have the credibility to tell them what our Friend has done for us and is ready to do for them.

If we are to love others as Christ has loved us, the brokenhearted are the focus of our concern. As He has been with us, so we are to be with people who are hurting— not sympathetically aloof, but empathically involved. Loving as Christ loved means to identify, listen, understand, and comfort.

By this all will know that you are My disciples, if you have love for one another.

John 13:35

The more I study and meditate on Jesus' commission in the new commandment, the more aware I am that the broken things we think are too broken to mend are what keep us from loving one another as He has loved us. Broken dreams, plans, and hopes, coupled with broken relationships, harden our hearts. The painful memories of the past make us determined never to be hurt again or get into a position of being disappointed. When we have failed or life has tumbled in on us, we tend to develop cold, calculating attitudes. We build walls to protect us from further heartbreak.

When this happens to us, the Lord's challenge to love, to be to others what He's been to us, becomes lovely sentiment for someone else. The Lord cannot use us in love's service; the seed of His word cannot penetrate the hard, unplowed soul-soil. But once He "sets the coulter deep and wakes our soul from sleep" we can receive the seed of His truth and hope. It will grow in the cultivated ground of heartbreak and will be watered by the tears of repentance and joy. Then we will be indefatigable in our love for others, like the Lord. We will be able to forgive before forgiveness is asked. We will be capable of initiating reconciliation regardless of our rights or our defensive need to be justified.

That's what Jesus meant when He said, "By this all will know that you are My disciples, if you have love for one another" (John 13:35). The world is still waiting to see that quality of authentic love. If the church of Jesus Christ ever modeled that, we could change the world! Wouldn't it be wonderful if we could offer the slogan, "We weld relationships through the healing of broken hearts"?

This is My commandment, that you love one another as I have loved you.
John 15:12

In all the varied experiences of a broken heart, the Lord is most concerned with our healing. The brokenness of a contrite heart is our gift to Him out of our suffering; a new heart filled with confidence and hope is His gift to us. Oscar Wilde was right when he wrote in "The Ballad of Reading Gaol," "How else but through a broken heart / May Lord Christ enter in?" My teacher and friend James Stewart of Edinburgh puts it this way: "It is when a man strikes rock bottom . . . that he suddenly finds he has struck the Rock of Ages."

A broken heart must lead us to a point at which we surrender to our Lord the cause of the shattering experience. Our disappointment with ourselves, other people, life itself, or even God must be relinquished to Him. Until we are broken of our tendency to try to heal ourselves, He cannot help. Next, accept His reconciling love for the bitterness of what you have done or others have done to you. Receive the Lord's indwelling Spirit as a constant companion. Then thank the Lord for the rebirth of hope and the desire to live again. He heals the memory of the pain and focuses our attention on what He is going to give us—a new beginning.

Now Jesus' commission flashes with the new light of wisdom. If we are to love others as He has loved us, the brokenhearted are the focus of our concern. As He came to bind up the brokenhearted, so must we— by His power and not our own. But how He ministers to us in our broken things gives us the key to understanding how we are to love others. Here again His presence, perspective, peace, and power give us our strategy. As He has been with us, so we are to be with people who are hurting—not sympathetically aloof, but empathically involved. Loving as Christ loves means to identify, listen, understand, and comfort.

I want to remind you to stir into flame the strength and boldness that is in you.

2 Timothy 1:6 TLB

$\mathcal{A}$ cold Christian is a contradiction of terms. Coldness or even aloof coolness is simply an outward sign of the absence of Christ's fire.

When Christ's fire does burn in us a new verve and vitality are expressed in all we do. We become cheerleaders for others and tackle tasks with an assurance of unlimited spiritual power to see us through. People with Christ's fire burning in their hearts are fun to live with. Their radiance lights up the dullness of life's routines.

The fire of Christ's love is the secret of their effectiveness in communicating their faith to others. They don't need slick evangelism brochures or constant guilt-producing challenges from their pastors to reach out to others. Reaching out comes naturally, and therefore is winsome. Because they care profoundly, they want everyone to know the Lord and receive His Spirit. But instead of being firebrands, they are people who are branded with the fire of Christ's character and compassion, and that leads them into both social responsibility and personal involvement with people who need the Lord.

What happens to a church when its membership is filled with authentic, "on-fire" Christians? It becomes a loving and forgiving fellowship. Worship is alive with praise and joy. There are no fire doors around the pulpit to confine the blaze of the Spirit burning in the exposition of the Bible. It spreads to the pews and out into all the classes and groups of the church. The leadership of the church becomes an incendiary force rather than a society of spiritual firefighters. The church as a whole becomes a warm fire to attract others. Acceptance and inclusiveness abounds. When visitors gather around the fire, the dry kindling of their own hearts is set afire.

Then He said to them, "Follow Me, and I will make you fishers of men."
Matthew 4:19

*B*efore going fishing in rivers and lakes, I find it necessary to check out my bait. If I'm going fly-fishing, I want to have with me lots of different kinds of flies. There's nothing more frustrating than standing in a river and watching other fishermen catching fish with a type of fly that I left at home. When I go fishing on a lake or in the ocean, I take my whole box of lures along. That way I'm prepared for anything.

The same is true in fishing for people. People's needs are different, but of primary importance in witnessing to others are our own experiences of grace in the struggles and challenges of life. All that we've been through stands as preparation for the opportunities to share our faith. And Christ is constantly arranging those opportunities.

It is important to remember, though, that our responsibility is not to try to model perfection. Nor are we required to have all the answers. That would put people off anyway.

Fishing for people is really taking time to be a friend. Often, that friendship may have to be a one-way street for a time. Most people are primarily interested in themselves and their own needs and hopes. When we are willing to be a giving friend with no demands, people begin to feel loved. They know they can count on us for a steady flow of affirmation and encouragement. Over time they become convinced that we are for them and will not change our attitudes about them when they fail. They also know that we'll be the first to cheer their successes. Our goal is to become the kind of person others would turn to when they face difficulties or want to express delight. Having earned the right, we will be able to share how Christ has helped us to grapple with problems or to discover the joy of living at full potential.

I will give you a mouth and wisdom which all your adversaries will not be able to contradict or resist.

Luke 21:15

*H*ave you lain awake at night going over what you are going to say to a person the next day? Or have you ever sat scheming for hours how you would word what you were going to tell someone? Have you ever found that what you prepared didn't fit? Often we blurt out our carefully prepared statements with little sensitivity about how the person is feeling at that moment. It isn't a bit surprising that we are misunderstood so often.

The only way to avoid that is to trust Christ for the special kind of preparation He provides us for resolving misunderstandings. Everything we go through prepares us for solving future problems. Daily prayer and Bible study condition our thinking and attitudes. Experience of the Lord's gracious patience with us makes us more sensitive to the needs in others. The Lord is constantly teaching us in the ups and downs of life. He knows the future and is getting us ready for what He knows is ahead of us.

When a misunderstanding disturbs us we can spread it out before the Lord. He will direct our thinking to passages of Scripture that reveal His truth. He will remind us of what we've learned from Him in similar conflicts. He will give us profound, forgiving love for people who are troubling us. We will be given a new empathy to sense what may be causing the people involved in the misunderstanding to talk and act in ways that have hurt us. It's then that we can commit the outcome to the Lord, trusting Him completely.

The result of this preparation is that we are set free of the need to justify ourselves with defensive statements. We can enter into conversation with people who have hurt us, be prepared to listen attentively, and when the timing is right, respond spontaneously, drawing on all the Lord has done to prepare our thinking and attitudes.

But when they arrest you and deliver you up, do not worry beforehand, or premeditate what you will speak. But whatever is given you in that hour, speak that; for it is not you who speak, but the Holy Spirit.

Mark 13:11

*W*hat Father John Powell prays before giving a talk could well be our preparation for attempts to straighten out misunderstandings. "May what I say be less of a presentation and more an act of love."

Often when my wife Mary Jane knows that I have a misunderstanding to work out on a particular day, before I leave home in the morning she asks, "Lloyd, are you prepared?" I know she is not referring to the preparation of a canned monologue or well-rehearsed phrases, but the preparation of quiet with the Lord. Years of working with people have taught both of us that we can't make it without that!

The same is true for opportunities to share our faith. The Lord prepares us for what He has prepared. The way He helps us in our troubles prepares us for the troubled people we meet who desperately need His love and power. Here again canned speeches miss the mark. People are put off when we shift into the honed phrases of overused jargon. But when we really listen intently to people's problems we will discover we've been through the same or similar difficulties. Then we can draw from our own real-life experiences of how the Lord stepped in to help us. That usually gives us an opportunity to help people to commit not only their specific problem but their whole lives to the Lord.

After a time like that we look back and realize we could not have been effective communicators without the training in living the Lord had allowed in our lives.

And we are aware of something else. We were not alone. The Lord was there with us guiding exactly what we were to say.

These things I have spoken to you, that in Me you may have peace. In the world you will have tribulation; but be of good cheer, I have overcome the world.

John 16:33

I want to share eight discoveries about relationships and communication with others that have helped me.

1. People do not care about how much we know until they know how much we care. It is what we are and what we do to express love that creates a climate for openness for what we say.

2. People will understand what we say only after they know we understand them. That means taking seriously their ideas, values, hopes, and dreams, as well as their needs, problems, and distresses.

3. People will listen only when we've taken time to listen to them. Usually we are thinking so much about what we are going to say when it's our turn to speak that we don't really hear what the other person has said.

4. People are like harbors and each is his or her own harbormaster. Most people are concerned about themselves and what they are experiencing. But when they feel we care about them, they will open up.

5. People can hear six times faster than we can talk. So when it's our turn in a conversation, get to the point!

6. People will misunderstand. Three elements are involved in every conversation: the one who speaks, what is said, and the person who listens.

7. People are slow to admit they were wrong or precipitous in their judgments. For this reason, the ball is always in our court as a part of our ministry of reconciliation.

8. People will not always respond to our best efforts. Honor their right to continue to misunderstand you. When your convictions and integrity are involved, don't change who you are just to please.

But may the God of all grace, who called us to His eternal glory by Christ Jesus, after you have suffered a while, perfect, establish, strengthen, and settle you.

1 Peter 5:10

*T*he tragedy of coercive bad moods is that eventually we are the ones who suffer. Moods meant for others always boomerang. They fly back and hit us in the soul. They cut off the flow of God's grace. We become all the more miserable. Prayer is stifled and joy is a stranger to us. And yet, for a Christian, joy is no option.

That presses us on to the cure of moodiness. As negative moods are caused by our perception of conditions, condemnation, and conditional love, just so battling through to joy means confrontation, confession, and commitment.

Confrontation means getting in touch with the mood, analyzing its causes, and admitting responsibility for it. No one or no situation can control our moods without our permission. It is often helpful to ask, "Why am I feeling the way I am?" Dare to be ruthlessly honest.

The next step is confession. This means not only telling our Lord about our mood, but confessing our need for Him to help us experience fresh grace, the Lord's unmerited and unlimited love. Joy is the result of God's presence and power. Whatever the cause of our dark mood, the brightness of grace can dispel the darkness. We all desperately need to know that God loves us and will not let us go.

The cross is the source of our victory over our moods. It is the sublime assurance that there are no limits to the Lord's forgiveness. But also, there is nothing too great for Him. The grace that flows from Calvary into our hearts gives us the assurance that there is power available to us. Our God can bring good out of all we go through.

He is also able to save to the uttermost those who come to God through Him, since He always lives to make intercession for them.

Hebrews 7:25

Self-confidence is based on the reliability of the self. But if the negative experiences of the growing years or the lack of esteem from others has deprived us of feeling good about ourselves, we may spend the rest of our lives devoid of self-confidence. Even the most secure person finds it difficult to endure hardships and failures that shake his or her confidence.

The problem with self-confidence is that the self is not consistent or constant. Now we are at the core of the issue. We all blow it too often for us to put our ultimate trust in ourselves. We collide with life's difficulties and seeming impossibilities. Often, we find that we are inadequate and insufficient when faced with the needs of people. We realize we can't love selflessly. The stress of life robs us of peace of mind. Pressures mount. Disappointments engulf us. We realize we don't have what it takes.

The reason is that we were never meant to be self-confident. We were created for a relationship with the Lord. He alone can give us an authentic, lasting confidence for living. His ability can fortify our disability. He is the same yesterday, today, and tomorrow. What He has done, and is ready to do for us, provides the constancy and consistency that motivates the complete trust of genuine confidence. It is the confidence of knowing our ultimate destination is assured and all our needs in getting there will be met.

That's the confidence-building assurance of the "He is able!" assertion in Hebrews 7:25. Christ is able to save to the uttermost, completely and perfectly. He has saved us. He saves us in each day's stuggle. And He will save us when our earthly life comes to an end. So let's live today with confidence in Him!

> *Now this is the confidence that we have in Him, that if we ask anything according to His will, He hears us. And if we know that He hears us, whatever we ask, we know that we have the petitions that we have asked of Him.*
>
> 1 John 5:14–15

*C*hrist-confidence replaces self-confidence as we realize His ability in spite of our disabilities. He is able when we are unable. Ulrich Zwingli, the reformer, put it pointedly, "Our confidence in Christ does not make us happy, negligent, or careless, but on the contrary it awakens us, urges us on, and makes us active in living righteous lives and doing good. There is no self-confidence to compare with this."

The words *confidence* and *boldness* come from the same root in Greek. Christ-confident people have a boldness in living. The Book of Acts illustrates this. The fourth chapter is one of the most exciting examples. That quality of life the Sanhedrin observed in Peter and John, which identified them with Christ, was boldness. "Now when they saw the boldness of Peter and John, and perceived that they were uneducated and untrained men, they marveled. And they realized that they had been with Jesus" (Acts 4:13). The word for boldness, *parrhesia*, means "intrepidly daring, free to speak, unafraid of anything or anyone."

The boldness of Peter and John was not rooted in self-confidence, but in Christ. Their experience of Him was utterly reliable. They had been with Him in His ministry, death, and resurrection. His message had unlocked the truth. His death was an assurance of their salvation. His resurrection was a final validation of the ultimate power of God. His presence in them as indwelling Lord was the motivating power to attempt anything He guided.

Boldness was what the leaders of Israel remembered about Jesus and then were amazed to find it reproduced in the apostles. It should be the undeniably evident quality of Christians in every age.

Let not your heart be troubled; you believe in God, believe also in Me.
John 14:1

*M*ost people are so insecure that they will wait to be loved before they are free to love. But when our solitude in prayer has given us the liberating assurance of God's love, we can become primary, first-move lovers of people.

My friend Lloyd Umbarger lived in the home of Henrietta Mears, the great Christian educator. One day while he was watering the grass, he noticed a beautiful young woman coming to see Dr. Mears. After spending several hours with that powerful person-liberator, the young woman came out radiant. Lloyd asked her how she was doing. The young woman confided that she had come to see Dr. Mears about her feelings of loneliness and had confessed that she had few friends. "What did Dr. Mears say?" Lloyd asked. "Well," the young woman responded, "she asked me to name the qualities I would like in a friend. So I told her I needed people who accepted me, would not misuse me, on whom I could count in spite of everything, and who could share my hopes and dreams. Then Dr. Mears said an amazing thing. 'Go be that kind of friend to other people, and you will find that is what they will be to you.'" Powerful advice about being an initiative lover of people.

Jesus' way out of loneliness involves being part of a movement that is following Him in changing the world. He wants to give us the gift of solitude in which He can transform those things in us that keep us from having satisfying relationships with people, and He longs to enable us to be people who conquer loneliness by being wound-healers in others.

We don't have to be part of the lonely crowd any longer. Jesus walked the lonesome valley for us so we no longer need to walk it alone.

And if I go and prepare a place for you, I will come again and receive you to Myself; that where I am, there you may be also.

John 14:3

Our loneliness is a "homing instinct." Just as animals, birds, and fish have a homing instinct capable of leading them back to their original habitats, we have a loneliness to be at home with God. We've all heard of dogs or cats that found their way home after being lost at great distances. Pigeons are distinguished for their ability to fly hundreds of miles back to their homes; swallows make an aerial journey of thousands of miles each year and return to the exact nesting place they left. Salmon return to spawn in the very part of the river where they were hatched. The examples from the natural world are many.

God has placed the same instinct in us, and intimate communion with Him is our home. God came Himself to show us the way.

It was on the night before Jesus was crucified that He gave the secret for overcoming loneliness. His disciples were feeling the loneliness of impending separation from Him. They feared what was about to happen. Jesus' honest predictions about His death were about to come true. What He said to give them courage is our hope in loneliness.

"Let not your heart be troubled; you believe in God, believe also in Me. In My Father's house are many mansions; if it were not so, I would have told you. I go to prepare a place for you. And if I go and prepare a place for you, I will come again and receive you to Myself; that where I am, there you may be also. And where I go you know, and the way you know" (John 14:1–4).

What has that to do with loneliness? Everything. Jesus came from the heart of God to show us the way to the heart of God. That's the secret of healing loneliness, the homesickness for God. Remember the hymn: "Softly and tenderly Jesus is calling, . . . Come home . . . come home!"

Jesus answered and said to them, "Even if I bear witness of Myself, My witness is true, for I know where I came from and where I am going; but you do not know where I come from and where I am going."

John 8:14

*A*nyone who knows me knows that I'm no mechanic. Whenever I have to assemble a piece of equipment that comes with all the parts pre-packaged in a crate, I have a difficult time. I dump all the parts out on the floor. There's always a moment of decision: to plunge into the task or read the instructions. Recently I saw a crate that had a bold warning written on the side: "Be sure to read the manufacturer's instructions before assembling this equipment." Then, in smaller letters—"You will not be able to assemble this product unless you follow the instructions step by step." Why is it I always want to try it without the instructions? I usually end up with a pile of extra bolts and screws.

The manufacturer's instructions! You are probably way ahead of me in the parable I got out of that. I usually come to the end of my efforts with a poorly constructed article, extra parts, and lots of frustration. Then I have to go back, take it all apart, and start over following the instructions faithfully step by step.

The same is true for our lives. Our manufacturer, creator, and Lord revealed the way He wanted His people to live. When we had messed it all up He had to come and show us how to live in Jesus Christ. The Word of God, who created us, came to be the blueprint for how we were meant to live the years of our lives, here and forever in eternity. We'll not learn how to live with pressure until we go back to the manufacturer's instructions. When pressure gets to us, it's time to find out what's wrong. We've tried to run our own lives and it hasn't worked. When the pressure builds, and we holler "Help!" He's there to show us where we have overloaded the circuits and shorted out Him, other people, and the joy of living. When we consider how Jesus lived with pressure, we discover the secret of how He can help us today.

The next day John saw Jesus coming toward him, and said, "Behold! The Lamb of God who takes away the sin of the world!"

John 1:29

Separation from fellowship with God has consistently resulted in the feeling of guilt—specific guilt for definite sins, generalized guilt for the root sin of separation. The feeling of guilt is a sure sign of an uneasy state of grace. Guilt is the absence of love—the refusal to receive love and love God in return, the failure to love ourselves as we are loved by Him and to love others graciously as He has loved us. The question remains: If we feel distant from God, who moved? We did!

That's why He Himself came to us in His Son. He came to His people who could no longer come to Him. His purpose was to expose His loving heart. There was a cross in the heart of God before there was a cross on Calvary; the eternal grace of God was revealed on that treacherous Friday afternoon outside of Jerusalem.

How else could He do it? What else could He say that would penetrate the guilt-ridden hearts of men and women? The cross was love to the uttermost, grace's ultimate entreaty. As the Lamb of God was nailed on the cruel cross, His words echoed from the heart of God, "Father, forgive them, for they do not know what they do" (Luke 23:34). Indeed, they didn't know what they were doing. The people who crucified Jesus did not realize that the ultimate sacrifice for humankind's sin was being enacted once and for all, then and for all time.

After the Resurrection, when His disciples and followers looked back on the cross, they could exclaim with awe and wonder, "That's how much God loves us!" The cross became the center of their gospel message. It invaded the guilt-infested hearts of people and became the power that transformed their lives. The same good news sets us free of guilt today.

He has taken it out of the way, having nailed it to the cross.

Colossians 2:14

It's a challenge to forgive and then forget. We can take comfort in the assurance that we don't have to take it alone. The same Savior who called His disciples to take up their crosses and follow Him did not carry His cross alone to Calvary! Simon of Cyrene was conscripted into service to carry the heavy crossbar the final steps up Golgotha. Why was Matthew so careful to include this in his passion account? To show the humanity of Jesus? Surely Jesus could have carried that cross alone. The One who performed miracles and healed the sick was not lacking in power to carry His cross! There's a profound meaning here for us. If Christ was willing to be helped to carry His cross, should we refuse His help in carrying ours?

We will never be alone to carry our crosses if we accept His uplifting help. Our cross is to serve people. Often that begins by forgiving them and forgetting what has been done.

Christ can and will give us the healing of our memories. He's done it for me countless times. I've seen it happen in thousands of people with whom I have prayed that the gift of a divine amnesia be given. When we believe that nothing is impossible for the Lord and tell Him of our inability to forget, He is ready to blot out all the anguish and pain of a debilitating memory.

Paul challenged the Colossians to nail their sins to the cross. The same should be true for our memories. In ancient Greece a nail driven through a charge list against a person and displayed publicly meant exoneration. The apostle maximizes the imagery by calling the Christians to do the same. Nail it to the cross! When we do, the same love exposed on Calvary floods the tissues of our memories, expunging the remembrance of harbored sin—our own first and then those of others we have hoarded so dangerously.

Recapitulation, Resurrection, Regeneration:
Three momentous words;
Words of great hope.
Christ's death and resurrection are
recapitulated in us when we surrender
our lives to Him
We die to self-sovereignty; we are born again.
A new person is raised up in us,
we are a new creature.
A new creation.
Old things pass away, the new has come.
We are ready to be filled with the Holy Spirit.
Our regeneration begins.
Each day we are filled afresh.
Our transformation continues.
We have been called, chosen, destined
to be made like Christ.
Fear of death is gone;
All our physical death can do to us
is to release us to a fuller realization of heaven
we have begun to experience now.

Therefore we were buried with Him through baptism into death, that just as Christ was raised from the dead by the glory of the Father, even so we also should walk in newness of life.

Romans 6:4

*B*ecoming and growing as a Christian means passing from death to life.

How can we be sure it's happened to us? Here's a series of tests. Do you have a freedom to live without resistance and reserve? If you were to die physically today, are you sure that your death would be nothing more than a transition in living? Have you ever made a complete and unreserved surrender of your negative instinct of destruction? Do you have a positive excitement about living? Is joy the vibrant emotion of your heart? Can you love yourself and others deeply, warmly? Are you free of death?

To be sure of all this, I want to invite you to your own funeral. Picture your old self in the coffin—the old person intent on self-limitation and negative resistance to life. This is the moment of the death of death for you. Let go of your death grip on life, of all the debilitating patterns. Then picture the lowering of that old self into the grave. Gone from sight and feeling forever. Now invite Christ to live His resurrection life in you. Picture your new person motivated by the will to live. How will you act? What will you do? How will you express Christ's love? Hold the picture. You have been born anew! D. T. Miles once said, "The resurrection that awaits us beyond physical death will be the glorious consummation of the risen life we already have in Christ!"

Someone once said, "Don't take life so seriously; you will never make it out alive." Not true! We will live forever. But how we live now determines where, how, and with whom. If we have come alive in Christ now, then we need not take life too seriously. We will live each day with gusto and joy.

For I determined not to know anything among you except Jesus Christ and Him crucified.

1 Corinthians 2:2

Calvary is not only an assurance of the Lord's love and forgiveness, but the healing of our broken dreams and wishes. The cross is not only the death of Christ for us, it is the summons to our death to ourselves. To be crucified with Christ means that we say with him, "Not my will but Your will be done." Mending begins with that.

I have never known a broken heart that was not healed when the person unreservedly surrendered the hurt to our Lord. As a man said to me recently, "If my heart had not been broken, my pride would never have been shattered, and I would never have discovered the deeper levels of the Lord's love when we have a contrite heart."

Go back over the broken things and see if the truth holds. Broken dreams force us either to cynical despair or a new trust in God and His strategy for us. Broken hopes for loved ones force us to let go, to stop playing God either as their strength or their comfort, and to release them to the Lord's amazing capacity to bring good out of evil. Our concern over health must finally bring us to the brokenness of praying, "Whether I live or die, I am the Lord's. Here, Lord, is my body. Heal me according to Your plan for now and eternity. I praise You that I belong to You. I am more than this frail body that I relinquish to Your complete control." The same is true in grief. There comes a time when we must give the broken pieces of our shattered emotions to him. He is the Lord of the living—here and in heaven. The brokenness of grief can open us up to the Lord as never before. When our hearts are broken by other people, there's no place to go but to the Lord to ask for the power to forgive and to be an agent of reconciliation.

He will baptize you with the Holy Spirit and fire. . . . [T]he chaff He will burn with unquenchable fire.

Luke 3:16–17

*T*he chaff in us is burned out by the fire of the Holy Spirit. Our chaff is anything that keeps us from our Lord or any other person. It is the attitudes that cripple, the values that demand false loyalty, the habits that incarcerate us. Our chaff also includes memories of past failures for which we will not accept forgiveness and forget, the plans for the future that could never receive our Lord's blessings. Most of all, it is willful self-centeredness and determination. We are loved just as we are, true, but the Spirit will never leave us there. His work in us is to recreate us in the image of Christ. Once He comes to live in us, he begins to move out into every area of our minds and hearts. He's never finished with us.

Recently I passed through a very difficult and painful period of seeing myself realistically through the eyes of a couple of people I love very much. The only place I could go with the data was to prayer. The Spirit was firm and yet gentle. Then He gave me the power to do something about it. The amazing thing was that just before this need for change was brought to my attention, I had been feeling very secure and at peace, as if my growing in Christ had finally reached a quiet maturity. Not so! Chaff I hadn't realized was there had to be burned away. And it will be like this for as many years as I have to live on earth.

Closely related to the burning of chaff out of us is the galvanizing of our relationships by the fire of the Holy Spirit. Welding takes white-hot fire. So do deep, inseparable relationships. The fire in my heart coupled with the fire in yours make us one. Christ prayed that we might be one. His living Spirit in us is indefatigable in making this possible.

If you then, being evil, know how to give good gifts to your children, how much more will your heavenly Father give the Holy Spirit to those who ask Him!

Luke 11:13

*J*esus wanted His disciples prepared for Pentecost. Unless they had the kingdom as the basis of their life plan, the power soon to come upon them would not be used for the purpose intended. He had to be sure that they understood what had been the theme of His parables and one of the essential reasons for His death and resurrection. He had come to call a kingdom people—reconciled, forgiven people in whom He could live. Opening ourselves completely to the sovereign reign and rule of the Lord is an essential prelude to Pentecost.

Recently a man in my church came to talk to me about how to receive the power of the Holy Spirit. He had observed the deep joy and contagious love in some people who openly identified its only source as the Spirit's indwelling, artesian power. He wanted what they had. The man thought that spiritual power came through having the right "experiences." I affirmed that receiving the Spirit's power was preceded by a surrender of our wills and then all our relationships and responsibilities. We took an incisive inventory, including attitudes, prejudices, broken relationships, and then looked at his marriage, money, job, and plans for the future. He discovered that he was running his own life and not attempting anything big or adventuresome enough to need the Spirit's power. That shocked and stunned him. But the same Spirit for whom he longed was at work, and He helped this man through the painful process. The first thing it required was checking those decisions about time and money that precluded doing the Lord's will. He did receive what he was looking for—and so much more: a freedom to live a daring life of adventure in the kingdom. The King's power is for the kingdom people!

And He said to them, "Go into all the world and preach the gospel to every creature."

Mark 16:15

The dynamic power of the Holy Spirit will be given in constant flow as long as we are engaged in communicating our faith. We are to be conduits or channels, not reservoirs or holding tanks. Who in our lives has missed both the abundant and eternal life because of our silence? Are we willing to be made willing for the basic, undeniable calling of every Christian?

The Lord's power will not be squandered on us for long if we refuse to be channels of His grace as witnesses. And where? "Jerusalem, and in all Judea and Samaria, and to the end of the earth" (Acts 1:8). Not only the extent, but the quality of the Lord's movement is implied. Jerusalem for the disciples would not be easy, with conflict over Jesus' death and resurrection. To announce that Jesus is alive would not win a popularity contest with the Sanhedrin. Judea, somewhat easier. But Samaria? The area was filled with half-breeds who had been the subject of hundreds of years of prejudice since the time of the Exile. Yes, Samaria too. And to the end of the earth. The Spirit of Christ would reach all nations.

For us the focus of our mission is at home in life's most intimate relationships where people really know us. It has a focus at work and in the community where the consistency of our life and witness can be observed. But it also means our nation and the world. Most of all, it includes wherever we are or are sent. But don't wait for a call to be a missionary or a clergyperson. Start with the people at hand. Wherever life leads, there will be people waiting whose lives mysteriously are being prepared for the serendipity of meeting the Savior or growing in Him because He arranged for us to be in the right place at just the right time.

No one can say that Jesus is Lord except by the Holy Spirit.
1 Corinthians 12:3

*F*aith is not a humanly initiated capacity. It is utterly futile and guilt-producing to tell ourselves or anyone else that what we need is faith or more faith. We can't produce it! When our minds are invaded with the assurance of God's forgiveness and acceptance, He gives the gift to respond. That response is expressed in the elements of faith—acceptance, surrender of our lives, a commitment of all that we have and are to serve Him as Lord of our lives, and an openness and willingness to be filled with His Spirit. Are we alive in the abundant life with the confidence of eternal life because of that faith?

The Holy Spirit who gave us the gift of faith to believe the gospel also gives us a gift of applied faith for the specific needs and challenges of life. It is the confidence that nothing is impossible for the Lord. Has our being filled with the Spirit given us this bold quality of faith?

The Spirit of the resurrected Lord is the healing power available to Christians today through the Spirit's gift of healing for the physical, emotional, personal, interpersonal needs of our lives and the people for whom He guides us to pray. First we are to pray in order to know what to ask and then to ask it with the gift of confident faith. Have you ever asked for the gift of healing?

The advanced gift of faith gives us the courage to pray in the name of Jesus. That clarifies what is in keeping with all we know of what He said, did, and does. Unless a prayer request glorifies Him, His name cannot be used nor His power released. But once the rightness is established, we are given the release of His Spirit to ask for and expect what He has pictured for us as the focus of our prayers of intercession and supplication. Have we discovered the power of Christ's name?

To them God willed to make known what are the riches of the glory of this mystery among the Gentiles: which is Christ in you, the hope of glory.
Colossians 1:27

A Christ-captivated life enables us to live an extraordinary life. We are not limited to the confines of our own intellect or talent. The secret is Christ in us. Paul discovered that and communicated the wonder of the transferred life when he wrote to the Colossians about the mystery hidden for ages but now manifested in Christ's people: "Christ in you, the hope of glory" (Col. 1:27). Glory is manifestation. Christ manifests Himself in us and transforms us into His own image. The secret of the Christian life is not only that we have been *with* Jesus but that He *is* in us! There should be daily amazement—first in us and then in others—as to what we are able to discern, dare, and do. Christ in us is the inner source of wisdom beyond human sagacity, discernment beyond comprehension, love beyond our cautious affection, truth beyond our experience. The deeper we grow in Christ, the more people will be forced to wonder.

There will be changed lives around us because of Christ in us. The greatest miracle is in the conversion and transformation of a person with whom we have shared the love of Christ. When we give ourselves away in caring, costly relationships of affirmation and encouragement with those who do not know Christ, He uses us to model His power and introduce them to Him. People will live forever because of the Lord's ministry to them through us.

Christ will get the glory. We can enjoy being a channel of His grace. All the compliments and adulation go to Him. Our reward is a boldness in knowing who we are, whose we are, and for what we were born. People will see . . . be sure of that. They will wonder what has happened to us; they will marvel at what has happened around us; and then, finally, they will realize what is happening in us. Jesus. There can be no other explanation!

Thanks be to God, who gives us the victory through our Lord Jesus Christ.

1 Corinthians 15:57

*W*inning is not controlling and manipulating people to get what we want. It isn't being "top dog" or always rising to positions of power. It's not financial success and security or simply receiving the cheering accolades and approval of people.

The kind of winning I'm talking about is much more profound. It is an inner quality that transforms our outer attitudes toward life. For Christians, winning is fulfilling the purpose for which we were born. It is being the person the Lord intends for us to be. Winning is living at peak performance, to the maximum level of our individual capability. We never realize our full potential until we experience this sublime joy of knowing that we are loved and cherished by the Lord and receive the fullness and freedom of His Spirit.

True winning, then, is desiring, discovering, and doing the Lord's ultimate will and following His daily guidance. Winning is living in the liberating assurance that we are sons and daughters of God and have been chosen to fulfill a unique destiny.

The good news for us, though, is that, as Christians, we are running a race that we've already won. We don't compete to win the Lord's acceptance or affirmation. That's already been given in full measure. Instead, we are called to run with Him as winners who have been given the crown of victory.

This is the confidence we are to have as we face life's opportunities. In our personal relationships, in our work, and in the accomplishment of the particular assignments the Lord gives us, we are meant to live with full faith that, in His own way and timing, His plans and purposes will be accomplished through us. He wants to enable us to win in our calling to love others profoundly and succeed in the work He gives us to do.

For the law of the Spirit of life in Christ Jesus has made me free from the law of sin and death.

Romans 8:2

*I*n his second imprisonment just before his execution, the apostle Paul, reflecting on his life in Christ, gave us a motto for winning, "I have fought the good fight, I have finished the race, I have kept the faith" (2 Tim. 4:7).

These words, inspired by Jesus, are the words of a winner. They spur us on in our present lap in the race of life. There's no need to put ourselves down as losers. Living life in Christ is winning in itself. We can say with Paul, "I can do all things through Christ who strengthens me" (Phil. 4:13).

For a Christian, there's no such thing as a no-win situation or relationship. We are called to be faithful to our Lord. Even when that means difficulty, we win in seeking to do what He guides and in expressing the joy, love, and hope He provides. The results are up to Him. Instead of piling up one more self-incriminating failure to mock us when the next big challenge comes along, we will press on knowing that in the end we will experience an ultimate victory that will be the climax of a lifetime of winning.

Jesus invades the inner being of each of us. His healing touch reaches the child of the past in us with acceptance and affirmation. He tenderly exorcises the crippling memories or negative criticism that makes us feel inadequate. He communicates His vision for what we can be, living at the full potential of His power in us. We feel the surge of courage. No longer do we need to will our own failure. We are sons and daughters of God, crowned with glory and honor and free to live without the fear of winning.

Little children, keep yourselves from idols.

1 John 5:21

*J*esus' parable of the wicked vinedressers helps me to understand my most dangerous idol. Remember the story? The owner rented out the vineyard with its abundant vines, its many wine presses and vats, a protective wall, and a tower. All the vinedressers had to do was enjoy the vineyard and its profits and at the end of five years pay a third of the produce to the owner. That was the rub. The self-possessed and determined vinedressers began to believe and act as if the vineyard were theirs. They had worked it, fertilized, pruned the vines, and arduously harvested the crops. "The vineyard is ours! What right does the owner have to claim any of the produce? It was our sweat and labor that developed the vineyard." When the owner's delegation of servants came to collect, the vindedressers and cast them out of the vineyard. When the owner's son came, they killed him, hoping to possess the inheritance forever.

This parable of self-exposure of the heart of God was told by Jesus during His last week in Jerusalem before He was crucified. It helps us to come to terms with what He believed to be His mission in Israel, the vineyard of God, and in our hearts. The transition from His to ours to mine is never immediate but grows over a long time. We may even invite the Lord into the vineyard and share the tithe of our efforts, but He is still little more than an honored guest in the vineyard. We are convinced it belongs to us!

But there's one thing the Lord will not be: He will not take His place on our shelf of beautifully displayed idols. He is Lord of all and demands to be Lord of all in our lives.

That makes me want to say, then pray, and finally sing with abandoned commitment the words of Andre Reed's hymn:

> Holy Spirit, all divine,
> Dwell within this heart of mine.
> Cast down every idol throne;
> Reign supreme, and reign alone.

But you shall receive power when the Holy Spirit has come upon you; and you shall be witnesses to Me in Jerusalem, and in all Judea and Samaria, and to the end of the earth.

Acts 1:8

*W*e are on the edge of a momentous outpouring of the Holy Spirit. If we dare to experience the same prelude to power the apostles experienced, we will be ready for a new Pentecost, the rebirth of the church, new fire for burned-out church people, and the expulsive power of uncontainable enthusiasm and excitement.

What Jesus did to get His disciples ready for Pentecost is what He longs to do in you and me. He took a confused, disunified, equivocating band of followers and forged them into a movement. Let's look at how He did it. Luke tells us vividly in the first chapter of Acts.

First of all, Jesus wanted His disciples to be sure of Him as the leader of the movement. He wanted them to know that He was the same Lord who had called them into discipleship, ministered among them, and was crucified and raised for them. But He wanted them to know something more: that He would always be with them through the Holy Spirit. They had to know this; they had to be sure. After He ascended, He would return. The same Spirit who had dwelt in Him, whom they now experienced in this incisive interface of preparation, would return. The Holy Spirit would be the Lord's continuous activity among them, His living presence in the present tense.

That's what we need to know. Christ is alive! He is here with us. He wants to come not just around, or among us, but within us. In keeping with His assurance, "Behold, I send the Promise of My Father upon you; but tarry . . . until you are endued with power from on high" (Luke 24:49). The remarkable "Acts," not just of the apostles, but of the Holy Spirit through them, are available today and are to be everyday Christianity among those who join His movement to change the world.

They ate their food with gladness and simplicity of heart, praising God and having favor with all the people. And the Lord added to the church daily those who were being saved.

Acts 2:46–47

*M*oss Hart gives us a motto for a thrilling life in his play, *Light Up the Sky*. One of the characters talks about his excitement and expectation for a show about to open: "We're sticking a Roman candle into the tired face of show business tonight . . . and the sparks that fly are going to light up the theater like an old-fashioned Fourth of July."

That's what we should be about—lighting the darkness, sticking a Roman candle into the tired face of boredom whenever and in whomever we find it. Boredom will be a thing of the past if we spend ourselves being sure no one around us is bored.

You may have resisted the idea that your life is boring. It may never have occurred to you that the blandness, dullness, and sameness of your life—the ruts of routine—are really boredom. But if life is not exciting, if you don't feel a sense of adventure, if you are not delighted by the possibilities of tomorrow, if you've given up to the eventuality of sameness, then you are bored. This could be the last day of boredom for you. Discover the joy of an intimate relationship with Christ; become a celebrant of yourself, other people, and life; lose yourself in people and their needs. Dare the impossible; expect the surprising infusion of the Holy Spirit— and I can assure you that you will never be bored again. Then you can rejoice with Christ, the Life, and say with Paul, "For me to live is Christ!" Your experience of the adventure will be as Jeremiah expressed it—fresh every morning and all through the day and night.

Allow me to reword a travel-agency advertisement: "Escape the ordinary, the usual, the predictable, the boring. Take an eternal journey with Christ!" It will be a thrilling life—all the way up.

*In the name of Jesus Christ of Nazareth, rise up and walk. . . . Men of
Israel, why do you marvel at this? Or why look so intently at us, as
though by our own power or godliness we had made this man walk?*

Acts 3:6, 12

The name of Jesus was the secret of the boldness of the apostles. The
Lord had promised that He would be with them and whatever they asked
in His name would be given them. It was in the name of the Lord Jesus
that they had healed the lame man in Acts 3 who now stood with them
before the Sanhedrin as a living testimony. And yet it was with a super-
cilious, mocking tone that the high priest had asked by what name they
had performed the miracle, implying that it had been by some magical
formula or incantation of an exorcist. Peter's response was more than the
Sanhedrin had bargained for.

At that time, the word *name* meant the nature, personality, authority, and power of a person. The name was the counterpart of its bearer;
his character and essence. In Hebrew, the name of God was synonymous
with His presence. Second Samuel 7:13 speaks of the name of God dwelling in His sanctuary. Jeremiah quotes God as swearing by His name. The
biblical name of God denotes His attributes. Jesus came in the name of
the Lord and sent His disciples out to preach and heal in His name. To
speak or act in the name of another was to invoke his presence and
power.

Note that when Jesus healed or did a miracle, He did not do it by
God's name. He was the name! Immanuel, God with us. The authority
and power that were in Him were now delegated and entrusted to the
apostles and the church. By His name—His presence—they were empowered to do what He had done during His messianic ministry.

The power of the living Christ was at work through them. The actual manifestation of healing quickened their faith. That explains the
boldness before the Sanhedrin. Personal experiences of the power of the
name working through us make us unafraid, ready-for-anything people.

Nor is there salvation in any other, for there is no other name under heaven given among men by which we must be saved.

Acts 4:12

*B*oldness is the result of the conviction not just that Jesus saves but only that Jesus saves. The key word in this verse is *salvation*, the free gift of deliverance from sin. It actually means healing and health, wholeness and oneness. The magnificent word stands for everything Jesus Christ came to be and do for us. Through His life, death, and resurrection we are reconciled to God. The cross was a one-time, never-to-be-repeated sacrifice for the sins of the whole world. When we accept His atoning death for our sin, we are forgiven and set free of guilt and self-condemnation. We are born again, beginning life anew as a loved and forgiven new creature. When we let God love us, a new creation begins, the past is forgiven and healed, the future is open to amazing possibilities of freedom and joy. We come alive—now and forever. The Holy Spirit comes to live in us, and the healing process of making us whole people begins. We can dare to be ourselves as loved unreservedly by God. His grace—unlimited favor and acceptance—makes us graciously affirming and loving. We cannot contain the ecstasy and delight we feel. Others are blessed with an unqualified acceptance. A lively hope springs up within us. Problems are only the prelude to fresh discoveries of the Spirit's potential. The aching needs in our hungry hearts are fed by a daily, moment-by-moment companionship with the Holy Spirit. Layer by layer, He penetrates into our psyches, reorienting and reconstituting us around the mind of Christ—His wisdom, disposition, and intuition. The will to destroy is replaced by the will to live the abundant life and share it with others. No other religion or cult can promise that!

> *Great is my boldness of speech toward you, great is my boasting on your behalf. I am filled with comfort. I am exceedingly joyful in all our tribulation.*
>
> 2 Corinthians 7:4

Opposition crystallizes boldness. Difficulties deepen our determination. Conflict forces us to clarify the irreducible maximum of what we believe.

In Acts 4:18, the Sanhedrin commanded Peter and John should not "speak at all nor teach in the name of Jesus." The ruling was a gift from God! Startling? Perhaps. But look at it this way: The prohibition against speaking and teaching in the name of Jesus solidified the apostles and the church in courageous witness in a way that could never have happened without opposition. Peter and John had to decide whether to be obedient to God or to the Sanhedrin. Now they could understand existentially what Jesus had meant when He had challenged them to seek first the kingdom of God and put Him first, before family, friends, recognition, or popularity. I know of no truly bold person who has not experienced the sharp razor's edge of that decision. When we know who we are and what we are to do because of prolonged time in prayer, we can play to the right audience. Pressure comes in our lives when we equivocate and try to please everyone. Our insecurity often makes life a popularity contest and we must win people's approval at all costs. The cost is always exorbitant.

We live in a time when strong convictions about anything are suspect. Our need to be liked drains our pertinacity. C. S. Lewis says about a character in one of his novels: "Mark liked to be liked. There was a good deal of spaniel in him." There may be a good deal of solicitous spaniel in all of us. But when the issues are focused, we are forced to discover the real center of our security in Christ.

Praise God for opposition! Lives are not changed without it, parishes are not renewed without its pain, and we do not become the toughened disciples we were meant to be without its honing discipline.

Christ's offer to us in life's challenges is,
"Take courage!"
Authentic courage is something we
take because
the Lord has taken hold of us.
He has a tight grip on us.
He will never let us go.
Not now;
not ever.

For we cannot but speak the things which we have seen and heard.
Acts 4:20

One reason for the boldness of the early Christians was not just that Jesus saves but that only Jesus saves. An exclusion led to a bold inclusiveness. When we believe that our Lord is not only the best of good men, or one savior among many, we are filled with an urgency that expresses itself in boldness. Recently a woman jumped from a burning building into the net held by sturdy firemen. Later she was asked, "How could you do it? Where did you get the courage?" She answered, "I had to do it. It was my only chance!"

That's the way the disciples felt. They would agree with E. Stanley Jones's blunt alternative: "Christ or chaos." Through Christ's cross and indwelling power we are reconciled to God, renewed in self-acceptance, released from guilt and self-justification, reunited with others in accepting love, and reconstituted as agents of hope in the world. No other religion or cult can promise that!

Now we can understand boldness: it was clear vision, absolute certainty, strong conviction, and unflinching courage. Contemporary Christians and the church of our time have no greater need. How shall we find it? The prayers of the early church give us the secret of the source of strength.

What an amazing response the church gave to Peter and John's report—not fear, nor wavering trepidation, but prayers. We need to consider this prayer as a model, for it gives an outline of how they sustained their boldness.

It's a great comfort to know that God's faithful people have always been in trouble. In fact, it's a sure sign that we are obeying God rather then men. So what's new about persecution for righteousness' sake? Jesus called it blessed.

And when they had prayed, the place where they were assembled together was shaken; and they were all filled with the Holy Spirit, and they spoke the word of God with boldness.

Acts 4:31

$\mathcal{V}$ery late one evening, I told a friend that I was going down to the church. He playfully, but pointedly, drew attention to the error in my terminology. "Oh, are there Christians meeting together at this hour for study and prayer?"

He had me. What I said was not what I meant. I should have said, "I'm going down to the building where the church often meets." To go to church is not to go to a place, but to gather with a particular kind of people with a peculiar purpose and a very special power.

For Luke, writing his account of the acts of the Holy Spirit, there was no such confusion. The first time he used the word *church (Acts 2:47),* it was drenched with meaning. The early Christians had been called out, called to the Lord and called into fellowship with each other.

Belief in Christ as a gift of the Holy Spirit galvanized the early Christians in thought, affection, and life purpose. They believed that Jesus was the Christ, that God had raised Him from the dead, that He was present with them in the Holy Spirit, that He was their absolute Lord of all life, and that their purpose was to share His love with each other and the world.

The soul is the life verve in us. When Christians are of one soul, it means that the Holy Spirit who lives in each has brought unity of direction and goals. We breathe the same "life breath" spiritually and are guided in a unified functioning together. Through the Holy Spirit we are fellow participants in Christ and in a life of mutual love, sharing, and caring.

Go, stand in the temple and speak to the people all the words of this life.
Acts 5:20

*I*t's interesting how advertisers and opportunists of all kinds use the words *the good life* to sell everything from beer to suburban living. They know how to touch the raw nerve in all of us. In one week I found 360 uses of *life* in advertisements. We all join the chorus to sing the lusty words with gusto, "I love life, and I want to live!"

But what is life and what does it mean to live with a capital L? Some of us have been given the privilege of tasting and touching all that we are told will bring happy living and have found the promises oversold. No place, position, personality, prowess, prosperity—or even person—is able to pull it off for us. There is still a longing for something more.

Our quest for life is not new. It has been aching in the heart of man for a long time. That was the voracious hunger of people in Jerusalem when the church was born. The reason for the eager response to the early Christians was that they modeled and mediated a quality of life that was attractive, magnetic, and powerful. People who heard them talk about their new life in Christ, empowered by His living Spirit, wanted what these Christians had found. Their vibrancy, their love and acceptance of each other, and their indomitable vision and purpose created a hunger in people to taste the quality of life they exemplified. The life they were living with the resurrected Christ and with each other demanded an explanation—and a response. The indicative mood of the church's life created an imperative mood of response. People wanted to live the way the Christians were living. What a response! Believers were added to the church, healing power was unleashed, and Jerusalem was shaken by a pervading spiritual revival.

And with great power the apostles gave witness to the resurrection of the Lord Jesus. And great grace was upon them all.

Acts 4:33

*L*ife is the balanced symmetry of our relationship with one another. We often speak of the "life" of a church or the "life" Christians share together. Because of Christ's life in a believer, there is a totally different quality to that believer's relationship with fellow believers. Christ's love, forgiveness, esteem, and hope become the basis of our union. A part of the proclamation of the Christian life is the miracle of fellowship, unity, and oneness. Since most people's problems come in their relationships, often the most forceful aspect of presenting the gospel is to share with people what happens when Christ's grace is the basic ingredient in our attitudes and disposition. There can be no question that the effectiveness of the early church in evangelism was caused by the love the Christians shared. "My, how those Christians love one another!" was the telling response of the world.

Our task is not to argue, philosophize, or cajole, but to live a life that demands explanation. Is there anything about us that would force people to say, "Now that's living! That's the way I wish I could live!" When we consider sharing our faith as imparting life, what a difference it makes. Then the emphasis is on Christ and not on theories about Him that we try to force upon people.

If we are to live a life in Christ that demands explanation, it's not only the observable quality of our lives, but evidences in our lives that must show there is a power at work in us. People must be forced to wonder and then to know that there is something more than personality prowess or healthy maturity, that there is something, Someone beyond ourselves enabling us to live the life that attracts attention.

Go, stand in the temple and speak to the people all the words of this life.
Acts 5:20

I heard a man explain the influence of a television producer who is a member of our congregation. "I watched him for months. It was not so much what he said. We hear a lot of people in our industry talk about some new fascination over a philosophy or religious idea. Neither was it the way he reacted in crisis, though he is consistently strong and calm. But that could have been explained by his healthy childhood or successes in the industry. No, it was more than that. It's the way I feel when I'm with him. Long before I asked him about what he believed—and note, I had to ask him—he made me feel of value, like I was the only person alive when he talked with me. He is so free! But I sensed he had not always been like that. I just had to find out what made him tick! Finally, late one evening at an after-production party, I got him in a corner and said, 'Hey, friend, you are something else! How did you find what you've got?' Then he told me about Christ in the most unreligious, nonpious way I've ever heard. I didn't feel the way I usually do when people talk about Christ. We've talked a lot since then. I've made a start; I can now say that I'm a Christian. Church people usually turn me off. But this guy was irresistible!"

That should be happening to us constantly in our relationships. Our task is to know Christ so well and to grow so deeply in Him that we don't have to sit around worrying about how to witness. If we allow our Lord to live in us and spend our energies cultivating friendship with Him, we will be witnesses. The Lord Himself will position people in our lives because He knows we're ready.

I suggest that we need the same reorienting challenge that was given to the apostles and a release from some prison of the past or present to back it up. The two must always be kept together: the Lord's clear word and the undeniable evidence in our lives of an opened prison door.

Go and stand in the Temple, and tell the people all about this new life.
Acts 5:20 TEV

*T*he word *life* is used to summarize all that happens between and among those in whom Christ lives. When we speak of "our life together," we employ the word *life* to define what happens when two people or a group are in a place with some level of communication as persons. When we say a party had life, we mean that something happened that gave it zest and vitality. Or when we say that the life of a church is dynamic or inspiring, we are trying to put into words a spiritual something that occurs. Actually, it's not something, but "Someone."

People are interested in life and desperately want to maximize the years of their living, however stifled that desire can become by the pressure of living. People have an inherent life-wish in their psyches. Christ appeals to that and then shows people what real living is all about.

A word about the prisons from which He releases us to go tell *all about this new life*. There are those prisons of our own making—reserve, fear of being criticized, lack of daring courage. Secondary loyalties to people and positions can keep us from pulling out all the stops. So can anxiety about failure. But by far the most tightly locked prison in which many communicators live is their own lack of freedom in living the abundant lives themselves. There's a direct ratio between fresh discoveries of new life in Christ and vital communication of it. There is no prison worse than sameness. The best gift we can give is to concentrate on being all that life entails in our own study of Scripture for the adventure of a Spirit-filled life. We won't be able to control what happens to and around us. But the Spirit will be in control. The Spirit wants to set us free!

We are His witnesses to these things, and so also is the Holy Spirit whom God has given to those who obey Him.

Acts 5:32

Obedience is the secret to spiritual strength. We must obey what Christ has said in His message; we must obey what comes to us from reading His Word; and we must obey the deep inner voice of His guidance for particular situations and relationships. How do you know if you're being obedient? I find it helpful to ask myself the following questions:

1. Am I living consistently as much of Christ as I know?
2. Am I living out the implications of what I discover daily in the Scriptures?
3. Am I refusing to do what I feel I should to be faithful to Christ? Has He already told me more than I acted on?
4. Am I consciously inhibited from speaking about my Lord because of fear of rejection or of being considered foolish, unintellectual, or uncultured?

The power of the Holy Spirit is released by obedience. There is no other way. We cannot expect the joy and energy of His infilling if we are saying no to what we know from our prayers we should do.

Obedience is like a thermostat. It opens the flow of the Spirit for the needs around us. The cold of the world calls for the heat and warmth of the fire of the Holy Spirit within us.

Joy is the undeniable mark of the new life. We are not expected to be perfect, or never fail, or be free of life's pressure problems. But joy should be the identifiable evidence that Christ is alive in us and we are facing reality with His guidance, interceptions, and undiminishable strength.

A joy-filled life will always demand explanation, and we will be ready. We have been released from the prisons of a life that is not life at all, to live a new life in Christ and to tell all about it to those God has made ready to listen.

And they stoned Stephen as he was calling on God and saying, "Lord Jesus, receive my spirit."

Acts 7:59

*W*e are told that Stephen was "a man full of faith and the Holy Spirit." The two dimensions belong inseparably together. The greatest gift of the Holy Spirit is faith. It is the gift that makes all other gifts possible. This gift not only liberates a person to respond to the gospel, but frees him or her to dare to believe that all things are possible through Christ. Faith first produces the new life in Christ and then a new life of daring in the believer. The Holy Spirit in Stephen had given him the courage to surrender his life to Christ and then to anticipate expectantly Christ's intervention in all situations. The power of faith produced a viable relationship between Stephen and the living Christ. Whatever else we admire about this fearless, unpurchasable saint, we find the ultimate taproot of our admiration in his audacious faith.

On a human level, Stephen was not naturally any greater than you and I. The difficulties he went through brought out what the Lord had worked into his character.

If we are willing to be as open to the Holy Spirit as Stephen was, then we will be trusted with the kind of difficulties and challenges he was. But we won't see this as trouble; we will be able to allow life to happen to us fully. Instead of resisting reality, we can befriend it, knowing the Lord will use it. That could make all the difference for you and me for today and all tomorrows.

Our prayer needs to be: "Lord, give me Your Holy Spirit; pour into me faith, grace, power, wisdom, and freedom to believe You can do signs and wonders in and around me. Then give me whatever challenges You can use to bless others and expand Your church. And I ask only one thing more: May at least one person see in my face the face of an angel. There are lots of Sauls who are watching, Lord. Help me to obey and be faithful!"

And when Simon saw that through the laying on of the apostles' hands the Holy Spirit was given, he offered them money.

Acts 8:18

*W*e cannot expect the Holy Spirit's power until we have opened our hidden hearts to the Lord. A sorcerer named Simon had said that he believed in Christ and was among those who were baptized. Yet his inner life was still untouched. In it were bitterness and compulsive patterns of rebellious self-will. Simon was still in charge of Simon. He wanted a spiritual high while his heart was still low-down; he wanted gush without grace through repentance and forgiveness.

Simony is a word that comes from that spiritual sickness. Historically, it meant the buying and selling of position and office within the church. But there is also a subtle simony in all of us. We all would like to have a spiritual radiance without repentance. We want life without having to change our lifestyle. Hidden sins; fantasies we could never tell anyone; broken, hostile relationships; determined patterns of thought that contradict the gospel; habits; selfish attitudes that emaciate the people around us—all these lurk within most of us, while at the same time we say we want Christ as Lord of our lives and His living Spirit as the power of our living. We are willing to pay handsomely for the worst and best of two worlds—not only money, but religious activity, self-generated goodness, oblations of overactivity, and manipulative kindness—all so we won't have to let down the moat bridge of the castles of our carefully protected, secret hearts. But the very things we hide are the point of entry for the Holy Spirit. When we confess them, accept forgiveness, and turn them over one by one, the Spirit takes their place. There must be something, Someone, to fill the emptiness. Only His Spirit, the Holy Spirit, can do that!

Then the Spirit said to Philip, "Go near and overtake this chariot." So Philip ran to him, and heard him reading the prophet Isaiah, and said, "Do you understand what you are reading?"

Acts 8:29–30

I want to share with you what I believe is the secret of an exciting life. People who have discovered it are some of the most attractive, winsome people I know. Their lives are distinguished by an eagerness and earnestness. This secret is the source of the unquenchable enthusiasm I feel about living.

The mysterious origin is traceable to two words: guidance and obedience. This is the belief that the Holy Spirit actually can guide our thoughts and that obedience can appropriate His power to do what is guided. The Holy God, creator of all, Savior and Lord, will use you and me! We can cooperate with Him in accomplishing His plans and purpose in people and situations.

R. H. L. Sheppard found this secret: "Christianity does not consist in abstaining from doing things no gentleman would think of doing, but in doing things that are unlikely to occur to anyone who is not in touch with the Spirit of Christ."

When I first read these words, it was like taking hold of a live wire. I couldn't let go. A current of electricity surged through me. "That's it!" I thought. There's the secret: not just abstinence, but affirmation. A Christ-honed conscience can guide our morals, ethics, and personal behavior. That's maintenance, but what of adventure? That begins when we love the Lord with our minds and dare to believe that He can invade the tissues of our forebrain to guide our thinking, imagination, and will. When we are filled with the Holy Spirit, there is an inspiring indistinction between His thoughts and ours. He becomes the Lord of our intelligence, the generator of the mind's potency for possibilities we never dreamed could be. Couple that with the will to act on what He guides, and you have the secret of exciting living.

And they were not able to resist the wisdom and the Spirit by which he spoke.

Acts 6:10

A woman I know was almost hysterical about what was happening to her daughter and her grandchildren because her son-in-law didn't believe what she did. He couldn't escape the nagging with which she pressed her urgent desire for his conversion. One day, a new thought invaded her mind. "Be to your son-in-law what you hope he will become. Leave his conversion to the Lord. Stop sending tracts and literature. Think of five things you like about him, emphasize them and affirm him." From the time she dared to accept that guidance, things began to happen in the young husband's life.

A young woman said: "Now that I believe God can plant thoughts in my mind, I have begun to follow orders. I can hardly believe the results. When I am guided to speak to people and say what I am led to say, they keep responding, 'That's just what I need to hear today!'"

These stories of real people dramatize the secret of an exciting life. Added to them are countless examples of wisdom, direction, vision, and creativity I see mediated in the church by people who are under the Spirit's guidance. Things that no amount of human intelligence alone could develop are envisioned and realized. At work, people are finding capacities to solve problems and greet the possibilities of the future as never before. They are open to the guidance of the Spirit. I am amazed also at the remarkable things that can happen when people get the needs of a city on their minds and ask for the Spirit's guidance there. The Lord of intelligence is giving strategies for solutions that would never occur without Him.

The secret of an exciting life is really no secret at all! It's written across the pages of the Book of Acts. You and I are to be the subjects of the new chapter God wants to write today.

Then the churches throughout all Judea, Galilee, and Samaria had peace and were edified. And walking in the fear of the Lord and in the comfort of the Holy Spirit, they were multiplied.

Acts 9:31

A leading senator asked me a very penetrating question. "What do you feel is the greatest need in our country?" My response was immediate, "For the Christians in America to discover the power of prayer and for the church to become a praying fellowship."

I told him I believed the power and guidance of God were available for our nation if the people of God would unlock the limitless resources of intercession for our leaders and the problems of our nation. His retort stung. "You'll have to make Christians out of the Christians before that will happen!"

I encouraged him to go on. "Well," he said thoughtfully, "the name *Christian* is so culturalized it no longer means very much in America. People use it to indicate what they are not more than what they are! We need some new name to describe someone who really knows Christ and lives out his faith. If people who call themselves Christians staked their lives and their ethics on Christ, I agree, this nation could be turned around."

I thought a lot about that afterward. Long before the followers of the resurrected Christ were called Christians, they were called "those belonging to the Way." That vivid designation cuts to the core of what I feel the senator was trying to express. But we do not need a new term; we need to return to the original one. The early church exemplified a quality of life in fellowship with Christ, each other, and the world that earned the compliment. Before they had carefully worded creeds, elaborate church organization, and professional clergy, Christ's people startled the world with the consistency of belief and behavior and the congruity of the ethos of Christ and their ethics.

But in every nation whoever fears Him and works righteousness is accepted by Him.

Acts 10:35

*W*e all have agendas. Some of them are open for others to see; some are hidden. They list what we want, when we want it, with whom and under what prescribed conditions. Agendas are necessary to help us focus our goals and move steadily and effectively toward them. When you know a person's agenda you can discern what he thinks is important, what values dominate his direction, or what reservations hinder his development.

Congregations also have agendas. They are a composite of what the majority of members believe a church should be and do. What we have experienced previously or found meaningful is usually the basis of a congregation's agenda.

There is nothing more crucial for Christians than to ask, "What is the Lord's agenda?" The question forces us to consider what His next steps are for us. That requires prayer, study of the Scriptures, and faithful seeking of His specific direction. It demands a persistent query: "Lord, what's next?"

The early church had a difficult time getting on the Lord's agenda. He had made it clear prior to Pentecost and the birth of the church. But the church had been reluctant at each step to adopt this agenda.

There will be times our willingness lags and we would like to evade responsibility. That's just why the Lord's agenda is so crucial. It sustains us in the midst of emotional ambiguity. The Holy Spirit is the source of our motivation. He will guide and direct all our days. What the Lord's agenda envisions, He will empower. When we are open, He will give us what we need. We can move on steadily toward our goal.

Then Barnabas departed for Tarsus to seek Saul. And when he found him, he brought him to Antioch. So it was that for a whole year they assembled with the church and taught a great many people. And the disciples were first called Christians at Antioch.

Acts 11:25–26

*W*henever we pass through "dry periods" or feel shelved from active duty for a time, we are to accept what is happening as an ordained interval of preparation and be confident that the Lord has not bypassed us. If we trust Him and listen to what He wants to say, as well as learn from what He allows us to go through—be sure of this—He will use us more effectively than ever before. Sickness, times of inactivity, or other changes of circumstances that alter our usual schedule and involvements can be used by the Lord to prepare us for what He has prepared. "Lord, teach me; show me Your way; help me to grow in knowledge of and love for You!" That's the humble prayer for the hiatus. Then we can begin to see things from His priorities and planning. Nothing is wasted for God. What we go through, what we face in life's excruciating disappointments, or what we are forced to learn when we get quiet enough to listen are all preparation for future ministry with people.

There is only one thing to do: Focus on Christ! He is all we need. But is He enough for you?

Paul's long time of preparation between his conversion and the beginning of his ministry got him ready spiritually and intellectually for what the Lord had waiting for him to do. The prolonged time at Tarsus made the apostle ready to proclaim the gospel at Antioch and then to the world. In the ebb and flow between preparation and participation with the Lord, the issue is trust. If we trust Him, He will use the preparation to get to us so that subsequently He can get to people through us and our participation. The Lord is never in a hurry. When He's finished with us at Tarsus, there will be an Antioch, and it's worth waiting for. The people we live with or work among will be blessed. The power of Christ through us will help them to assume the name of Christians!

Peter was therefore kept in prison, but constant prayer was offered to God for him by the church.

Acts 12:5

*P*rayer is not just to get God to do something, but to help us realize what He has done already. It is not an argument to convince God of what we need, but a conversation in which He shows us our need to recognize what He has previously done and is presently doing. It enables us to enjoy what He has entrusted to us.

Prayer is focusing on the gifts of God. Of all gifts He gives us, the most precious, and at times the most perplexing, are the people in our lives. Intercessory prayer for people is not for the purpose of getting God to change His mind about them, but for us to discover His mind for our relationship with them. Talking to God in prayer not only puts us in touch with Him but puts us in touch with people. When we share our concerns about people with the Lord in prayer, He shows us how to share ourselves with those people.

When most of us think about prayer for people's needs, our minds leap to something we want God to do or change. We immediately see the yawning gap between what they are and should be, what they have and what they need, what they have done and ought to do. We envision prayer as the bridge between what is and ought to be. We have learned that there are abundant resources of God for people if we will pray. That is good. But I want to focus on the power of prayer for appreciation as well as anticipation. There is a profound level of prayer that goes beyond remission for what is past or requests for what we long to be for the people we love. In-depth prayer for people liberates us to enjoy them right now, where they are, as they are. William Law was right: "There is nothing which make us love a man so much as praying for him." Prayer-born love frees us to recognize that the person is himself God's greatest answer to prayer.

*We know that God's nature
is unchangeable;
are we sure that His will is equally so?
Is the wish, the submitted wish
of a human heart,
able to alter the counsel
of the Almighty?
Can the humble request
of believing lips
restrain, accelerate, change the
settled order of events?
Can prayer make things that are not
to be as though they were?
Yes,
a thousand times yes!
Intercession is the mother tongue
of the whole family of Christ.*

Dora Greenwell

Continue earnestly in prayer, being vigilant in it with thanksgiving.
Colossians 4:2

*W*e seem to find comfortable security in persistent, preoccupied praying about a problem. The familiar feeling of distress over a difficulty or a need becomes more satisfying than the answer. This is especially true when the answer demands that we incarnate the prayer we have prayed and become part of God's answer for a person. Often the prayers complain more about people than they confess our trust in God. We complain to God about what needs to be changed or corrected in a person. But then we find it demands too much when we are asked to affirm the changes that occur.

A father I know prayed ceaselessly about his son. The young man's emotional problems were of grave concern to him. Then one day, he shared the problem with a friend. The response was not what he expected. "Unless you are willing to spend time with your son, all the praying will miss the mark! You are the answer to your own prayers. He needs *you!*"

To see is to behold, to admire, to honor. Elizabeth Barrett Browning in *Aurora Leigh* said, "God answers sharp and sudden on some prayers, / And thrusts the thing we have prayed for in our face." That's what happens when our prayers for some change or adjustment in a person's life are answered, not only in the particular thing for which we prayed, but when, in response to the Lord's love, we are thrust face to face and heart to heart with the person. That's what we all want most of all, isn't it? In answer to our problem-oriented prayers, the Lord gives a person-centered answer. The answer keeps knocking until we accept the person himself as God's gracious gift.

Therefore let it be known to you, brethren, that through this Man is preached to you the forgiveness of sins; and by Him everyone who believes is justified from all things from which you could not be justified by the law of Moses.

Acts 13:38–39

*T*he memory of past failures is like sand in the gears of our effectiveness. We are in the present what we have been in the past. The careful computer of memory records all the things we have done or have had done to us. We cannot wipe them out with redoubled efforts at goodness or self-justification. All that we have done to ourselves and others haunts us until we are forgiven. But the forgiveness must be radical and deep by the One who has authority to forgive. Only an incarnate God upon the cross can do that. "Forgive them, for they do not know what they do" (Luke 23:34). But we knew, Lord! The voice of love that paid the price for our sins responds, "Neither do I condemn you; go and sin no more" (John 8:11). Can it be true? All that we have said and done, forgiven? Yes, even before we ask. It is love's priority and power to forgive.

The syndrome of failure, forgiveness, and repeated failure was finally broken in my life when I realized that I was forgiven even before I sinned, that His forgiveness was given before I asked for it and my often reluctant request was grasping for a reality that had been finished for me on Calvary. The cross did not change God's attitude toward me; it revealed His unchanging nature. That finally melted my compulsive, repetitive pattern and gave me a first experience of freedom. But there was no deep personal freedom until I forgave myself. The reason I kept on doing the things that caused me guilt was because I could not be as gracious to myself as God had been. Arrogant pride! I was playing God over my own life. I was shocked when a friend helped me see this. The bars of my own "guilted cage" kept me locked in and unfree. Then one night in prayer I felt the Lord very near and powerful. "Will you love Lloyd as much as I do?" He asked. "Forgive him! I have."

Paul and Barnabas, who, speaking to them, persuaded them to continue in the grace of God.

                                                    Acts 13:43

*F*reedom covers all dimensions of time. We are free to take a backward look and receive forgiveness for ourselves and others. We can take an inward look to see those things that fester in us and make us insecure, and then accept the healing righteousness of God. We can take an out-ward look to people and dare to shower them with the overflow of our Christ-oriented self-delight and acceptance. We can take a forward look, knowing that the future is not an enemy, and meet each challenge, knowing that power is available. Realized forgiveness is but a prayer away. That's the bottom line for a blessed life!

Paul's stirring message of freedom in Christ won him a hearing from the whole city of Antioch. That marked an end of an era and the begin-ning of a new age. The Gentile frontier was unmistakably open, and pio-neer Paul was eager to break the trail. He pressed on with freedom because he knew the Lord went before him to prepare the way. Luke shows that those who believed had been prepared to respond: "Now when the Gentiles heard this, they were glad and glorified the word of the Lord. And as many as had been appointed to eternal life believed. And the word of the Lord was being spread throughout all the region" (Acts 13:48–49).

But life on the new frontier was never devoid of two conflicting re-alities for Paul: the hospitality of the Gentiles and the hostility of the Jews. The Gentiles were responsive and the Jews persistently dogged his tracks, disturbing his ministry and dissuading his converts. But freedom in Christ provided joy in the midst of difficulty and persecution.

The bottom line of the gospel is freedom expressed in joy, for us as well as Paul.

Now the Lord spoke to Paul in the night by a vision, "Do not be afraid, but speak, and do not keep silent; for I am with you, and no one will attack you to hurt you; for I have many people in this city."

Acts 18:9–10

Recently a man said to me, "I can take anything if I know it will end. There's a limit to the short-range difficulties I can face. What gets me is when I get into a problem that won't quit. Just when I think it's over and I can relax a bit, I get hit by a new wave of frustration. I don't know how long I can hold out unless I can see that I'm going to get to the end of the thing!"

We all feel that way at times. Most of us can empathize, if not with the application of our convictions to our work, certainly in our relationships, challenges, and difficulties of other areas. We can endure brief vicissitudes; it's when they drag on endlessly that we are tempted to give up hope.

When my strength is depleted, when my rhetoric is unpolished by human talents, when I am weary, the Lord has a much better tool for empathetic, sensitive communication. The barriers are down. When I know I can do nothing by myself, my poverty becomes a channel of His power. More than that, often when I feel I have been least efficient, people have been helped most effectively. It's taken me a long time to learn that the lower my resistances are and the less self-consciousness I have, the more the Word of God comes through. There is less of the club of judgment and more of a cross of grace. In a time like that I need to hear what I am saying more than the listeners; the result is that they hear what I may have blocked from them before.

Are you feeling weak or fearful right now? Thank God! Now's the time to speak and not be silent. It's a blessed time of productivity—a gift from the Lord. Embrace the troubled moment; make it a friend. Whatever you do, the glory will go to Christ and not to you. That's where it belonged all along!

So now, brethren, I commend you to God and to the word of His grace, which is able to build you up and give you an inheritance among all those who are sanctified.

Acts 20:32

$\mathcal{T}$he other day I heard a man's maturity in Christ described as tender toughness. At first the words seemed contradictory. How could this person be tough and tender at the same time? Wouldn't one cancel out the other?

We all know tender Christians. They are warm, emotional people whose love enables them to express assurance and compassion.

But there is also a toughness we admire in some followers of the Master. They are distinguished by determination and directness. They seem to know who they are and where they are going, because they know whose they are and what they are to be and do. They are on the move toward a clearly defined goal.

The problem is that most tender Christians need more toughness and most tough Christians need more tenderness. The man whose maturity was complimented had both. My experience of him confirmed the accolade. He had the tenderness of grace. Life had pounded softness into him. He had been hard and judgmental until successive failures and tragedies had brought him to the healing love of our Lord. The "new creation" gave him a capacity to affirm and encourage others. His own brokenness and sense of fallibility was expressed in gracious sensitivity to others. But, thank God, he has never lost the other half of grace. He is a man under orders who is determined to seek and do God's will as he sees it. No one dissuades him from his direction. He sees reality as it is, and when it comes to following Christ, living in the Scriptures, and spelling out the implications for his life and society, he is tough. This unpurchasable man has tender toughness. We are all meant to be like him.

I kept back nothing that was helpful, but proclaimed it to you, and taught you publicly and from house to house.

Acts 20:20

*I*t is shallow love that desires to keep life smooth and easy for people. By word, suggestion, or outright resistance, we can keep people from doing what God has willed for them. That's frightening. Not one of Paul's associates, fellow disciples, prophetic seers, or faithful prayer partners volunteered, "Paul, I affirm your vision. I know what will happen in Jerusalem, but I am for you and willing to go with you. Don't turn back or stay here in safety. I would not bend your heart or crush your determination. Praise God, you know what you are to do, and I am for you!" But Paul's friends never said anything like that. How very tragic, after all they had seen the Lord do in them and around them.

Tender toughness, that's what spurred on the indomitable apostle. His purpose was clear. What he would be called to do and suffer in Jerusalem was "for the name of the Lord Jesus." That means literally, "under the guidance of, in keeping with, and for the sake of the Lord." When a person exposes any vision, dream, or plan to the pure illuminating light of that perspective and it stands the test, he or she can seek to fulfill it with joy and courage.

All this centers on a serious analysis of our own relationship with the Savior. Has His love made us creatively tender toward others? Has His indwelling Spirit enabled us to be tough about ultimate issues? Tenderness without toughness is sloppy sentimentality. Toughness without tenderness is harsh intractability. But together, they make the courage- producing combination of Christian maturity. Thank God, He gave Paul both. He would never have made it to Jerusalem and on to Rome without them! We may have more of one than the other; only the Lord can tell us. He alone can tenderize the tough and toughen the tender. He is ready to do both.

*Now when we heard these things, both we and those from that place
pleaded with him [Paul] not to go up to Jerusalem.*

Acts 21:12

*W*hen Paul and his companions reached Tyre, they sought out the
disciples of Christ there. Paul knew that they were there and sought
them out for fellowship and mutual encouragement. What happened
when they were together may make us wonder how much encouragement they were to Paul.

Luke tells us they stayed at Tyre seven days. At the end of the time,
the Tyrean Christians told Paul "through the Spirit" not to go to Jerusalem. Conflicting guidance? Hardly, if the Spirit was the same Spirit. I
think the Spirit revealed the dangers ahead for Paul. The people inter-
preted this as a prohibition and told Paul that he should not go. But Paul
had received orders from the Spirit to go and also had been given a clear
picture of what going would mean. He did not argue or spend a long time
discussing guidance. He simply followed what he knew he had been told
to do.

Often loved ones and friends get the same guidance as we do, but it
is channeled to us through the grid of their own fears of their concern for
our safety. We can't imagine that trials and difficulties could ever be the
Lord's will for people we love. Success, ease, and peace without conflict
have become the false signs of the Spirit's blessing. He often wills these,
but they can never become the sure signs that His will is being done.
Success is doing what the Lord wills, ease is living in the flow of His
Spirit, and peace is often discovered in outwardly turbulent circumstances. It is equally dangerous to think that we are doing the will of the
Lord only if we are suffering or facing trouble. Paul's guidance was to go
to Rome by way of Jerusalem. With raw courage and determination, he
forged ahead, kindly accepting his friends' counsel, but not veering from
his clearly set course.

To all the saints in Christ Jesus.

Philippians 1:1

*N*ow there's a real saint!" is an expression we use to pay a person a very significant compliment. By it we mean that a person is living out his or her faith in spite of adversity or troublesome circumstances. We also refer to the apostles and great Christians of antiquity as saints. Often we read of the Roman Catholic Church elevating a person of another period of history to sainthood who had a vision of God and had performed certain spectacular, miraculous acts. But seldom do we think of ourselves as saints. And yet this is one of the great New Testament designations of a Christian. It is the term Paul used in his greeting to the church at Philippi: "To all the saints in Christ Jesus who are in Philippi."

If we were addressed as Saint John or Jean or Sam, we would probably respond, "Oh yeah? You should know more about me and you wouldn't use the term so loosely."

Sainthood is not status. It has nothing to do with our achievement or impeccability. Rather, it reminds us that by grace alone God elected and set us apart to be His people. I think we should use the term more often because it clarifies for us that our goodness has absolutely nothing to do with earning what can only be received as a gift.

Consider the saints at Philippi. When we picture that church gathered together to listen to the reading of Paul's letter, we see an astonishing mixture of humanity. The church was a classless, inclusive, nonsexist fellowship of very different kinds of people. And they were all saints—holy people—not that they were perfect, but because they were called and appointed to be God's people.

God's love and presence are not given to a special few but to those who will open themselves, surrender their will, and be obedient to whatever they are guided to do.

Grace to you and peace from God our Father and the Lord Jesus Christ.
Philippians 1:2

*W*ow, God! Wow! It's too good to be true! But I know it's true for me now. Thank You for loving me just as I am and for replacing that uneasiness and fear I have always felt with a peace like I have never known before!"

This prayer was prayed by a brilliant young woman who had asked me, "What is God like?" She was astounded by what I shared with her.

Paul gives us the answer in his greeting at the opening of his letter to the Philippians: grace and peace. What is God like? Grace! What happens to anxieties and fears when you experience grace? Peace! Paul's experience of God—his theology, message, and now his deepest yearning for his friends at Philippi—could be summed up in these two powerful words.

Grace tells us what God is like in His attitude and action. The Greek word was used to express unreserved love for another out of pure generosity of heart and with no thought of reward. For Paul, grace was rooted in the cross. When we see what we have done with the gift of life, ourselves, people, the world; when the anxiety of separation from God because of our willful rebellion finally gets hold of us; and when the knowledge that God loves us in spite of all that we have done or been amazes us—that's grace! It means forgiveness, acceptance, and a new beginning we never deserved.

Peace is the result of grace. It literally means, "to bind together." In other words, the peace that comes from unmerited, unearned love can weave and bind our fragmented lives into wholeness. The civil war of divergent drives, which makes us feel like rubber bands stretched in all directions, is ended. The Lord is in control. He has forgiven the past; He is in charge of the now and shows the way for each new day.

So, grace and peace to you!

He who has begun a good work in you will complete it until the day of Jesus Christ.

Philippians 1:6

Can people change? Is it really possible for human nature to be changed? Is the promise we hold out to people that they can be different really true? What do we mean when we say that the old person passes away and we become an entirely new person in Christ?

These are serious questions being asked today.

Paul believed in the power of God to change human personality. Our verse for today expresses a powerful combination of affirmation and encouragement. He recognized the beginning and challenged the incomplete. How very sensitive!

Behind Paul's confidence was his trust in Christ. He knew that the power of Christ was the life-changer. The words *began* and *continue* are sacrificial words. They designated the beginning and end of a sacrifice.

People want to become the best we affirm them to be. Negative lambasting never changed anyone. Our improvement programs for people are not shortcuts to growth but sequacious paths on which they get lost. Paul believed that the shortest distance to personality change was a direct line to Christ. He knew that if he could assure the Philippians that Christ was at work in them, it would awaken grateful humility, out of which a new daring and aspiration would grow. It is in personal relationship with Christ that we change and become more like Him.

I know this in my own life. It was because Christ had begun to work with me and gave me the gift of faith to respond that I started the Christian life as a college freshman. Radical changes in my personality and my relationships have taken place since then. I am not the man I was a few years ago; nor am I now what Christ will make me in a few months, tomorrow—today!

It is right for me to think this of you all, because I have you in my heart, inasmuch as both in my chains and in the defense and confirmation of the gospel, you all are partakers with me of grace.

Philippians 1:7

*I*n spite of what I am at times and all that I have yet to discover, God takes delight in me. The result is a new delight about the people in my life.

One morning when I was studying this verse I was overcome with the realization of how delighted Paul was in the expression of his feelings for the Philippians. He knew all the problems and differences they were having, but his letter was written in the context of affirmation that they were "his people" regardless of what happened. It's one thing to talk about grace, something else to incarnate it. There is no evidence that he would hold back his feelings of joy over them until they measured up.

One thing I have come to realize is that I often break the first Commandment in my judgments. God created me in His own image. I return the compliment by the idolatry of making approval and acceptance a commodity to be bartered for the performance I want from other people. After brooding over this passage for a long time, I took an honest inventory. I realized that my feelings of delight were often measured out to match my standards.

The secret of Paul's delight in the Philippians was in his experience of God's delight in him. But there's also a subtle twist in the grammar of this verse that presents a fascinating picture of what the church should be. The expression, "Because I have you in my heart" could just as accurately be translated, "Because you have me in your heart." The Philippians were delighted in Paul, and this gave him courage throughout his ministry.

Who in your life and mine needs our delight? Life is short! Could it be that someone in our lives will never have that liberating experience? Why?

For God is my witness, how greatly I long for you all with the affection of Jesus Christ.

Philippians 1:8

One of the authentic tests of people in Christ is their inclusiveness. The deeper we grow in Christ, the broader is our reach to enfold others who may express their faith and action differently. There is a tender lack of judgmentalism in a person who has suffered and experienced the forgiveness and new life in Christ.

How could Paul be so tolerant of people who preached Christ out of jealousy and ambition? I think it was because of the apostle's passion for Christ, trust in His power to innovate good out of failure, and acceptance of his own humanity. Paul wanted Christ to be made known in every possible way. He knew that he could not reach everyone. Others, for whatever motives, could get through to some he could never reach. He also trusted Christ to bring good out of the mixed natures of people. The patience of our Lord is magnificent in the way He waits for us to respond in different ways. Think of the strange ways that people are brought to Christ. What is abhorrent to us may be just the answer for someone else.

Paul could admit his own mixed motives. The New Testament is full of the evidences of his humanity: his curt dismissal of Mark, his conflict with Peter, his discord with the church in Jerusalem. Yet Christ had done great wonders through him. He knew that he was in transition and had only begun to grow in grace.

Often people who have known life's pain and disappointment are able to express initiative love to others who fail. The flip side is that usually the things we see in others that we don't like are exactly what trouble us. When we listen intently to our criticism and judgments, we usually can tabulate what's wrong inside ourselves.

As we go through this day, let's make a conscious effort to evaluate the people whom we cut off because of their manner, style, ideas, or the expressions they use.

For I know that this will turn out for my deliverance through your prayer and the supply of the Spirit of Jesus Christ.

Philippians 1:19

A friend of mine was deeply troubled and exhausted, yet he had responsibilities he could not ignore. Some very rough days were ahead of him. "Listen," I said, "every time you tighten up and get anxious, remember I am going to pray for you once every hour these next few days. Remember, I've taken the burden for you and will consistently talk to our Lord about it. Go ahead and relax!"

When I heard from him some weeks later, he told me about an incredible freedom he had found during those days of pressure. When things got tight, he remembered I was praying and it gave him courage.

Paul asked the Philippians to pray for him. He said that their prayers and the help of the Spirit of Jesus would deliver him in his need. The unstudied rush of Paul's thoughts in today's Scripture gives us an insight into his deepest feelings about the power of prayer. He has two sources of strength: the Philippian prayers and the help of the Spirit of Jesus. Could it be that when he thought of their prayers he also thought immediately of the thing for which he most needed them to pray? The help of the Spirit—that's the supreme prayer we can pray for another.

We cannot explain it, but there are resources of God's power that are released only when we pray. Prayer is the language of partnership with God in His continuing work of reconciliation. We pray, not to change, but to discover the will of God. Prayer draws us into fellowship with God and the people for whom we pray. He motivates in us the desire to pray for the very things He is more ready to give than we are to receive. The purpose of prayer is to unify us with God and each other.

According to my earnest expectation and hope that in nothing I shall be ashamed, but with all boldness, as always, so now also Christ will be magnified in my body, whether by life or by death.

Philippians 1:20

*I*f you had five uninterrupted minutes with our Lord, what would you say to Him and what do you think He would say to you? The value of this question is that it focuses our deepest desires and reminds us that those five minutes are available anytime.

One of the most liberating discoveries I have made in my own relationship with Christ is that He is *for* me and not against me. He wants the best for me! That's often difficult to accept because I am very demanding of myself. Whatever I desire to improve my life, Christ wants for me more.

The purpose of prayer is relationship, not answers. Anything we might receive as a result of praying is meager in comparison to our Lord's greatest gift . . . Himself.

In this attitude, Paul asks for three things: that he never fail his duty, that he be full of courage, and that he will bring honor to Christ. The fascinating thing about this prayer is that our Lord wanted that for Paul even more than Paul wanted it for himself. Christ was on Paul's side, but these qualities were gifts to be received, not prizes to be achieved. Paul did not want to be ashamed by failing in those last crucial days. He longed for boldness in speaking out for his Lord. His longing was to glorify Christ, to manifest his power, to be conspicuous in his witness. All of this he longed for whether he lived or died.

As I think about Paul's eager expectation, I know what I want for my life today. I long for the same things. I want to be faithful, to be bold, and to reflect Christ's love and power in all my duties. What about you? There's just enough time today to do the things He wants us to do in the way He wants us to do them.

My earnest expectation and hope [is] that in nothing I shall be ashamed, but with all boldness, as always, so now also Christ will be magnified in my body, whether by life or by death.

Philippians 1:20

*D*o you ever find that the memories of past failures and hurts lurk in you? The resentments of the past, the broken relationships, and the troublesome reminders of our failures can rob us of the joy of living right now.

But what about worry over the future? Often our concern about what will be blocks out zestful enjoyment of what is now. Blaise Pascal said, "We are never living, but only hoping to live; and, looking forward always to being happy, it is inevitable that we never are so." We live our lives on a deferred-payment plan. I agree with William James, "We do not live, nor enjoy life now, but wait for some future event or occurrence."

The bonds of Christ enabled Paul to live fully immersed in the now. In these words, "As always, so now," we hear Paul desiring to be the Lord's man in the present moment, completely alive to what the Lord was seeking to accomplish in that hour. He was free to actualize, to see the situation as it was; he was free to relationalize, to enter into relationships of gracious caring; and he was free to realize, to be sensitive and aware of what the Lord was seeking to do through him.

For Paul, newness was nowness. He was part of Christ's "now" breed. He believed that the old had passed away through the forgiveness of the past. The new had come! The manifestation of his being a new creation in Christ was that he could live fully in the moment at hand.

*A saint
is one
who makes it easy
to believe in Jesus.*

Ruth Bell Graham

For to me, to live is Christ, and to die is gain.

Philippians 1:21

*Y*ou have no right to force me to think about death. I came to the Easter service to hear about the resurrection, not to be challenged about my own dying. I want to know how to live, not how to die!"

The man was disturbed. His directness made way for conversation about why death was so unsettling to him. In the Easter sermon I had asked each person to picture his or her life—responsibilities and relationships. Then I asked, "What if you were told that you were to die today? How would you feel about it? Do you have the assurance that death would only be a transition in living for you? Do you know the reality of the resurrection for yourself—not just for Jesus so long ago, but through Him for yourself?"

The man was shocked by the realization that though he believed in Christ, he was afraid of dying. He could not say with Paul, "To die is gain." Fear about death and dying is evidenced by our customs for the funeral and our efforts to evade the eventuality of our own dying.

We cannot live—really—until we come to grips with death. Paul had died to himself and his own willful design for his life long before he made this statement in prison. Death was not an ending for him but the beginning of the next phase of eternal life that had begun when he turned his life over to Christ. "I have been crucified with Christ. It is no longer I who live but Christ who lives in me."

Once we have faced the fact of death, accepted Christ's promise, "Because I live, you shall live also," we are ready to turn back to the challenge of living with new zest and abandonment.

My Easter Christian picked up the challenge. We talked at length about his life. Now he doesn't have to wait until Christmas to come to church again. He's there every Sunday!

For to me, living means opportunities for Christ.

Philippians 1:21 TLB

𝒜 few years ago I visited the ruins of Philippi in northern Greece. There in the excavated jail where Paul and Silas had been imprisoned, I sat alone, recapturing the time when the two adventurers sang psalms until the earthquake of the Lord's intervention set them free at midnight. I sang all the hymns I knew and then sang my way through the psalms, some of which I was sure they had sung. On the wall is a plaque with the words of Paul's confession, "For to me, to live is Christ, and to die is gain" (Phil. 1:21). It occurred to me that that affirmation is more than a statement of purpose. It is a strategy for survival. For me to live abundantly, I need Christ. And I need Him in those areas where I often think I should be able to handle life on my own, rather than to depend on Him. An alternative wording of Paul's admission could be, "Christ is the source of life, way beyond what I could accomplish for Him on my own strength."

So often I am like Peter at the foot-washing in the Upper Room: It's difficult to receive. But when I realize what I miss because of pride, I join with Peter in saying, "Wash all of me! I need You, Lord. Reach down into my inner heart and heal those things I have kept from You."

The kingdom of heaven means the reign, rule, and resources of God. When we surrender our lives to Christ and accept Him as Lord and Savior, we become citizens of His kingdom now and forever. But it is as we acknowledge our need for Him in our lives and relationships that we realize more and more of the power of His Spirit in our spirit. The kingdom is already ours, but humility enables us to enjoy the limitless strength and wisdom that are stored up for us. It is good news that we don't have to make it alone; the grand assurance is that we will never face a need that is too big for the Lord.

And being confident of this, I know that I shall remain and continue with you all for your progress and joy of faith.

Philippians 1:25

*W*e hear a lot about goal-oriented planning, management, and task accomplishment these days. Peter Drucker coined the phrase, "Management by objectives," and reminded us that we become the goals we set.

Paul clarified his ultimate goal—to live in Christ. Nothing could ever dissuade or destroy this reason for his being. In that context he could evaluate the long-range goals in his ministry. Should he remain alive, it would be to take the next step of strengthening the churches he had begun and take the next strides in expanding the kingdom to unreached areas. He had a reason for living on, even though death would be a pleasant beginning of a new phase of his life in Christ. We observe a man sorting out the priorities of his immediate decisions on the basis of how they would bring him closer to his long-range and ultimate goals.

The cause of confusion in the lives of many Christians today is because immediate tasks are put in the category and given the importance of ultimate or long-range goals. We are pulled from demand to demand with little basis for sorting out what's most important. Also there are many who get long-range and ultimate goals mixed up.

My ultimate goal is to be a man "in Christ"—to love and serve Him with all that I am and have. The long-range goal is to do that by the ministry of communicating Christ to others. On the other hand, my immediate goals deal with the people and program that demand attention right now. No cause, however strategic, should ever be elevated beyond a short-range classification. Like Paul, we can decide on the value of any one challenge by how it will bring us more closely to our real purpose.

And being confident of this, I know that I shall remain and continue with you all for your progress and joy of faith.

Philippians 1:25–26

*P*aul rejoiced over the Philippians and knew that they would rejoice over him because of his encouragement to them. This is a delightful picture of Christian fellowship: mutual rejoicing in each other as friends in Christ.

It's a wonderful experience to know that people rejoice in us. There is no finer compliment than for a person to say, "You are a source of joy to me. I thank Christ for you!" Knowing how much that means to us should motivate us to express our gratitude to others for what they mean to us and what they have done to bring joy to us.

At the same time, our goal should be to be the kind of persons in whom others can rejoice. Paul wanted to be with the Philippians again so that he could encourage their progress and joy of faith. Think of the people of your life. What can you do or say today to help them make progress and realize more of the joy of Christ?

The first step is to pray for and about them. Christ will help us discern what people need. He will give us empathy for their struggles and show us how to affirm their strengths. The second step is to share their hurts and hopes. The third step follows naturally. People open up to those who express how much they care. We can help them talk out their problems and challenges and come to clarity about what is the Lord's best for them. Then our responsibility will be to encourage them as they act on His guidance. The fourth step is to keep in touch. A note, a phone call, some consistent contact will help them know that we have not forgotten. They will be assured that their concerns are on our hearts and in our prayers. Most of all, they will know that we rejoice in them and are their cheerleaders, and we will have the delightful experience of knowing that they rejoice in us. Today's the day to rejoice in people Christ puts on our agendas and to be people in whom they can rejoice.

Therefore if there is any consolation in Christ, if any comfort of love, if any fellowship of the Spirit, if any affection and mercy, fulfill my joy by being like-minded, having the same love, being of one accord, of one mind.

Philippians 2:1–2

A man who recently had found new life and authentic joy in Christ began a search for a church where he could grow in his faith. As he made the rounds of churches in his Midwest community, he was shocked by what he found. He was disappointed by the lack of enthusiasm and excitement about Christ and the adventure of discipleship. Most of all, he was alarmed by the absence of unity and the conflict over secondary issues. Many churches need to get back to basics.

Note the gracious but pointed way Paul deals with the need for renewal in the Philippian church. He draws the Philippian Christians into an incisive inventory and then makes his point. In a way the apostle asks, "Has Christ supported you? Has His presence strengthened you? Have you known the affection, sympathy, and love of Christ?" The implied question is, "Do you have this kind of support, strength, and affection for one another?"

Do you see what Paul has done? He has helped us to return to the basic motivation of the Christian life—Christ Himself. There is a direct ratio between our consistent, fresh experiences of Christ's grace and our ability to be gracious to one another. Without that we will fall back into power struggles. Behind most divisiveness there is a struggle for control. That struggle can be camouflaged behind all sorts of causes and theological emphases.

Paul calls us back to Christ as the only basis of our unity. He helps us rediscover our central purpose of knowing Him and reaching a world that desperately needs Him. Often the things that divide Christians have little to do with this purpose. Lack of unity is a sure sign that we need to stop trying to control others and renew our commitment to seek the mind of Christ and His control of the church. Only then can we be of one mind and love and accord.

Let nothing be done through selfish ambition or conceit, but in lowliness of mind let each esteem others better than himself. Let each of you look out not only for his own interests, but also for the interests of others.

Philippians 2:3–4

*W*ait a minute, Paul. Do you realize what you have asked us to do in these verses? That's impossible in our culture! Have you ever found yourself thinking these thoughts? A sure sign that the Scriptures become God's personal word to us is that they hit us where we are living, cut right into our value system and character, and we sense the Holy Spirit transforming our lives.

Selfish ambition? A deep desire to boast? How do we develop healthy ambition used for creative purposes, or develop healthy self-appreciation without manipulating people as a means to our ends? The other day I attended a meeting with a group of leaders. My expectation for a time of mutual care and encouragement was bitterly disappointed. Everyone around the table was intent on impressing the others. They boasted about their accomplishments, even about their victorious Christian lives. *The disturbing thing was that no one was listening.* I kept asking myself, Why can't we listen to each other? Christ has called us to be enablers of each other to draw out the gifts and potential of what He has given us!

Paul's challenge to look to the interests of others actually means, "To fix attention upon, with desire and interest in." That's the rub, but it's also a great opportunity! If we could pray the words of this Scripture for our lives today, it could be a beginning of a new life for us. But there is a price: It would require an incisive inventory, and in today's Scripture Paul gives us the basis for that inventory. As you take inventory of your own life, notice that living out today's Scripture takes energy and involvement, time and inconvenience.

Go ahead—write it out! Take inventory on how selfishness and self-glorification get in the way of your relationships with others and the Lord. Then get on your knees and imagine yourself nailing your inventory to the cross—and leave it there!

Who, being in the form of God, did not consider it robbery to be equal with God, but made Himself of no reputation, taking the form of a bondservant, and coming in the likeness of men.

Philippians 2:6–7

*T*his is the body of the Lord Jesus, broken for you, and I am willing to be broken open for you. This is the cup of the new covenant in Christ's blood, making a new relationship between us. As Christ was poured out for us, I am willing to have my life poured out for you." These are the words the elders said to each other as they broke bread and passed the cup in a very moving communion service at a recent retreat. In that moment, they became the church as it was meant to be—a self-emptying fellowship.

The character of a self-emptying church is here in Philippians 2:6–7. It is known as the *kenosis* passage. *Kenosis* is the Greek word meaning "to empty," and proclaims the nature of the self-emptying humility of the Son of God as He became incarnate in humanity. Here is both motive and method of the Christian life. What those elders said to each other is an extension of the incarnation. Jesus gave Himself totally for us, and that's the way we are to live with each other!

Immanuel, God incarnate, God with us emptied Himself and thus became the essence of a servant, "being born in the likeness of men." He felt what we feel, suffered what we suffer, and revealed to us what life was created to be in self-giving, person-centric, sacrificial love. That self-emptying is the same way He wants to live His life through us every moment of every day.

Christ was not pretending or playing a part. Christ was not just a human being with generous ideas of good will and mercy. Christ was fully human and fully God, and what He is now to us in daily living is focused in what He revealed in Jesus of Nazareth.

Empty your cup for others and it will always be full. Break yourself open for others and you will become whole.

Let this mind be in you which was also in Christ Jesus.

Philippians 2:5

$\mathcal{T}$he man leaned forward intently. "I want what my wife has found! I'm not sure what it is, but it has changed her disposition." The man's wife had been a very difficult, demanding person. Her needs kept the family up and down emotionally like a yo-yo. Even though she was a nominal Christian, the demands she made on herself spilled over in dissatisfaction with her husband and children.

A group of women who met together to share their faith, study the Bible, and encourage each other invited the man's wife to join them in their weekly meetings. In these warm, caring disciples the woman witnessed what Christ could do to love and liberate a person. She realized she did not know Him personally; she also knew she was miserable and wanted to change. One day during a visit with one of the group, she turned her life over to Christ, accepted Him as Lord and Savior, and asked Him to change her disposition. The result of that prayer was a dramatic change in her attitude. It was some months later that her husband came to see me. The change in his wife astounded him and he wanted to experience what she had found. Through his wife's example, he too prayed to receive Christ's love and joy.

One of the distinguishing marks of a Christian is his or her disposition. Our disposition is the outer manifestation of Christ living within us. The Greek word for "mind" in Paul's challenge, "Let this mind be in you which was also in Christ Jesus" is *phroneite*. It means thought, attitude, or disposition. Paul wanted the Christians at Philippi to have Christ's attitude and disposition of humility, servanthood and compassion. The people around us are watching to see what He can do in their lives. We were meant to radiate His love, communicate His joy, care for others unselfishly, and uplift them with hope. So how's your disposition? Would it motivate others to want to have a relationship with Christ?

*He humbled Himself and became obedient to the point of death, even the
death of the cross.*

Philippians 2:8

"Don't try to sneak around Golgotha!"

I shall never forget these words spoken by Thomas Torrence to a class
at Edinburgh. The temptation to ignore the cross in an understanding of
God or in the living of life is always beguiling. At the foot of the cross
we are forced to see things as they are.

The cross was in God's essential nature before it was displayed on
Golgotha. It was not an afterthought, a result of circumstances, or an
expression of the worst that the anger and hostility of humankind could
do. God being who He is and humankind being what we are, it could not
have been different. Our end run around Golgotha is caused by our unwillingness to admit we need something that drastic to save us from our
self-centeredness.

The question that must be answered every day is: If I had been the
only person alive would the cross have been necessary? Dear friend, hear
this—what God revealed of His forgiving nature on the cross is still His
attitude toward us today. That's why the cross is the center of our faith
in every age and in every day of our lives. The Christian life begins and
is renewed at the cross. Nothing can ever be the same after Golgotha—
the once, never-to-be-repeated sacrifice for our sins. God has closed the
door on humankind's efforts to be good enough through religion or self-
effort.

The cross was then and is now. If it was not then, it cannot be now.
But if it is not now as a radical daily rediscovery, what it was then is
robbed of its liberating truth and power for us. We, too, have a cross—
the death to self-generated, self-centered plans and images. The cross
means obedience to seek and do God's will in all our responsibilities and
relationships.

By facing it head-on and accepting the reality of Golgotha we have
been given the free gift of eternal life in Jesus Christ!

There's no sneaking around Golgotha!

And being found in appearance as a man, He humbled Himself and became obedient to the point of death, even the death of the cross. Therefore God also has highly exalted Him and given Him the name which is above every name.

Philippians 2:8–9

One of my favorite quotations is from John Arthur Gossip: "If we would help people to be valiant in their Christian living, we should be ringing out over the world that Christ has won, that evil is toppling . . . that nothing can for long resist our mighty and victorious Lord. That's the tonic we need to keep us healthy, the trumpet blast to fire our blood, and send us . . . happily on our way, ready and eager to face anything, laughing and singing and recklessly unafraid, because the feel of victory is in the air, as our hearts thrill to it."

That's exactly what Paul was trying to do for the Philippians and for us. The dramatic, doxological language about our Lord's exultation puts fire in our being. Paul wanted his readers to feel both the humiliation and consequent exultation of Christ. What he implies is that if the Philippians give up their practice of self-aggrandizement and prefer one another in love, God will raise them up and defend their cause. Remember the context: This is Paul's description of Christ's inner disposition. It was so they might "have in them the disposition which was in Christ."

This leaves us with a challenge for today. Our responsibility is obedience; God's response is exultation. Resurrection is God's answer to the worst that life dishes out. We are raised with Christ when we begin a new life that is eternal fellowship with Him. Death is defeated and no longer paralyzes us with fear. Daily resurrection happens when Christ brings good out of the worst circumstances. We can dare to say with Mary Shelley, "If winter comes, can spring be far behind?"

What amazing freedom that gives us for today. We don't need to defend, boost, or glorify ourselves. Leave that to God.

Christ is risen! He is risen indeed!

Therefore God also has highly exalted Him and given Him the name which is above every name, that at the name of Jesus every knee should bow, of those in heaven, and of those on earth, and of those under the earth, and that every tongue should confess that Jesus Christ is Lord, to the glory of God the Father.

Philippians 2:9–11

*J*esus is Lord! Do you believe that? The greatest need of the church in America is to rediscover this basic creed of the early church: Jesus is Lord! God has called us to Himself in Christ. Our response is make Him the Lord of our lives. That means response, trust, and surrender of all we have and are. This is enabled bythe Holy Spirit's gift of faith.

For many of us, the missing ingredient is the will. It is possible to rationalize the existence and power of Christ without *relationalizing* His Lordship and experiencing His power. The commitment of the will unlocks the joy and adventure of following Christ. It means that we seek out His will, determine His priorities for us, and make hard choices of faithful obedience. To join with the great company of heaven and earth to "confess that Jesus Christ is Lord" is to fulfill our destiny.

Renewal takes place in a church when people who rejoice in their Savior are committed to Him as Lord. This means the experience of His presence and purpose in every facet of life. The bold new breed of Christians in today's church are those who are excited about their faith because of fresh experiences of the Lord at work in their daily lives. He has become the intervening, inspiring Lord of their marriages, struggles with identity, problems of vocation, tensions of relationships, and fears of failure.

The name that is above every other name is God's own name Yahweh, the Lord. The Father has exalted Christ and made Him reigning Lord of the Church. Through the name of Jesus Christ our Lord we have direct access to the Father and His limitless power. When we confess Him as our Lord, He gives us supernatural power to do what He commands.

Make today a day to constantly repeat the five words of power and hope: Jesus Christ is my Lord!

Therefore, my beloved, as you have always obeyed, not as in my presence only, but now much more in my absence, work out your own salvation with fear and trembling.

Philippians 2:12

*D*o you ever have difficulty getting people to do what you want? Do you ever wish you had some kind of power over your family or friends so they would do what you say just because you have asked it?

All of us have responsibilities of leadership in some area of life—in our homes, among our friends, or in some professional capacity—and every leader needs support. Paul gives us the key to great leadership in the passage above. Before he asks the Philippians to obey, he refers to them as "my beloved." Actually the Greek text means "beloved ones." The word refers to the love that is God. This is the love that is a gift of the Holy Spirit that motivates sacrificial love of oneself for others. Paul had demonstrated this love for the Philippians in concrete ways. He had earned the right to ask them to obey because he had their confidence and trust.

This leaves me with some penetrating questions. Think of the people in your life:

1. Do you love the people you lead? Do they know it?

2. Have you demonstrated tangible evidence of your care?

3. Do they know that you will *their* ultimate good?

4. Do they share in formulating the direction you give them?

5. Have you helped them set realizable goals that you help them inventory consistently?

6. Do you stand with them in costly involvement?

7. Are you vulnerable enough to admit your own failures so that an ambiance of grace is communicated and lived?

The other side of this Scripture for today is a challenge to consider what kind of follower you are. Openness to the thought, insight, and direction of another is a sure sign of maturity.

To be a great leader is to be a servant who follows Christ and walks with Him as He takes us to the needs of others.

Work out your own salvation with fear and trembling; for it is God who works in you both to will and to do for His good pleasure.

Philippians 2:12–13

$\mathcal{T}$he formula for cooperating with God is this: To love God is to let God love you; to let God love you is to be completely open to what He wants to do in every part of your thinking, feeling, and attitude.

That's what I believe Paul is talking about in today's Scripture. God is always at work in us. He chose us, loved us, and gave us the gift of faith to respond. He persists in us and will not let us rest at any stage of growth. God knows what He is doing with us. Even the desire to want what He wants is a gift. We can trust Him at every point, in the difficulties and the delights of life, because He will weave them into His ultimate plan to make us like His Son and prepare us to live with Him forever. So we can relax and enjoy the journey! God will not leave us unfinished or incomplete. Therefore, we can enter into each new day with the confidence that He will make us willing to be willing to do His will.

Cooperating with God is threefold: discovering where we need to grow; being open to being changed; and receiving His power to act. Here are some questions that I find helpful in discerning how.

What's the thing in me that makes it most difficult to be open to Christ today? Where have I grown recently and where do I most need to grow in personality, relationships, and responsibilities?

To ask these questions is a sign that God's work of giving us willingness is well on the way. Our Scripture tells us that a further part of God's work is to make us able. That's cooperation! So, why not let God love you?

Yes, and if I am being poured out as a drink offering on the sacrifice and service of your faith, I am glad and rejoice with you all.

Philippians 2:17

Our task is not to define the terms of our sacrifice for Christ. Faithfulness to Him clarifies the form and gives the force of our discipleship. What is sacrificial for one of us may require little of another. Our Lord is the focus. We are to keep our eyes on Him, not what others are doing.

Today's Scripture is a live wire. It jars us with the realization of how little our faith costs us. But an orgy of paranoid masochism will help no one. A creative urgency to get on with obedient times with our Lord and faithful following of His marching orders will get us into sacrifice soon enough.

Paul wanted to affirm the Philippians in their troubles. Their suffering was validated by the joy they experienced out of the profound realization of grace in their difficulties. Joy is always the outward manifestation of the inward experience of God's unchanging, gracious love. The joy Paul shared with the Philippians was no easy happiness, but a result of the endurance of painful problems through the sustaining power of grace.

This passage leaves us with two questions: Where in my life is Christ calling me to give up my security, safety, and comfort to be offered up on the altar of the needs of people and our world? How can I be a libation to encourage and affirm this quality of giving in others?

We can be a libation of affirmation and encouragement to help each other know it's all worthwhile because Christ has won the victory for us. We do not need to repeat Golgotha but to incarnate its implications. That will mean sacrifice, but it will be according to the guidance and direction of our Lord.

For I have no one like-minded, who will sincerely care for your state.
Philippians 2:20

*J*esus told us that within us would flow rivers of living water. There's a dry and thirsty land, a desert parched for love, in the people around us.

We wonder if Timothy was there with Paul when he wrote about him to the Philippians. Did he overhear Paul's dictation to his scribe? What an encouragement that would have been to him! Paul was not a capricious flatterer, motivated by insecure solicitousness. He was able to be direct and honest with his companions about things they needed to change, but he was also free to express his feelings of love.

As I write this, the faces of all the love-starved people I have known march before my mind's eye. If only they had had a parent or a significant friend in the formative years to express warm, accepting, emotional, and physical love. The unblessed children of unexpressive parents are everywhere. Disturbed husbands and wives bear the marks of the absence of healing affection upon their faces and in the frustrations of unfulfillment. Why are we so inhibited in expressing our feelings? Some are afraid they will not be received; others have tried and been rebuffed or misused; others have not had a deep feeling of being loved; others are just too concerned about their own inverted need to be loved; others are blocked by self-centered shyness; and still others withhold their love until the other person meets their standards or judgments.

Here's a good way to focus this for each of us. Ask yourself the questions, Who are the people in my life who need to know they are loved? What is it in me that holds back my feelings? Do I want to be different? Do I really believe that Christ in me can break through my reserve and speak and touch and heal with warm affection? How we answer that could change our lives!

If we could but show the world that being
committed to Christ is no tame,
humdrum, sheltered monotony—
but the most exciting adventure
the human spirit can know,
then those who have been standing
outside the church and looking askance
at Christ will come crowding in
to pay allegiance,
and we may well expect the
greatest revival since Pentecost.

James S. Stewart

But you know his [Timothy's] proven character, that as a son with his
father he served with me in the gospel.

Philippians 2:22

*P*aul had some great things to say about Timothy that become a personal challenge to us. Timothy had been to Philippi with Paul on his first
visit and had gone ahead for the second visit. Now he was to be sent back
again to give comfort. *Timothy* means "good comfort," and he had lived
out his name. He was the only one left with Paul who was free enough
of concern about his own affairs to give himself to the cause of Christ.
Timothy knew that there was enough time in any day to do the things
God wanted him to do.

Most of us are overly concerned about our own affairs. Our time fills
up with a daily round of demands and responsibilities. How do we know
what's important? For Timothy, it was the cause of Christ. This challenges us with a question: "Is what I am doing advancing the cause of
Christ or have I asked Christ to bless my causes?" There were some great
men around Paul at this time—Mark, Luke, Silas—surely they were busy
for Christ. Yes, but perhaps too busy to hear the cry of human need.

I had this experience the other day. A man poured out his heart to
me. He confessed a sin that had hung him up for some time. After we
talked it through, we prayed. Then I looked him squarely in the eye and
said, "My friend, God loves you and forgives you." Then he said, "You
know, I knew that, but I needed to hear it and feel it from someone else."
We all know how he felt.

Exactly! God made us that way. We need each other. His greatest
gifts are usually held for us to be given through others because His purpose is that we depend on Him and that we be interdependent with one
another. Your name may not be Timothy, but what that name means,
"good comfort," can be the purpose of your life today.

Rejoice in the Lord. For me to write the same things to you is not tedious, but for you it is safe.

Philippians 3:1

*P*roblems and rejoicing. We don't think of them together, do we? Paul's exhortation is repeated often: Rejoice in problems. He doesn't seem to mean, "Rejoice that you have problems," but "Rejoice when problems come along." What does this mean?

When you get whacked with a problem, open yourself to a deeper relationship to the Lord. Don't focus on the problem but on the Lord's presence and power.

I am convinced that rejoicing comes simply from the realization that the Lord is present and will find a way to use every problem for our growth and His purposes. It's actually feeling that repetitious movement of the Holy Spirit stirring up joy within us. That's why joy is indomitable and independent of circumstantial evidence.

Most of us have an inadvertent gear that shifts into place when a problem hits. Some get frantic; others remain stoic. Some run off in all directions searching for solutions. Others pretend there's no problem. Many of us pout, "All I ever get is problems." And others shout, "Somebody up there forgot me!"

I have often entertained the distorted thought that someday I would be free of problems. Not so. Problems are the evidence of the Spirit of God continuing His creative purposes. Wherever He is at work, another force—the power of evil—is also at work. Conflict between the two causes our greatest disturbance. In every problem our task is to become receptive to what the Lord is seeking to create in that situation and to rejoice that He's at work and His joy flows out of the inner depths of our being. We know that our Lord will win! Rejoice!

Who worship God in the Spirit, rejoice in Christ Jesus, and have no confidence in the flesh.

Philippians 3:3

*T*ears were streaming down her face as she left the church. The theme of the service had been unqualified love: God's love for us and the need for us to love the people around us unqualifiedly. The illustrations in the sermon had been painfully personal and many of them had dealt with relationships with family and friends. God had given this woman a great gift: He had shown her the agonizing portrait of her life. She was rankled, horrified, and then disturbed by the dolorous emotional condition she had created in her house.

Later when we talked in depth, she gave me a handle to understand her problems. She said, "I've been an 'iffy' Christian. You know, I will love you 'if.' I will accept you 'if.' I will give myself 'if' . . ." Her whole life had been developed around this manipulative syndrome. It was her way of getting what she wanted.

The term "iffy Christian" has lingered in my mind. Many of us suffer from this syndrome. It's a combination of criticalness, withheld affirmation and acceptance, and a deliberate attempt to see obstacles and not opportunities.

In Christ, God has made us "right" with Himself. He has forgiven our sins through the cross and loves us unswervingly. When we will not accept this and try to establish a righteousness of our own (that is, seek to win God's love by our goodness or perfection), a righteousness deficiency develops and the "if" syndrome shows in our relationships. We commit the ultimate blasphemy: We play "God" with ourselves and others and then perpetrate the worst crime of relational living . . . we judge and criticize and receive people only as they meet our ever-increasing standards of qualification.

If you are an "iffy" person, you've got lots of company. We can all make a new start today with a fresh experience of God's unqualified love. That's the only hope of healing the syndrome.

*That I may gain Christ and be found in Him, not having my own
righteousness, which is from the law, but that which is through faith in
Christ, the righteousness which is from God by faith.*

Philippians 3:8–9

*T*oday's passage is a profound analysis of the difference between guilt
and grace, frustration and freedom, manipulation and maturity. Paul
seems to be answering the basic question, "Why do we do what we do?"
He says, in substance, "It is not that in our own resources we are adequate—our ability comes from God who has qualified us to share a new
kind of relationship. Trying to fulfill the letter of the Law leads to guilt,
the death of the soul; the Spirit of God alone can give life to the soul."

Aldous Huxley said that a man's worst difficulties begin when he is
able to do what he likes. Not so. Our real difficulty begins when what we
come to like is motivated by a fatuous compulsion of a sense of guilt. A
life motivated by guilt becomes a guilted cage. We become entangled in
the tender trap of doing what seems good because we feel badly; we are
driven to do the right things for the wrong reasons; we are immobilized
in reaction and unfree to act; we are the victims of turbulent, inner
thoughts and seldom feel inner peace. Our accomplishments never
match our expectations. The people of our lives feel the pressure of our
unfilled dreams and often feel that what we do for them or with them is
the result of unsatisfied psychic demands. We are not free!

The liberating truth of today's Scripture is that we are set free from
the necessity to live to please God. We already are pleasing to Him. He
declared that once and for all in the cross. Now what we do can be an
expression of praise rather than a condition of His approval. What a difference!

Today, let's consider the things we do and why we do them. Tradition, custom, habit? These may be fine. But do we think God will love
us more for them? How much do we do as a free expression of love because of what He's done for us?

That I may know Him and the power of His resurrection, and the
fellowship of His sufferings, being conformed to His death.

Philippians 3:10

*W*hen we are driven by ambition, we will drive ourselves and the people around us. This is when we make dangerous compromises of our values. The entangling alliances of life result. We use people to get to our ends.

Paul exposes a different ambition that reorders all others. He wanted to know Christ and experience the power of His resurrection. This then reordered everything else. He had been through all the false ambitions as a Hebrew Pharisee and then as a vigilant Christian worker. Now in prison near the end of life, he ended up where he wished he could have begun: with no other ambition than Christ Himself.

I have spent a lot of time with people who knew they were about to die. A question I like to ask is, "If you could do it all over again, what would you do?" So many have said, "I would spend more time with Christ."

There are two parts to Paul's clarified ambition: to know Christ and experience the resurrection. To know Christ implies interpersonal relationship, not facts. This is expressed in actual experience of His resurrection. The cycle of death and resurrection is interwoven into all of life. In every situation, with every person, in every decision or plan, there is the moment of death. Once we let go of our grip on life, the gift of God can be given. Our Lord wants to give us His direction, insight, and power. But not until we die to our own plan.

To share in Christ's sufferings means that we become involved with people to care for them even at the cost of our own convenience or comfort. But Christ, not helping the people, is our ambition. Once He is central, then, inadvertently, we relive His death and know His resurrection, and what we do with people is less manipulating and more liberating.

What about you? What are your ambitions? Really!

Not that I have already attained, or am already perfected; but I press on, that I may lay hold of that for which Christ Jesus has also laid hold of me.
Philippians 3:12

*H*ow often we get hung up on a petulant perfectionism over the details of living that has little to do with Christ's purpose for us. Most perfectionism is initiated in a desire to be good and adequate enough to earn God's love. Paul knew he had that so he could get on with the real business of being "in Christ"—to keep on working toward his purpose in experiencing Christ and His resurrection power.

Paul knew that he was not spiritually mature. There was so much more to discover, learn, and experience. How very challenging! Here is the most spectacular Christian who ever lived confessing his need to continue to grow in maturity. This is a true test of greatness: the acknowledgment of the need to keep on growing.

No one would ever say that he has learned all that was to be learned or that he now was spiritually mature. But I wonder, at times, about our passive resistance to growth. I meet few people who are voraciously hungry for more knowledge and experience of Christ. Our habits and time expenditure betray how much we believe that we need to grow. What are we involved in right now that is an expression of our hunger and thirst for more of Christ?

Satisfaction is a sure sign of an impasse in our growth. The evidence of the Spirit's work in us is an urgent dissatisfaction with our present level of growth. But how do I know where I need to grow in Christ?

Dare to ask yourself the honest question: "How have I grown and where do I need to grow?" Then pray that Christ will show you where He wants you to grow.

Brethren, I do not count myself to have apprehended; but one thing I do, forgetting those things which are behind and reaching forward to those things which are ahead, I press toward the goal for the prize of the upward call of God in Christ Jesus.

Philippians 3:13–14

The goal for Paul's race was Christ. Christ was the finish tape for him. The verse means that he stretches forward, running "flat out," toward the goal. This imagery is illuminating. Just as a winning runner forgets the opponents around or behind him and looks only at the goal, Paul forgot the past and focused on the next steps toward the goal. Remember that Paul was in prison when he wrote this. He had an indomitable trust in the Lordship of Christ over past and future time. He longed to become more like Christ in every thought and action.

The race of the Christian life is the only race that is run knowing we have won already. We belong to Christ and our life in Him can only be more exciting as we press on. That gives us the vitality of a second wind.

There is nothing more disappointing than a runner who drops out of a race or a Christian who slacks up because he thinks he has reached the finish line. We always have a future and press on. The more we concentrate on Christ and live with attention riveted on Him, the more, inadvertently, we become like Him in thought, value, attitude, and character. "Therefore we also, since we are surrounded by so great a cloud of witnesses, let us lay aside every weight, and the sin which so easily ensnares us, and let us run with endurance the race that is set before us, looking unto Jesus, the author and finisher of our faith, who for the joy that was set before Him endured the cross, despising the shame, and has sat down at the right hand of the throne of God" (Heb. 12:1–2).

Brethren, join in following my example, and note those who so walk, as you have us for a pattern.

Philippians 3:17

*H*ow would you like to reproduce what has happened to your faith in the lives of others? Do you have the feeling that you would like everyone to discover what you have found? Can you say to the world around you, "Hey world, this is living! This is life as it was meant to be lived!"

Unless we believe that what's happened to us in our relationship with Christ ought to happen to everyone, then probably too little has happened to us. If we don't believe in what's happened to us, nobody else will.

But Paul goes even deeper than that. With alarming audacity, he says, "Keep on imitating me." That to me is the great test of the dynamic of our Christian experience. If we are not so excited about what we have found that we want everyone to experience it, then we have not found very much.

Many Christians never get on with sharing their faith because all that they think about is what is wrong in their own lives. "I am not worthy," we say. Of course we're not. If we ever thought we were, we would be completely unusable by our Lord. What He wants to expose to the world and have others imitate in us is our dependence on Him and the joy and love His Spirit can produce in us.

After Jesus had washed the disciples' feet, He said, "I have given you an example, that you should do as I have done to you" (John 13:15). We are to allow Christ to produce His life uniquely in each of us. His love, character, and passion for people's need is to be reproduced in us. When it is, we become an example to others.

How about an experiment today? Let's live through the day with an acute sensitivity to our actions and reactions, our feelings, and our handling of difficulties. Would we want others to live like that? Can we say to the people in our lives, "Keep on imitating me"?

Rejoice in the Lord always. Again I will say, rejoice!

Philippians 4:4

*P*aul had found the certainty that enabled him to rejoice in all circumstances. We read today's verse with amazement. Paul is in prison, a death sentence hangs over him, concern for the churches besets him, and yet he says, "Rejoice!"

This is more than a passing parenthesis in Paul's advice to his friends in Philippi. Actually he is giving his cherished fellow Christians a secret of how to live in problems, difficulties, and frustrations. He knew of the dangers ahead for the church everywhere. He was not being flippantly pious with easy advice. Instead, he was helping them to discover an aspect of their life in Christ that could liberate them when things got tough.

Here's the secret of victorious living Paul's words unlocked for me. When things get tough or difficult or downright impossible—rejoice. I have found that the same emotional channels that can contain and transmit discouragement and despair can be used for praise. When I surrender a particularly troublesome time, dare to thank God for it, and rejoice that He will use it for my ultimate good, I find that my attention is shifted from all the bad eventualities to God's possibilities. I know one thing for sure: God is faithful, nothing is ever so bad that His good cannot be brought out of it. I agree with Albert Einstein when he said, "I shall never believe that God plays dice with the world."

The transition point from discouragement to encouragement for me is in rejoicing. The more persistently I rejoice, the more my emotions are shifted away from the outward manifestation of tragedy to the inward movement of God's Spirit. Just as discouragement is contagious, so, too, rejoicing is creatively infectious. Years of experimentation have trained my emotions to move more quickly to praise. My motto, based on this verse, is "Regardless . . . Rejoice!"

Let your gentleness be known to all men. The Lord is at hand.
Philippians 4:5

One day my granddaughters were playing the what-are-you-going-to-be-when-you-grow-up? game. After each had told what she wanted to be, they all turned to me, "How 'bout you, Papa—what are you going to be when you grow up?" Good question. I'll never be fully grown until I get to heaven and Christ totally conforms me to His nature.

Yet as we mature in Christ, according to Paul, one thing we are to be known for is a conspicuous gentleness. An outward evidence that He lives in us is "gentleness," *epieikeia* in Greek. The word signifies an attitude of open reasonableness, and moderation and graciousness are also implied. A consistent experience of the grace of the Lord Jesus frees us of defensiveness. We are open to grow, so we don't have to defend what we are; we are willing to change, so we can take creative criticism; we are yielded to the Lord, so we don't have to defend our turf; we are dependent on Christ's power, so we don't have to face the battle with evil alone.

The startling thing about Paul's admonition about gentleness is that it is to be conspicuous. Make your gentleness known. Model it, express it, tell others about it! Why? Because doing this destroys combative competition. When we pretend we know everything, people want to expose our lack of knowledge or experience in some area. Pious perfectionism baits people; they have to pull off the mask. Posturing strength is a sure way to get people to tell us about our weaknesses.

On the other hand, if we are open, receptive, teachable people whose only source of power is Christ, whose only purpose is to glorify Him, and whose only relational strategy is *affirmation* of others—then we can grow. This gentleness is quick to admit needs and constantly willing to receive Christ's remedial correction and molding power. Let your gentleness be known today.

So now, brethren, I commend you to God and to the word of His grace, which is able to build you up and give you an inheritance among all those who are sanctified.

Acts 20:32

The Lord's will is that we become all that He intended us to be. His grace is for our growth. We have been programmed for greatness. Holiness is belonging to the Lord and being remade in his image. The word *saint* also has its root in the word *holy*. It means to be set apart, called, chosen, belonging to the Lord. His purpose for us is that we grow intellectually, emotionally, and volitionally. We are meant to be grown-up saints!

A boy asked his dad, "What's it like to be a grown-up saint?" We should be able to respond like his dad did, "I'm not what I used to be; I'm not what I ought to be; but praise the Lord, I'm on my way to becoming all that I was intended to be."

Paul longed for his friends in Ephesus to grow up in Christ, to be sanctified. Imagine the urgency he felt as he looked into the faces of his converts. Among those there must have been some of the disciples of John who had received the Holy Spirit. Surely a transformed silversmith was there. Leaders of the city who had received Christ were certainly among them.

We picture these among the new humanity in Christ now entrusted with the leadership of the church. Paul knew that what the Lord had begun in them would be continued.

Growth in Christ takes place as we give Him away to others. That always involves giving ourselves and what we have to help them discover what we have found. In actuality, it is blessed both to receive and to give. In fact, we cannot give away what we have been unwilling to receive. The more we receive of Him, the more we have to give of what people really need—love, forgiveness, and lasting care.

Brethren, if a man is overtaken in any trespass, you who are spiritual restore such a one in a spirit of gentleness, considering yourself lest you also be tempted.

Galatians 6:1

*T*he hardest time to be gentle is when we know we are right and someone else is obviously dead wrong. It is equally difficult to be gracious when we hold professional or personal power over others. It's so easy to be harsh and unbending. When we are, it's a sure sign of our own insecurity. But the greatest temptation for most of us is when someone who has failed us or himself has admitted it, and his destiny or happiness is in our hands. We hold the power to give or refuse a blessing.

Recently, a dear friend hurt me in both word and action. Each time we met, the tarnished relationship expressed its dullness. I had that juicy relish of being misused and misunderstood. I almost began to enjoy the leverage of being the offended one. His first overtures of restitution were resisted because of the gravity of the judgment I had made. He had taken a key idea I had shared with him in confidence and had developed it as his own before I had a chance to use it. The plagiarism of ideas had been coupled with the use of some of my written material, reproduced under his name.

I realized that however right I might be, the spiritual need of this brother was most crucial. The most difficult thing was to surrender my pique and work through the hurt. He felt as badly as I did.

Life is short. I will be dealt with by God for my failures also. Finally, the Lord got me where He wanted me: to deal with this man as He had with me when I failed Him and the people I love. For a brief time, I felt the gentleness of the Lord, that sweet mixture of justice and grace. His word to me was clear and undeniable, "Lloyd, why is it so important to you who gets the credit, just so My work gets done?" I gave up my right to be what only God could be as this man's judge and savior. The gentle attitude began to flow.

Be anxious for nothing, but in everything by prayer and supplication, with thanksgiving, let your requests be made known to God.

Philippians 4:6

This is a sick world in which there are disturbed people. People around us are often the cause of what happens. Selfishness in people causes pain and distress. When we are the cause of a problem, it's healthy to be able to admit it. But if we make ourselves responsible for everyone else's slights and oversights, we will become anxious about life. Our hostility against ourselves will develop into a habitual, conditioned pattern of response. Only Christ can help us own our real failures, disown them in His forgiveness, and press on. Then we can acknowledge the failures of others and forgive them as we've been forgiven.

Healthy Christ-motivated love for ourselves is expressed in creative self-expression. When we feel good about ourselves, we are able to communicate our needs and allow the people around us to help us. We are able to express our feelings without attacking people or blaming them; thus we free them to respond without being defensive. But a feeling of not being loved for the unique miracle each of us is results in diminished self-esteem. This in turn can lead us to suppress our emotions, and unexpressed emotions can fester into hostility and anxiety.

Anxiety is eccentricity—being ex-centric or away from the center. When we suppress our negative emotions, we are in effect taking punishment into our own hands. Since we have not learned to vent our anger creatively, we invert it on ourselves. There's a great difference between being sacrificial lovers of people and sacrificing ourselves for our own and others' failures. The one is self-abandonment, to which we are called as Christians; the other is merely self-blame.

The Holy Spirit wants to take us back over the years for the healing of those debilitating memories that depleted our self-images and developed the syndrome of self-condemnation. He exposes them to us if we are willing. Then He heals them with assuring love. We are given Christ-esteem.

The peace of God, which surpasses all understanding, will guard your hearts and minds through Christ Jesus.

Philippians 4:7

The only cure for worry about the future is to habitually practice the presence of Christ, envisioning Him commanding, controlling, and conditioning every situation.

The resurrection is our tangible source of hope. Jesus went to the cross in complete trust that God would bring good out of evil. The empty tomb is our assurance of a sublime confidence. There is nothing, absolutely nothing, including death, that can ultimately separate us from our Lord.

There's a famous painting in which the artist depicts the great contest between Faust and Satan. Faust gambled for his soul. The painting pictures the two sitting at a chessboard, the devil on one side and Faust on the other. The devil leers with delight over the checkmate of Faust's lonely king and knight.

Contemplation of the painting leaves one with the conclusion that Faust is completely beaten and at the mercy of Satan. Faust's expression is one of hopeless worry. The devil gloats with superiority. But one day a world-famous master of chess went to the gallery in London to view the picture. He spent hours meditating over the seemingly impossible situation it depicted. He paced back and forth. Then, to the utter amazement and surprise of the other art viewers in the gallery, he shouted a discovery that echoed around the marble corridors. "It's a lie!" he blurted out. "It's a lie! The king and the knight have another move!"

And so with our worries about the future. There's always one more move we never anticipated. Whenever we are tempted to say, "There's no solution. I'm finished. There's no hope. I'm beaten," we discover that God has a move we could not have imagined.

And let us not grow weary while doing good, for in due season we shall reap if we do not lose heart.

Galatians 6:9

One rejection can tip the scales weighted with hundreds of affirmations. Satan's trick is to preoccupy us with a rejection so that we forget the positive responses. As a young pastor, before I discovered the security of Christ's indwelling Spirit, one cranky comment from a church member after the Sunday morning worship would obsess my mind to the exclusion of dozens of people who told me that the sermon had introduced them to Christ or helped them in their living of the adventure in Him. I would brood for hours on Sunday afternoon.

One day a friend of mine said bluntly, "Lloyd, you're going to have to learn how to deal with rejection if you want to work with people." I had an overall low-grade spiritual fever that was doing what a slight physical fever does—I was not sick enough to go to bed, nor well enough to be effective.

This was part of what led me to my search for the power of the Holy Spirit. Finally, the Spirit broke me open to people and their needs. I became aware that often criticism was a plea for help from people. In other cases, it was legitimate objection to areas where I needed to grow. In the very least, it was an invitation to be taken seriously.

As I grew in dependence on the power of the Holy Spirit, I became less sensitive. I was the most surprised of all. The secret was in discovering the causes of people's resistance. In most cases the Lord had put a solid hook into people's souls, and, if my calling was to fish for people, a tug on the line was a sign that the fun of landing the person had begun. As an enthusiastic fresh- and salt-water fisherman, I'm always delighted when a fish really takes the bait. These kinds never leap into the boat! They have to be worked with for a long time before they can be brought alongside and netted.

The authors of the Westminster shorter catechism were convinced about the powerful relationship of both knowing and enjoying God. They firmly believed in the sovereignty of God. For them God was in charge of history and the life of the individual. In 1647 they wrote their stirring thoughts about the majesty of God in the catechism. "What is man's chief end?" they asked. And they answered, "To glorify God and enjoy Him forever."

*Command those who are rich in this present age not to be haughty, nor to
trust in uncertain riches but in the living God, who gives us richly all
things to enjoy.*

1 Timothy 6:17

*E*njoying God begins with the sheer delight of knowing and receiving
His unmerited favor and unqualified love. We rejoice with unrestrained
praise for who God is as our Father; respond to Him with uncontainable
adoration for all He has done, is doing, and will continue to do for us in
and through Jesus Christ; and we receive with unlimited gratitude His
gift of power, guidance, wisdom, and hope through His indwelling Spirit.

At the time I'm writing this, my youngest granddaughter, Bonnie
Ghlee Ogilvie, is five years old. One weekend my wife Mary Jane and I
had the privilege of having Bonnie stay with us. I eagerly came home to
enjoy being with my granddaughter. When Bonnie saw me, she ran toward me and leaped into my arms.

And, oh, how I enjoyed cuddling that lovely lass!

Do we dare to assume that God longs for the same response from us
throughout our lives? Is that too sentimental? Or is it too exalted?

A lad said to his dad, "Papa, you're great! I just want to be with you!"

I felt the same thing at dawn today about my heavenly Father as I
began my morning devotions.

One of the most liberating discoveries of my life is that I was born
and reborn to enjoy God and know the inexplicable delight of His enjoying me. Of course, I've known His judgment as a part of His gracious
care. And He is continually calling me toward His best for my life. He
offers me limitless encouragement to press on in the quest to do His will.
What a dynamic motivation it is to know that I can bring joy—the essence of enjoyment—to Him!

And because you are sons, God has sent forth the Spirit of His Son into your hearts, crying out, "Abba, Father!"

Galatians 4:6

*T*he secret of enjoying God is discovering that what provides Him with enjoyment in us is also what produces lasting enjoyment for us. There's no greater enjoyment in life than bringing delight to our Father, and His delight is that we understand and know Him.

God has written His signature in the natural world and has given us the capacity to recognize and appreciate the splendid beauty. He has entrusted to us loved ones and friends to share the pleasures of life. With providential care, He has arranged circumstances of our lives for our ultimate good and has given us strength to live at full potential. His admonition is, "Enjoy!"

So that we might know Him personally, He has come in Jesus Christ to reveal His true nature. In Christ we experience His loving-kindness, judgment, and righteousness. We have been loved to the uttermost, forgiven, and made right with Him through the cross. Now God's admonition is, "Enjoy all I've done for you!"

But press on. God gently creates in us a desire to know Him. He gives us the gift of faith to accept His love. He woos us to Him. Our experience teaches us that His promises are true. He will never leave us nor forsake us. Our knowledge of Him grows. At first, the awesome truths about God and His nature seemed beyond us, almost incomprehensible. But then, as we come to know the Father personally in the intimacy of prayer, we grow in the assurance that He will never let us down. He gives us strength when we are weak, gracious correction when we fail, and undeserved grace when we sin. He lifts us up when we fall and gives us new beginnings when we were devoid of hope. Just when we think there was no way out of a difficulty, He opened a door of opportunity. *Now* God's admonition is, "Enjoy your Father who loves you!"

But the hour is coming, and now is, when the true worshipers will worship the Father in spirit and truth; for the Father is seeking such to worship Him.

John 4:23

I'm convinced that enjoyment is the ultimate stage of knowledge. When we set out to learn the basic truths of an intellectual discipline, we are confounded by all we don't know. Little by little, we become more secure in ideas and theories. Then one day, we suddenly realize that we have captured the subject and know how to use our knowledge. What was previously frustrating becomes enjoyable.

As a young doctor put it, "Lloyd, I'm finally enjoying the practice of medicine. All the years of education and internship are paying off. Now it's a joy to be a doctor!"

More profoundly, enjoyment of our faith grows in the same way. In the beginning, God seems distant and aloof. Biblical and theological terms are like a foreign language. Our prayers are strained and shallow. We try hard to be faithful and consistent disciples. And then, with the touch of the Father's hand, we discover how much He loves us and wants us to know Him personally. Secondary theories about Him are replaced by an intimate relationship with Him. None of our awe and adoration is lost as we begin to enjoy Him. Enjoying God is not an immature step of growth but the sublime stage of knowing Him. To really know Him is to enjoy Him.

God's enjoyment of us is never conditional as ours is with each other. He created us for a relationship with Him and is continually working to convince us of how precious we are to Him so that we might enjoy Him. He knows that if we deeply believed that He enjoys us, we'd spend our lives bringing joy to Him by enjoying our status as His cherished people.

Paul, an apostle of Jesus Christ by the will of God, to the saints who are in Ephesus, and faithful in Christ Jesus.

Ephesians 1:1

*W*e are to enjoy God and use things. Never turn this around.

The best correction to remember is that we've been called into saint-hood to serve. To be in Christ is to be in ministry. People become the primary focus. The more we enjoy being saints, the more the Lord's love, forgiveness, and sacrificial caring surge through us to others. Serving people is also the most creative motive for confronting and seeking to change the social problems and needs that others face. In this a saint is fearless!

Some time ago I attended a meeting of leaders who knew each other by profession or accomplishment, but not as persons. Before we began the meeting, the leader asked us to introduce ourselves with a word or a phrase. We could not say anything that might identify what we do. We had to use language that exposed who we are. What a challenge that was for most of the people whose activities and positions are the essential meaning of their lives.

How would you have answered? What's the one word that expresses the essence of you? Would it embarrass you if I said, "I'm Saint Lloyd John Ogilvie by the grace of God?" If so, you still may be laboring with some limited ideas about sainthood. I suggest you take the lid off your reservations. Accept your status. You belong to God. Calvary was for you as if you'd been the only person alive that Friday. Pentecost was for you as if you'd been the only one in the Upper Room. The gift of faith is offered freely to you. His gift liberates you to pray, "Lord, I believe in You and commit my life to You."

When you pray this prayer, a conviction will grow inside you. You will think: "Jesus is Lord! He is my Lord! I will live the rest of my life for His glory!"

Your sainthood is settled. Your status is secure. It's part of our inheritance. *Enjoy!*

Grace to you and peace from God our Father and the Lord Jesus Christ.
Ephesians 1:2

I've never met a dynamic Christian who said he or she found Christ, got His attention, and then began a relationship with Him. Rather, they say, "He found me! And even my longing to know Him, He birthed in my heart!" He uses everything that happens to us and around us to bring us to Him. Then Christ whispers, "You are loved now!"

But is grace only for the beginning of the Christian life? Certainly not. In fact, we could not live a day without a fresh supply of grace. Sadly, however, some of us try. We begin the adventure of the abundant life and then try to live on the impetus of our own intellect and physical strength. It won't work! That's when we need the next aspect of grace.

Just as Christ graciously created the desire to know Him, He constantly seeks to initiate a deeper relationship with us. He has to be the one to do it. When life becomes pressured, filled with problems and frustrations, we usually try harder to make things work out. When we get burdened down with our failures or sins, we put off seeking forgiveness. We try to be different or better to atone for what we've done, said, or been.

It's when we neglect His grace that Christ magnificently fulfills one of Isaiah's messianic prophecies, "It shall come to pass that before they call, I will answer; and while they are still speaking, I will hear" (Isa. 65:24).

The secret is that Christ motivates in us the desire to pray! He invades our minds with the realization of our need, guides us to the wording of our prayers, and intercedes on our behalf to the Father. When we are at last able to admit our need or confess our sins or seek help with problems, He breaks our bonds and frees us to cry out for help.

Blessed be the God and Father of our Lord Jesus Christ, who has blessed us with every spiritual blessing in the heavenly places in Christ.

Ephesians 1:3

Throughout His life Jesus Christ reached out to the broken, the lost, and the downtrodden. He also reached out to some up-and-outers. Through their secure exteriors he perceived that the inner child of their past was battered, frustrated, and without blessing. He blessed rich and poor. He went to the cross to set them free.

Have you every heard the Father say to you, "You are my beloved daughter, my beloved son?"

Then He calls you by name and says, "You are mine. I have adopted you."

When He loves us with the power with which He loved His Son, we begin to know the majesty of what it means to be blessed "with every spiritual blessing in the heavenly places."

The heavenly places are not a geographical location, but a spiritual realm. Though the Lord's Prayer opens with, "Our Father in heaven," the word for heaven in the original Greek is actually plural: "Our Father in the heavens." Our Father is both running the universe and here with us in Christ. He is inside us in the Spirit that we might know that we are loved.

Once, when I was praying through the meaning of this for myself, I closed my eyes and pictured the face of my dad. He smiled, but with his customary reticence was not able to say what I needed to hear him say in that moment: "Lloyd, you're all right. I love you. I bless you."

I almost wanted to cry out in the midst of the vision of my father's face: "Say it, Dad. Say it!" Sometime later in another time of reflection he did, and I felt blessed.

More important, I have seen the face of my heavenly Father in the face of Jesus Christ. Beholding Him I have heard the Lord and Creator of the universe say to me, "Lloyd, you are my beloved."

He chose us in Him before the foundation of the world, that we should be holy and without blame before Him in love.

Ephesians 1:4

I had a caddy in Scotland whom I asked, "John, where do you live?"

"I don't live here," he answered.

"Oh? I understood that you'd been here awhile," I replied.

"I've lived here for forty-five years," he said in his Scottish brogue, "but I no belong."

"Why not, John? How old are you?" I asked.

"Sixty-five," he said, "but I no belong."

I asked, "What would it take for you to belong?"

"I would have been born and lived here every moment of my life, but I no belong."

I thought of the religious people I know who are trying to live good, responsible lives, but because they have never accepted the Father's blessing through Christ, would have to say: "I don't belong." But they can. The blessing is offered.

We can take the inheritance given to us or we can refuse to accept it. But do you know what happens when you accept it? You can become a blesser. Only the blessed can bless.

You see, what happens through Christ is that the cycle of the generations is broken. He has intervened to bless us and fill that blessing-shaped void inside us. He makes us secure so that in our relationships with family, friends, associates in the church, and people at work we can become those who express blessing, value, esteem, and hope.

The acceptance of God in Jesus Christ really means the continuous "gracing" of us, the pouring out of this grace upon us in unlimited measure so that we can be gracious and affirming and uplifting of other people.

Do you know you're blessed? Being blessed is the greatest of all miracles. The Father says, "You are loved. You belong to Me. You are My blessed person."

In Him we have redemption through His blood, the forgiveness of sins, according to the riches of His grace.

Ephesians 1:7

*B*eginning with Adam, the sad tale of history is a long saga of rebellion, resistance, and recalcitrance. Yet God persisted amazingly in His blessings and love. He called Israel to be His chosen people and gave them His blessing. Throughout the Old Testament we see God wooing His people with love, yearning over them, intervening for their deliverance, and providing for their needs. In each period of this history we hear the loving heart of the Father calling out to His children. We hear His voice in the prophets who announced both judgment and mercy and predicted a time when God would send His Messiah. Those who listened to these prophets heard what Immanuel would come to do. He would be the Lamb of God for a cosmic atonement for sin.

In His holiness and love God could not wink at sin. He could not compromise either His justice or His mercy. Therefore, out of grace He sent His Son "to demonstrate . . . His righteousness, that He might be just and the justifier" (Rom. 3:26). God set the ransom price by His judgment of sin. By God's mercy, He came in Christ to pay the full price, and at the cross He exposed His heart. God abhors, condemns, and judges sin, and yet by the power of the cross, He forgives sinners—people like you and me!

We have all gone over the line in breaking the Ten Commandments and Jesus' commandment to love. We've brought hurt, pain, and suffering to ourselves and others by what we've done or said or refused to be. We've broken His heart. Yet even before we asked Him, He forgave us. He reconciled us. He exonerated us. We stutter out our yearning to be free in response to His cross, melted by His love and healed by His forgiveness.

That same voice that cried, "Father forgive them," from Calvary says to us with the commanding power of His cross-shaped heart, "The ransom has been paid for all time. And now in this propitious moment in your time it is a pardon for you. You are forgiven. You are free!"

Therefore I also . . . do not cease to give thanks for you, making mention of you in my prayers: that the God of our Lord Jesus Christ, the Father of glory, may give to you the spirit of wisdom and revelation in the knowledge of Him, the eyes of your understanding being enlightened.
Ephesians 1:15, 16–18

Our hearts have eyes. The eyes of our heart, our "inner eyes," give us the ability to perceive truth, to feel the emotion that truth produces, and to will the demonstration of truth in our own lives. Who we become outwardly depends on what our inner eyes are able to see.

Before conversion, our inner eyes are clouded over with cataracts blocking our vision. We cannot see ourselves, others, and life in the clear light of truth. Nor can we behold God's true nature or see the beauty of the world that He's given us to enjoy. We are spiritually blinded.

Conversion begins the healing of our heart-eyes by removing our spiritual cataracts. We understand what the cross means for our forgiveness, but we still do not perceive all that the Lord has planned for us and the power He has offered to us.

We need a supernatural lens implant in the eyes of our hearts. Our vision continues to be impaired.

How graciously Paul exposed this need in the Ephesians! He did not reprove them for their lack of vision, but shared what he was praying for them to receive. He confronted them only after he had affirmed their faith, their love for one another, and his gratitude for them. The apostle knew that affirmation must precede reproof.

Paul calls this lens the "spirit of wisdom and revelation." In some of the ancient Greek manuscripts the word *spirit* is capitalized, which is consistent with the unveiling of truth in the work of the Spirit within us. We have been created to know God and to think His thoughts after Him. With the lens implant of wisdom we can see things as God sees them, express the emotion of praise, and will to become cooperative in the fulfilling of His will.

That you may know what is the hope of His calling, what are the riches of the glory of His inheritance in the saints.

Ephesians 1:18

*J*esus often spoke about those who believed in Him as the Father's gift to Him. With wisdom-implanted eyes we see the interaction of the Father and the Son. Just as those who believed in Jesus during the incarnation did so by the Father's work in their hearts, so too Christians believe by the inheritance of the reigning Christ. By divine election the Father sets us apart and makes us part of the "legacy of the liberated" entrusted to Christ. Though we don't realize this prior to our conversion, this is why we are attracted to the gospel, drawn magnetically to the cross, and propelled irrevocably to the risen, reigning Christ to claim the promise of our ransomed freedom. With releasing joy we leave our bondage and fall reverently, adoringly at the feet of King Jesus. Now we are His to enjoy.

At this point our role changes. We are not only cherished subjects of the King's domain, but we are the conscripted troops of a conquering Commander's invasion of realms that belong to Him but resist His rule. We are called to be crack spiritual commandos for the invasion of the bastions of evil. With Christ in command, the powers of hell cannot prevail against us (Matt. 16:18).

Being part of Christ's inheritance is the essence of *our* inheritance: to belong to Him, to be called to serve in His battle for righteousness, and to know that we cannot ultimately be defeated with our substantial inheritance. You were elected to be given to the Son so that you could give your life to Him, so that you could be His gift to others and eventually lift you to heaven and present you to the Father.

Can you picture this at every stage? If not, ask for a lens to be implanted into the eyes of your heart.

But God, who is rich in mercy, because of His great love with which He loved us, even when we were dead in trespasses, made us alive together with Christ (by grace you have been saved).

Ephesians 2:4–5

*T*here are four words we all need to hear more than any other. I know I need to hear them. Years of feeling the pulse of people's hurts and hopes convinces me that you need to hear them. Hourly. Daily. Right now.

We wistfully long to hear these four words from one another. Our deepest yearning is to hear them from the Lord.

What are these four powerful, healing, liberating words? Listen, listen to the whisper of the Lord in your soul.

You are loved now!

Did you hear the whisper? Those words are the essence of grace and grace's heart companion, peace.

Recently I asked people to send me their most urgent questions. Questions of all kinds came pouring in, filling the mailbags. Some people asked personal questions about life, others asked theological questions about God and His will, while a few asked biblical questions about difficult passages. One person simply sent in a postcard with this question scrawled across the back, "Is there any word from the Lord?" We all ask this question.

The word He whispers is *grace*. We should not be surprised by His whisper because He *is* grace. He also is mercy, everlasting compassion, and healing love. Loving-kindness filled the Father's heart for His estranged people until at last His heart overflowed in the gift of His Son.

Grace is the love that Christ defined. He incarnated it, revealed it, communicated it, and went to the cross to redeem us so we could experience it. Now Christ is the grace of God with us.

He whispers in our souls, *"You are loved now!"*

For by grace you have been saved through faith, and that not of
yourselves; it is the gift of God.

Ephesians 2:8

I'll never forget as long as I live the first time I really experienced healing grace. I was a postgraduate student at the University of Edinburgh.
Because of financial pressures I had to accordion my studies into a
shorter-than-usual period. Carrying a double load of classes was very demanding, and I was exhausted by the constant feeling of never quite
measuring up. No matter how good my grades were, I thought they could
be better. Sadly, I was not living the very truths I was studying. Although
I could have told you that the Greek words for grace and joy are *charis*
and *chara*, I was not experiencing them.

My beloved professor, Dr. James Stewart, that slightly built dynamo
of a saint, saw into my soul with x-ray vision. One day in the corridor of
New College he stopped me. He looked me in the eye intensely. Then
he smiled warmly, took my coat lapels in his hands, drew me down to a
few inches from his face, and said, "Dear boy, you are loved now!"

Those words communicate the essence of prevenient grace, love
that's given before we either deserve it or ask for it. I think of these words
every day, and on some days, every hour. "Jesus Christ is the same yesterday, today, and forever" (Heb. 13:8). He is God's grace with us.

As I told my story of receiving grace to a man in my office who constantly met himself at the pass with stiff-armed self-judgment, tears
streamed down his face. Grace Himself, the Lord Jesus, worked in his
heart. Together we reviewed the salient passages of Scripture about grace.

Then I asked him: "Do you hear the whisper in your soul?"

"Yes, I do," he replied, beaming.

We got on our knees, and he accepted the gift of grace. He was on
the way, and he has not stopped growing since.

I became a minister according to the gift of the grace of God given to me by the effective working of His power.

Ephesians 3:7

Sometimes when my desk is piled high with work and I can't imagine meeting all the deadlines, I think, *Why am I doing all this?* I've learned over the years that the only way out of a dumpy mood like this is to reflect on the privilege of being alive, of being a recipient and communicator or grace, and of working for God's glory. Then I say to myself—and anyone else who will listen—"It's a privilege!" And it becomes just that.

Few things will transform our attitudes toward people who cause us tough times more than to think of the privilege we have of being stewards and servants of grace to them.

What about tough circumstances? We're not to think of problems as privileges, are we? No, but to tackle them with courage and wisdom from the Lord is certainly one of our finest privileges. We are prisoners of the Lord, not our problems. The central issue of any problem is discovering what the Lord wants us to do and then to do it as a privilege.

If we exercise our privilege of knowing the Lord and living with His guidance for our actions and decisions, we can count on His faithfulness. He will keep us out of many potential problems. When we stumble into problems because we did not listen, He will help us out of them. But there are other problems He uses for our growth in grace. Then, too, there are problems in the lives of people and society in which He calls us to be His agents.

But whatever the nature of the problem, our only questions are, What does the Lord want? What does grace demand of me in response? If I were not trying to conserve my pride, what would I do? If I saw Christ-inspired problem solving as a privilege, what would my attitude be? These questions are wonderful steps out of the dumps of tough times.

For this reason I bow my knees to the Father of our Lord Jesus
Christ . . . that He would grant you, according to the riches of His
glory, to be strengthened with might through His Spirit in the inner man.
                                                    Ephesians 3:14, 16

A brilliant and successful young actor asked me to pray for him.

"What do you want me to pray?" I asked, hoping that he would reveal his deepest longing.

"Pray that I will have courage in a world of compromise," he answered intently. We all echo this longing. We need courage for our own set of circumstances in a time when others are buckling under and losing heart.

What is courage? Courage is a creative compulsion that is the composite of compelling convictions that calls us to consecrate all our capabilities and conscripts us in a cause that cannot be compromised.

For us Christians, courage is a magnificent blend of the Lord's guidance in what we are to be and do. In other words, courage is Christ in our inner being—mind, emotions, and will.

We are all called to be overcomers. This means not only trying harder, but allowing Christ to work in and through us.

On the night before He was crucified, Christ said, "In the world you will have tribulation; but be of good cheer, I have overcome the world" (John 16:33). In the Greek, the word translated as "cheer" is *courage*. It is something offered that we must willingly accept.

Christ spoke these words before the cross and the resurrection. He was sure of overcoming, which means victory. He was confident of the Father's victory and now dwells within us to give us the same confidence. It is *His* confidence, not something that we conjure up on our own to please Him.

We pray, "Lord, I can't make it without Your power. Give me the gift of courage!"

He responds, "I am in you, around you, above you, behind you, and go before you to show the way."

Now to Him who is able to do exceedingly abundantly above all that we ask or think, according to the power that works in us.

Ephesians 3:20

*T*he Lord wants us to discover inner stillness that can be sustained in the fast-moving pace of our busy lives. I have often pondered what being "still" really means. I have falsely associated it with uninterrupted times of absolute silence alone with the Lord, away from the world's impertinent noise. And yet, so often when I carve out of my schedule a few days for quiet study and prayer, I discover that the absence of the noise of our culture does not assure stillness or quiet.

This is because of the noise inside me. I still hear the noises of demanding people and the sounds of unresolved problems. But there is a deeper source of discordant noise pollution. It comes from my urgent voice of self-will arguing with the Lord over what's best for me and for the people of my life or the problems I face. Stillness eludes me. I can't hear what the Lord wants to say in the inner voice of thought and inspiration.

Stillness is surrender. It's being willing to do nothing until we are able to allow God to do what only He can do and He has given us clear direction of what He wants us to do.

Letting go isn't easy. We think we know what's best for us. And we forge ahead before we have clear guidance from the Lord. We want the Lord's help but are reluctant to give Him complete control. That sets up more discordant noise than any amount of the turned-up decibels of our noisy world. It's the blaring pollution of petulant willfulness. We get pushy with the Almighty!

When the late Dr. Henrietta Mears, the great Christian educator, was asked what she would do differently if she had her life to live over, she said, "I'd trust God more." If that question were asked of me, I'd say the same thing except I would add "and sooner."

A Christt not in us . . .
is a Christ not ours.

William Law

And He Himself gave some to be apostles, some prophets, some evangelists, and some pastors and teachers, for the equipping of the saints for the work of the ministry . . . till we all come to the unity of the faith and of the knowledge of the Son of God, to a perfect man, to the measure of the stature of the fullness of Christ.

Ephesians 4:11–13

*H*ave you ever prayed for Christ to be formed in you? I've asked Christians this repeatedly. Over the years, few have answered yes.

Often we think of Christ as outside of us, as being out there somewhere. We pray, hoping for His strength and help in our struggles. We long for His inspiration for our minds and hearts and His intervention in our difficulties. We accept and plead for His power to be released in life around us. But when His fullness pervades us, our perception of the world around us and what He can do changes. He gives us the vision of what He will do and how we are to cooperate with Him.

The fullness of Christ includes His mind for our thoughts, His nature for the formation of our character, His person for the shaping of our personalities, His will for the direction of our wills, and His power for our actions.

Once we yield our inner lives to the formation of Christ in us, we can face the struggles of our outer lives. Each new challenge or difficulty calls for greater inner growth in His fullness. Our first reaction will not be to cast about for direction or solutions in the circumstances, but to turn to Christ. We can thank Him that out of the fullness of the wisdom, knowledge, and vision of His divine intelligence we will be guided in what to think and what to do. The otherwise disturbing pressures of life will become an occasion for the further formation of Christ's fullness in us. In greater degree, every day we will think and react in oneness with Him.

My little children, for whom I labor in birth again until Christ is formed in you.

Galatians 4:19

*W*hen we pray that Christ in His fullness be formed in us, we are relieved of three troublesome struggles of life. The first is our struggle with our human nature. It is a long, weary, grim battle to try to change ourselves. But when we honestly confess our defeat in trying to get better and ask for the fullness of Christ, He enters in and performs a continuing miracle of making us like Himself.

Second, we are freed from the struggle to be adequate. I know I am insufficient for the demands of life, but I also know Christ is all-sufficient. I cannot imagine any problem He cannot solve, any person He could not love, and any challenge He would not be able to tackle. And so, from within me, Christ is at work giving me what I could never produce without Him.

Third, we don't have to struggle with worries over what the future holds. What the Lord allows to happen will be used for the greater growth of His fullness in us. We can relax. Whatever we face will be an occasion for new dimensions of His character to be formed in us.

Think what could happen in the church if we made the fullness of Christ our united quest! So much of our limited vision, lack of love and forgiveness, and unwillingness to serve each other and the world would be transformed.

But this can happen only when we yield to this fullness individually. The fullness Christ offers needs to be preached, taught, modeled, and prayed for today. We need to experience and share the secret of Christ's fullness. If we were ever to pray that Christ be formed in us, lives would be ablaze with His love and power, and those outside the church would be drawn magnetically to seek the secret of our joy and freedom.

Be renewed in the spirit of your mind, . . . that you put on the new man which was created according to God, in true righteousness and holiness.

Ephesians 4:23–24

One New Year's Eve a good friend grasped my hand and looked me squarely in the eye. Instead of the usual, jolly "Happy New Year!" greeting, he said thoughtfully, "Lloyd, I pray that this will be the best year of your life."

How would you respond? What could make this year one of your best, a year with few problems, good health, and the accomplishment of your hopes and dreams? What year in the past would you consider one of your "best years"?

As I think about this, I am amazed to realize that one of the years in the past I would consider a really "best year" was filled with challenges, difficulties, and trouble. Does this surprise you? It shouldn't. Unless I miss my guess, you probably would agree that a truly great year of your past was one in which you faced and conquered some seemingly insurmountable odds. You were stretched to grow as a person and were stronger because of the mountains of adversity you succeeded in climbing. From the mountain peak you knew that the climb was worth it. Also, from your new, elevated vantage point you could see new mountains to climb.

The "best year" of my past was a year in which I made a momentous discovery. The Lord taught me to live in day-tight compartments. This year of my life was made up of great days, each of which I lived to the fullest, as if each were my last. The cumulative result was a year of spiritual power and growth in the midst of concerns that might have rendered it the worst year of my life.

So, in response to my friend's hope that I would have one of the best years of my life, I commit myself to living one day at a time, unreservedly open to the blessings the Lord has prepared.

Therefore we do not lose heart. Even though our outward man is perishing, yet the inward man is being renewed day by day.

2 Corinthians 4:16

$\mathcal{D}$own days have a way of accumulating into discouraging months equaling a dreary year. The problem is that these down days become habitual. We soon expect little from a new day and are not surprised when this is exactly what we get.

It's a shocking realization, but spiritually, nobody is a victim. No one can ruin a day for us without our permission. The one thing we have at our command is our attitude, which is determined by how we deal with what happened yesterday and our level of trust in the Lord for our tomorrows.

As we deal with pressures, difficult people, knotty problems, demanding deadlines, and frustrating situations in any one day, we discover the extent of the effectiveness of our faith. Lofty theories and carefully polished phrases may be fine for theological debates, but what we need is power for the battle of daily living.

Louisa Fletcher Tarkington expressed our longing for a new beginning:

> I wish that there were some wonderful place
> In the Land of Beginning Again:
> Where all our mistakes and all our heartaches
> And all of our poor selfish grief
> Could be dropped like a shabby old coat at the door
> And never put on again.

To make each new day a new beginning, we need more than zippy admonitions about self-induced "happy thoughts" and self-generated, self-improvement plans. I would not mock your daily struggles with life with more guilt-producing "oughts." Instead, I want to talk about what the Lord offers and provides to make each day truly a joyous new day.

And be kind to one another, tenderhearted, forgiving one another, just as God in Christ forgave you.

Ephesians 4:32

*T*he best way to create a climate of graciousness is to be ready to ask forgiveness ourselves when we fail. A person who admits his mistakes becomes a person to whom others can readily say, "I'm sorry!"

Giving and receiving forgiveness is really an expression of self-worth. We believe in ourselves as persons of value so much that we do not want to load our emotional systems with the virus of resentment. It's so much healthier to forgive and seek forgiveness. Anger, hatred, and resentment are life's most expensive emotions. They debilitate our spirits, tax our nervous systems, weaken our hearts, and confuse our minds. Eventually, unexpressed anger becomes the taproot of anxiety. It's turned in on ourselves.

A physician examined his patient thoroughly. All the tests were completed. He sat down at his desk to write out a prescription. The patient expected a powerful medication to cure his ills. All the doctor wrote was: "Your future happiness is dependent on being forgiven and forgiving!"

Our prayers for forgiveness also need to include what happens around us in society. There comes for us a time of creative acceptance of our part in the massive sufferings, wrongs, and injustices of our time. The Lord has called us to be people who allow our hearts to be broken on what breaks His heart.

When we allow ourselves to feel the needs of people, the segregation in our corporate heart, the toleration of unrighteousness, we no longer wring our hands and smack our lips in consternation. We say, "Lord, I'm part of it! I cannot expect of my city or nation any more than I do of myself."

Walk in love, as Christ also has loved us and given Himself for us, an offering and a sacrifice to God for a sweet-smelling aroma. But fornication and all uncleanness or covetousness, let it not even be named among you, as is fitting for saints.

Ephesians 5:2–3

I'm convinced that when it comes to sexuality, God's way is the most enjoyable way to live. Let me explain why I think so.

Paul calls us to live as if fitting for saints by giving thanks. Thanksgiving puts everything into perspective. When we thank God for any aspect of life, we immediately acknowledge that it's His gift to us. We also assume responsibility to use the gift in a way pleasing to Him. Sexuality is His gift. Continually thanking Him for it is the creative antidote to sensuality.

Sexuality is the totality of a man's manliness and a woman's womanliness. It is personality in expression of thought, word, and action. It is not simply sexual gratification or the distinctive physiology of the two sexes.

God gave us sexuality not just for the perpetuation of the species, but as an expression of His providence. Sexuality is a dynamic force that enables personality to attain its purpose of existing with and for others. It gives us verve, drive, and the will to be creative. Sexuality is nurtured in infancy and childhood in the bonds of family love. It grows in self-giving, reciprocal relationships with friends of both sexes. More than just a physical drive, sexuality is a profound mystery rooted in the human spirit.

Our sexuality is a delight to behold in both men and women. A human being filled with physical and spiritual beauty is a source of joy to God as much as a breathtaking sunrise. We are to thank Him for a healthy, attractive body, a charming, warm countenance, and the unique, never-to-be-repeated miracle of personality in another person. God wants us to enjoy being men and women and truly appreciate the sexuality of people of both sexes around us.

Sensuality is just the opposite. It results when we wrench physical sex from total sexuality. Sensuality is treating persons as objects. It's gratification in fantasy or action without responsive, loving, lasting relationship. Physical, sexual intimacy outside of marriage is not in God's plan.

See then that you walk circumspectly, not as fools but as wise, redeeming the time, because the days are evil. Therefore do not be unwise, but understand what the will of the Lord is.

                                                      Ephesians 5:15–17

*E*very day you and I encounter people in trouble—friends with heartaches beneath their polished surfaces, fellow workers who long for someone to care. The Lord has deployed us in our families, workplaces, churches, and communities so we can be used decisively when He wants to communicate His love, forgiveness, and sometimes confrontational truth. I have a friend who begins every day with the prayer, "Lord, make me usable, put me where I can be used, help me be useful so when this day ends, I won't feel useless!"

When Paul challenged the Ephesians to *redeem* the time, he used a term from the world of commerce meaning "to purchase or buy up."

Buying up the time is something like working on the floor of the stock exchange. Quick decisions must be made under great pressure with many distractions.

We need wisdom and discernment to know what to do or say to make the most of every opportunity. Paul reminds us of our purpose of buying up time—"because the days are evil." Indeed they are. No one needs to convince us of the influence of Satan over people and situations. And since his schemes are so subtle in holding back the forward movement of the kingdom of God, we need daily, hourly guidance and power.

The Lord has a strategy for each situation and relationship. Prolonged time in prayer prepares us for them. Often the Lord shows us beforehand what we are to say and do. Other times, He reveals His will at that moment. We don't need to excuse ourselves from a conversation or meeting for private prayer, for when we open the channel of our minds to the Lord daily we can expect the fulfillment of Jesus' promise, "The Holy Spirit will teach you what you must say."

[Speak] to one another in psalms and hymns and spiritual songs, singing and making melody in your heart to the Lord.

Ephesians 5:19

One of my wife Mary Jane's favorite old movies is *Singing in the Rain*. In fact, she had one of the old posters from the movie framed and hung on the wall of our kitchen. The poster shows Debbie Reynolds, Gene Kelly, and Donald O'Connor with umbrellas up, splashing through puddles, and singing with gusto. But the poster for *Singing in the Rain* does more than remind Mary Jane and me of the movie. We are urged to sing in the rain! We frequently experience clouds and rain in pressures and problems, and we need to reaffirm that they cannot diminish the joy of the Spirit.

It's what we sing that makes the difference. Paul recommends spiritual songs, hymns, and psalms. There's a wealth of all three to express the song in our hearts. How about, "This is the day the Lord has made, I will rejoice and be glad in it," or "Bless the Lord, oh, my soul and bless His holy name, forget not all His blessings," or "He is Lord, He is Lord, He is risen from the dead and He is Lord," or "In my life, Lord, be glorified"? The resources seem limitless.

I find it helpful to add to my morning devotions a psalm and a hymn or a contemporary spiritual song. One of them is sure to speak to my need and become my theme song for the day. Sometimes we have a repetitive thought that captures our mind for several days. Sometimes it's negative and depressing. Why not replace it with a song of joy that puts hope in our hearts and rhythm in our steps? It will help us claim the next amazing way that Paul suggests for having the time of our lives—all day long.

Bondservants, be obedient to those who are your masters according to the flesh, with fear and trembling, in sincerity of heart, as to Christ.

Ephesians 6:5

*M*ost of us will work 160,000 hours during our lifetime. If we take few vacations and work after hours, many of us will work about 200,000 hours. A housewife will work more than 290,000! Work can be either a drudgery or a delight.

In Ephesians, Paul speaks to slaves and to slave owners. At the time in which he lived more than sixty million slaves inhabited the Mediterranean area. Therefore, Paul spoke of the responsibility of slaves to their masters and masters to their slaves. But as he did, he dropped a bombshell into the world that eventually exploded into the emancipation of people from slavery.

Work can become a false god and the object of our worship. We can spend our whole lives trying to *find* our meaning in our work, rather than *bringing* meaning to our work. We can become workaholics, seeking to find our self-esteem in the approval of the people with whom or for whom we work.

How do you really feel about your work? When you get up in the morning, do you say, "Praise God, it's a new day and I can go to work"? I once said to a good friend of mine, "I'm really afraid that the church officers are going to discover what fun I'm having working and they'll cut my salary in half!" We don't usually think of enjoying our work as part of enjoying God. Is it wrong to enjoy your work? Or is it wrong to spend your life working at something that is not enjoyable?

The apostle Paul has given us a salient, powerful truth that cuts right to the core of how to glorify God in our work. He simply states that we are to treat the people with whom or for whom we work as we would treat Christ. To the employers, he says, Treat whose who work for you as you would treat your true Master in heaven. With this dynamic truth the church began to discover the true vocation of every Christian.

Be obedient to those who are your masters according to the flesh, with fear and trembling, in sincerity of heart, as to Christ; not with eyeservice, as men-pleasers, but as bondservants of Christ, doing the will of God from the heart.

Ephesians 6:5–6

*F*or Christians, success on the job is making the Lord the boss of our lives. We report to the Lord; we serve our employer. Everyone works for some human overseer. Some person is humanly in charge of every realm. Every team must have a captain. Someone bears the lonely task of stopping the buck. The laborer has the job supervisor, the supervisor has the department head, the president has the chairman of the board, and the board members have the investors. Even the self-employed person is dependent on others to utilize his services or assure his investments. We are all intertwined in the fabric of interdependence.

I met an old friend recently. Years ago I'd been with him when he accepted Christ as Lord of his life. As a part of getting reacquainted, I asked a foolish question: "Whom are you working for these days?" I asked this knowing that his work in the television industry often brought frequent changes of employers. "The Lord!" he responded with a smile. He went on to tell me that the most difficult challenge for him in becoming a vital Christian was to work for the Lord and express that allegiance by doing his best for his employer.

Paul would have been pleased by that. In Ephesians 6:6–7, he gives us the servant's secret of going to work for a new boss. "Don't work hard only when your master is watching and then shirk when he isn't looking; work hard and with gladness all the time, as though working for Christ, doing the will of God with all your hearts" (TLB). There it is: Work for a boss as if working for Christ. That changes both our attitudes and productivity. Our task is to work industriously and energetically as a part of our witness. We are called to excellence in honor of Christ.

Therefore, whether you eat or drink, or whatever you do, do all to the glory of God.

1 Corinthians 10:31

*P*eople often ask me, "What do you do for a living?" They expect me to give them the name of a job. I always respond, "Christ is my life. He is my living." The apostle Paul did not tell the Philippians, "For me to live is to be a tentmaker." He said, "For me to live is Christ." He brought the dignity of Christ's power to working with his hands as a tentmaker as much as he did to the preaching of the gospel.

I once heard of a terrible epitaph engraved on a man's tombstone. "He was born a man. He was reborn a Christian. He died a businessman." How tragic that his family could not have rearranged the epitaph to read, "He was born a man. He was reborn a Christian. He lived as a minister of Jesus Christ in the business realm."

I love to reflect on a fantastic statement made by George McCloud, a leader in the renewal movement in Scotland and throughout Great Britain. "I simply argue that the cross be raised again in the center of the marketplace as well as on the steeple of churches. I want to recover the truth that Jesus was not crucified on an altar between two candlesticks, but on a garbage heap at a crossroads of the world, a cosmopolitan crossroads where they had to describe who He was in Latin, in Greek and in Hebrew, where soldiers gambled and cynics talked in smut."

Christ died in a real world then and occupies a real place in our lives now. He must be at the center of the real issues in our life. The church is simply a place that equips us to handle these issues in our lives as believers in Christ.

And whatever you do in word or deed, do all in the name of the Lord
Jesus, giving thanks to God the Father through Him.

Colossians 3:17

I once had a secretary who worked for me because she felt led by the
Lord to take the job. Alice Sellers was indefatigable in her work. One day
I thanked her profoundly for all she had done for me. "My dear friend,"
she replied, "I'm not doing it for you! I am here on orders from the Lord."

Alice felt no need to please me. She was working for the Lord and
was playing her part on the stage of life for him. Paul would have affirmed
that.

Until Christ is securely in charge of our lives, our insecurity will
make us vulnerable, hungry for other people's approval. Our need to be
loved, accepted, and approved will drive us to comply with what people
want us to be and do. We can blame others, but the blame lies with ourselves. People climb on our backs because we have provided them the
saddle, the stirrups, and the sharp spurs.

We all admire people who know who they are and where they are
going, whose inner nerve center gives them a clear eye and a firm jaw.
They are selective of what they do on the basis of a clear agenda. There
is no vacillation or equivocation. If what we need from them is in keeping with what they know is best for them, they will do it; if not, they can
refuse without self-incrimination or fear of rejection.

Christ enables that healthy kind of self-acceptance. As we are loved
by Him, we can love ourselves. This creative self-preservation comes
from knowing our value to Him and therefore to ourselves. We are called
to be good stewards of the gift of life. It's caring deeply for one of God's
precious persons—ourselves. If we don't believe we are worthy of care
and preservation, we need a profound experience of Christ's love for us.

Finally, my brethren, be strong in the Lord and in the power of His might.
Ephesians 6:10

*T*here's someone who doesn't want you to enjoy God. In fact, he's working day and night to make you think that's an absurd idea. He knows that if you're intent on glorifying and enjoying God, he will lose the possibility of influence over you.

His name is Satan.

Satan has a very clever strategy. He seeks to trip us up by enticing us to think, say, and do the things that are contrary to God's clearly prescribed way of living in Him, and then to make us feel that we are unworthy of His grace.

Sometimes we repeat Dennis the Menace's explanation: "The devil made me do it." Do we realize what we're saying? We're acknowledging that Satan can influence our thoughts that prompt the hurting, destructive, negative things we do. And we're right. He can and does. He wants to keep us locked into a hedonistic kind of enjoyment that keeps us from grace-rooted, joy-oriented enjoyment that's expressed in praise, faithfulness, and obedience to God and His commandments.

Our minds and hearts are the battleground between God and Satan. While we as Christians cannot be possessed, we can be influenced. Satan can play on our unresolved psychological problems and spiritual doubts. He is able to influence us to do the things that make us feel we have finally done that which will make God stop loving us. We feel badly. And he laughs.

We say, "How could I ever have done that?" Or, "That's the one thing I thought I would never do!" Or, "I guess I'm not as far along spiritually as I thought." Self-doubt is followed by self-incrimination and remorse. We are put out of commission for a time.

Is there no hope? Must we continue vacillating? Yes, there is hope. And no, we don't need to remain helpless victims of Satan's influence.

Put on the whole armor of God, that you may be able to stand against the wiles of the devil.

Ephesians 6:11

*P*aul wanted the Christians to know that it is not just human nature that causes life's problems and conflicts. He challenged them to face the motivator of selfishness, divisiveness, negative thinking, and negative actions.

Our biggest battle is not against people, but demonic beings who can use people. When we give our lives to God and seek to enjoy His grace, we will become targets of the demeaning tactics of Satan. When a church is on the move, experiencing success in what really counts—changed lives and dynamic ministry of the laity in evangelism and mission in the community—watch out. Criticism, competition among leaders, factionalism, and just plain misunderstandings and organizational foul-ups distract from the forward thrust of revival. Or people become proud of the very programs or buildings or staff that God uses to bring growth and effectiveness. We quickly become defensive of "our way" and lose our freedom to grasp God's new direction for constant renewal.

Satan is delighted when we blame people or groups for divisiveness or debilitating conflict. He wants to remain anonymous so he can continue his diabolical derision undetected. His wiles and scheming are the problem. Paul says—*face the enemy*. But how do we do this?

Paul had observed firsthand the battle armor of the Roman soldiers. He saw how crucial each part was for protection. The apostle wants us to spend time each morning in the Lord's armory to get suited up for battle. Our thoughts and inclinations can be protected.

Every day we have decisions to make, people to deal with, work to do, and challenges to meet. What's more, we have temptations to face. We need to put on the whole armor early each day before we meet anyone or attempt anything. The wonderful thing about God's whole armor is that it protects every part of our being. Let's get suited up!

Stand therefore, having girded your waist with truth.

Ephesians 6:14

The belt of a Roman soldier's equipment was placed around his waist. It held his tunic in place. Without the belt, his tunic would flap about, interfering with his free movement and possibly tripping him. The belt also served as a brace for the lumbar region. It gave the soldier a sense of strength and stability. That's why Paul associated the brace of truth with standing.

Truth helps us to stand with strength as well as to take a stand with courage. He's talking about all the implications of truth from Christ the Truth. In Christ we have the ultimate truth about God, His grace and power. We know the truth that Christ died for our sins and that we are elected to be saints. We are loved and forgiven. In the commandments and in Jesus' teachings we have the truth spelled out for our daily decisions and living.

What's more, we have Christ's indwelling Spirit to guide us and give us strength to discern and do His will.

Abiding in Christ is the way we become braced with His truth. He constantly brings us back to reality—His truth about God, about us, about how life is to be lived, and about the specifics of what obedience to Him entails.

A friend of mine puts it this way. "Knowing Christ sure takes the guesswork out of living. I don't have to spend my energies thrashing about. The basics are so clear and if I'll listen in prayer, the specific marching orders are not long in coming. What a great way to live!"

We are called to love the Lord with our minds, to think clearly about His revealed truth, and to live our lives in congruence with it. Daily Bible study kneads into our minds and souls the truth we need for every situation.

If evil at its overwhelming worst
has already been met
and mastered, as in Jesus Christ it has;
if God has got His hands on this baffling mystery
of suffering in its direct, most defiant form, and
turned its most awful triumph into
uttermost, irrevocable defeat;
if that in fact has happened, and on that scale,
are you to say it cannot happen on the infinitely
lesser scale of our own union
with Christ through faith?
In heartbreaking things that happen to us,
those mental agonies, those spiritual
midnights of the soul,
we are 'more than conquerors,'
not through our own valor or stoic resolution,
not through a creed or code or philosophy,
but 'through Him who loved us'—
through the thrust and pressure of the
invading grace of Christ.

James S. Stewart

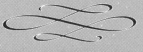

Put on the breastplate of righteousness.

Ephesians 6:14

*C*losely related to the brace of truth is the breastplate of righteousness. The truth about our righteousness with God by faith in Christ protects us from Satan's scheming efforts to make us insecure. He is the author of the lie that we should try to earn our status with God. The tenet that he's constantly trying to sell is that if we're good enough we can earn God's love, or if we work harder we'll earn our salvation.

Often we think Satan's influence is limited to ghastly things he tempts us to think or do. No, one of his most effective maneuvers is to encourage self-righteousness. If he can get us into his program of earning our salvation, he has begun to win in his effort to keep us from enjoying grace.

The breastplate covered a Roman soldier's chest and back from neck to waist. The purpose of the breastplate was to protect the heart and lungs from blows or the piercing penetration of an arrow, sword, or lance.

Our spiritual hearts, the zone of our feelings, need no less protection. The intellectual knowledge of our righteousness with God plus the gift of faith to accept it has a powerful effect on our emotional stability. The intellectual comprehension of it directly conditions our emotions.

Christ is our righteousness. He covers us with what Isaiah called the "robe of righteousness" (Isa. 61:10). Having this assurance we are protected from the roller coaster of emotional highs and lows.

Most of all, with the breastplate of righteousness in place, Satan will not be able to influence us with uncertainties about our relationship with God or get us off track by pushing us to strive for what is ours already. And with this security we will be motivated to righteous living.

Shod your feet with the preparation of the gospel of peace.

Ephesians 6:15

The shoes Paul observed on Roman soldiers were half-boots called *caliga*. They were made of leather, had open toes, and were tied around the ankles and shins with straps. The soles were thick and heavy and were studded with hobnails.

These shoes had been carefully designed to provide surefooted stability and to protect the soldier against sharp objects placed in a battlefield. Often an enemy would place in the ground sticks sharpened to dagger points to cripple an advancing legion.

You may wonder what a Roman soldier's shoes have to do with our battle against Satan's influence and particularly how these shoes can be associated with "the preparation of the gospel of peace."

The word meaning "preparation" in Greek is *hetoimasia* and denotes readiness or surefooted foundation. Both shades of meaning probably were in Paul's mind. In the Christian's walk, the unassailable peace of Christ does make us alert and surefooted in the slippery places. It also protects us from the traps and field spears Satan may have put in our way. The main thing Satan wants to do is put us out of commission. He can't do this when we are protected by peace.

Peace is the direct outgrowth of righteousness. Peace with God provides the peace of God. It is the profound assurance of our forgiveness and reconciliation with God through the cross. The estrangement and conflict is over. When this peace grips us, we are compelled to share it with others. We wonder if Paul had Isaiah's prophecy in mind, "How beautiful upon the mountains are the feet of him who brings good news, who proclaims peace" (Isa 52:7), when he wrote to the Ephesians. Satan can't harass a person who has peace and whose purpose is to share that peace with others.

Above all, taking the shield of faith with which you will be able to quench all the fiery darts of the wicked one. And take the helmet of salvation.
Ephesians 6:16–17

*T*he shield Paul is talking about was called a *scutum* in Latin. It was made with wood-covered linen and leather, with iron strips fastened to the top and bottom. Tall and oblong, the shield protected the whole soldier from the enemy. Its construction was designed to withstand incendiary arrows dipped in pitch and lighted before being sent from the archer's bow.

Most of us can readily understand what's meant by "the fiery darts of the wicked one." When our shield of faith is down, we are pierced by flaming arrows that ignite our impatience, anger, or desires. We can flame with indignation, defensiveness, or destructive criticism. Satan's fiery darts can also be sent into our conscience to set a blaze of guilt over unconfessed sins. Other flaming arrows instigate adultery in the mind with all the fiery passions expressed on the picture screen of our fantasies.

How can the shield of faith protect us against these incendiary arrows of Satan? I believe Paul is thinking of the gift of faith that trusts God with our needs moment by moment. A fiery dart can set aflame only the kindling of an unsurrendered need. Intimate, personal, ongoing prayer enables us to trust God with our concerns. When we see the flaming arrow heading toward us, we can lift our shield and make a fresh commitment to our Lord.

The helmet of salvation is closely related to the shield of faith. It protects our brain, not only from fiery darts but from destructive blows that Satan inflicts to hammer away at the security, stability, and safety of our salvation. Our thinking is constantly refortified by the special messages the Lord gives us. Our helmet guards our thinking against the invasion of thoughts of discouragement. With its protection we can be hopeful thinkers in a world of negative thinkers. Put on your helmet and hold your shield with confidence today.

And the sword of the Spirit, which is the word of God.

Ephesians 6:17

*T*he sword Paul had in mind was a short dagger used in hand-to-hand combat. For close encounters with Satan, we have the power of the Spirit to bring to mind just the right Scripture promise to cut off his attack. The term Paul used for "word" here is *rhema* rather than *logos*. Jesus Christ is the divine *logos*, God's incarnate Word of revelation of Himself. "In the beginning was the Word, and the Word was with God, and the Word was God. . . . And the Word became flesh and dwelt among us" (John 1:1, 14). *Rhema*, on the other hand, is used for a saying of the Lord that is particularly applicable to a specific need. The Scriptures are filled with these propitious promises. When we store them up in our minds, the Spirit brings just the right one to mind to claim victory over Satan's influence.

For example, when we are exhausted and need strength, the Spirit uses a *rhema* like Isaiah 40:31, "But those who wait on the LORD Shall renew their strength; They shall mount up with wings like eagles, They shall run and not be weary, They shall walk and not faint."

Or when Satan plays on our fears, Isaiah 43:1–2 becomes a sword of the Spirit: "Fear not, for I have redeemed you; I have called you by your name; You are Mine. When you pass through the waters, I will be with you; And through the rivers, they shall not overflow you."

Take a hold of Jeremiah 33:3 as a sword when you feel boxed in on all sides by what seem to be impossibilities: "Call to Me, and I will answer you, and show you great and mighty things, which you do not know."

When you're discouraged with your own efforts, listen again to Zechariah 4:6: "'Not by might nor by power, but by My Spirit,' Says the LORD."

Or, when you feel you have to take it all alone, let the Spirit remind you: "For He Himself has said, 'I will never leave you nor forsake you'" (Heb. 13:5), or, "Lo, I am with you always" (Matt. 28:20).

[Always pray] with all prayer and supplication in the Spirit, being watchful to this end with all perseverance and supplication for all the saints.

Ephesians 6:18

*T*he treasure chest of words from the Lord or inspired by the Lord seems bottomless. There's a promise for every situation and enough for every day of the rest of our lives.

Some time ago, I gathered promises for every day of the year. I had them printed and sent them to my friends all over the country. I encouraged them to memorize one a day to enrich their memory bank with hope.

A friend wrote me about the impact of these promises on his life: "I never realized the power of using specific words from the Lord in particular problems. It is as if these Scriptures were spoken just for me. When I claim them in my prayers, I receive courage."

Prayer is the way we put on the whole armor of God in the battle. This takes more than a brief morning prayer and a "Good night, Lord," as we're falling asleep. In fact, it requires conversational prayer under the Spirit's guidance throughout the day. He guides us to the words of the Lord repeatedly, hour after hour, and helps us claim a full suit of armor for each situation.

Our great need is for boldness. Paul asked the Christians in Asia Minor to pray that he might be given courage to speak boldly during his imprisonment in Rome, and he knew that they needed boldness as much as he did.

The source of that boldness came from Christ who had defeated Satan. Now, one name sends Satan cowering away with trembling and fear. One name alone can expel his influence and defeat his schemes. It is the name of Jesus Christ.

Claim your authority. Hold out the cross and say to Satan, "Stop meddling with Christ's property. I belong to Him. In the name that's above all names, the name of Jesus Christ, you have no power over me or this situation. In His name I intend to glorify and enjoy God!"

My brethren, count it all joy when you fall into various trials, knowing that the testing of your faith produces patience.

James 1:2–3

The first secret of stress management is to think about stress as a source of joy! That requires a new perspective, a different way of thinking. When Christ indwells our thinking, transforming our way of looking at life, we can then see the sources of stress as a prelude to a deeper experience of joy.

"Count it all joy when you fall into various trials" (James 1:2). In the midst of stress we are challenged to "count it all joy." The Greek word for "count" comes from the verb meaning to consider, to think. The implication of these words is that once and for all, now and forever, we are challenged to think through our trials—our stresses—until we perceive them as a source of deeper joy.

What an amazing insight! But look at it this way. The causes of stress are in what might be called the five C's: change, conflict, criticism, concerns, and crises. Add to these an overbooked schedule, unresolved tensions, and a troubled conscience, and we have a stress-filled life. But we also have the possibility of greater dependence on the Lord for guidance and the assurance of His intervention in our needs.

Joy is the result of grace. The two words come from the same root in Greek. When Christ's mind controls the cerebral cortex we know that we are loved regardless of what happens to us or around us. The stresses of life are the negatives that release the positives. They can be either the occasion of deeper trust, with the release of fresh grace, or the source of frustration. When we surrender our stresses to Christ, He uses them for our growth and His glory. We know that He will neither leave us nor forsake us. Joy springs forth from that artesian reservoir of grace. We *can* turn stress into a steppingstone! It all depends on how we think about it.

If any of you lacks wisdom, let him ask of God, who gives to all liberally and without reproach, and it will be given to him.

James 1:5

A man shared with me the stress he was feeling from church work. "I had to back off. Fussing with conflict between groups struggling for power in the church, raising budgets, and keeping the organization going, I lost the fire, the excitement, the joy of my faith. I lost track of why I was doing it all. There seemed to be a lack of adventure, of doing something we could not do without God's power. Why, I think He could withdraw His presence from my church and the people would not know it happened. Maybe He has. Oh, I go to worship, say my prayers, and try to live out my faith on my job and at home, but I'm tired of church work!" The man had done too much for too long, under too much pressure without clear goals and an adequate inflow of inspiration and strength.

Do you know the feeling? Have you ever felt that about your job, about marriage, or activities, or life as a whole? Who hasn't? What's the solution? For me, it's not just doing less, but doing the right things for the right reasons. It's having the freedom to say yes to some things and no to others because we have a clear understanding of our central goal. It's discovering that there is enough time and available spiritual power to do the things God wants us to do. It's trusting God to control our thinking and attitudes to employ our stress-coping mechanism to the maximum.

It's amazing that anyone living in A.D. 50 could have anything to say about burnout in the contemporary asphalt jungle. And yet James gives us the secret of living without the fear of burnout—energy, enjoyment, enthusiasm, and excitement: When we lack wisdom we can ask God to give us this gift of the Holy Spirit. He is more ready to give than we are to ask. He will give liberally and without reproach. He does not add blame to the stress we are feeling. Rather, He makes us wise in our management of time. When we ask Him, He gives us wisdom to reorder our priorities, spend time in prayer about our choices, and receive His strength to do what He wills for us.

257

If any of you lacks wisdom, let him ask of God, who gives to all liberally and without reproach, and it will be given to him.

James 1:5

*F*aith is the primary gift—before wisdom. Remember we cannot produce faith; it is engendered by the Holy Spirit. All we can do is admit our need, and even that is a result of the Spirit's activity. So my sense of this challenge by James is that the Spirit works in us giving us an urgent desire and hunger for God that supersedes our doubts. Then we become more sure of God's love than we are of our doubts. That's when we can doubt our doubts and ask for wisdom. We don't need to spend the rest of our lives being tossed to and fro like the waves of the sea driven back and forth, churned up by the wind. Our double mind, fractured by doubt, can become as single as God's liberality.

I know this to be true from my own spiritual and intellectual life. There have been times when doubt has disturbed my peace. I did not doubt God's existence, but I did doubt His power for problems and people. And then, when I least expect it, by the mysterious moving of the Spirit in my mind and heart, I begin to doubt those doubts and sense a longing to find a more intimate fellowship with the Lord. I want Him more than the false security of the doubt. Then I am given the faith-courage to ask for a hearing heart of wisdom. He has never refused that prayer that He Himself motivated. The gift of greater wisdom helps me see through the darkness of whatever caused the doubt. But most of all, I am filled with the inner light of God's presence and new confidence, vision, and hope begin to flow.

But let him ask in faith, with no doubting, for he who doubts is like a wave of the sea driven and tossed by the wind.

James 1:6

A pleasant, surface conversation with a brilliant intellectual at a party suddenly took on an unexpected dimension of depth. "Do you ever have doubts?" the research scientist asked intently.

"Of course," I responded. "Doubt can be creative as the prelude to intellectual and spiritual growth. The crucial thing is discovering what to do with our doubts."

"What do you think—is it a sin to doubt?"

"That depends," I answered with empathy, "on whether your doubt is dynamic or debilitating. There is an authentic doubt that delineates the demarcation line of where we need to grow. Dynamic doubt takes place in the context of fellowship with God; debilitating doubt holds Him at arm's length." I went on to explain that the issue is what we do with our doubts. The most important thing is to tell God about them and ask for the gift of wisdom to discern deeper truth in both our understanding and experience. I challenged the man to a thirty-day experiment. "Get back into prayerful communication with your Lord in spite of your doubts and ask for the gift of wisdom. In communion with Him, dare to doubt your doubts!"

It worked. At the end of the month, he came to see me. "You were right," he exclaimed. "I was holding God at arm's length with my doubts! Telling Him about them has broken the bind. I had put Him on the judgment stand when I needed Him most as an advocate in the battle for assurance against doubt. Sure, I still have doubts, but now I want to see them as a sign that there's a next step to be taken." Always doubt your doubts.

From childhood you have known the Holy Scriptures, which are able to make you wise for salvation through faith which is in Christ Jesus.

2 Timothy 3:15

*T*he heart for the Hebrews meant the intellect, emotions, and will. It was the core of a person's being. Solomon wanted his heart wholly and completely obedient to the will of God so that he could govern wisely and well. Solomon wanted to be receptive to all that God had to give.

But the young king did not want a hearing heart for his own enjoyment. He longed to be receptive so that he could discern what was right and do it. In asking for an understanding heart to obey, he was asking for the spiritual gift of wisdom. God answered his prayer and wisdom became synonymous with his name. The "wisdom of Solomon" punctuates his time of history.

Wisdom is our greatest need today. We need it for our responsibilities and relationships. It is the missing quality in most leaders, the lacking ingredient in society, the reason for the impotence and ineptness of most Christians.

We worship at the shrine of fact, place our oblations on the altar of knowledge, and bow down before our capacity to solve the mysteries of life. We live as paupers of the mind because we lack the power of wisdom.

True wisdom cannot be earned or acquired by human effort. Nor is it reserved for old age, nor the result of experience alone. We can have lived long and squeezed life dry and not have wisdom. Wisdom is a gift. It is imparted by God, imputed in communion with Him, and infused by His Holy Spirit. It is beyond acquired skills. Deeper than insight. More profound than learning.

Do you have the gift of wisdom? You can! The first step to greatness, effectiveness, and inner power for living is wisdom. You can receive the gift today. Right now. An understanding heart filled with wisdom can be yours!

You do not know what will happen tomorrow. For what is your life? It is even a vapor that appears for a little time and then vanishes away.

                                            James 4:14

*W*e have such a few years to do the things the Lord wants each of us to do. To miss that is to miss everything. I think that's what James felt when he went on to say, "For what is your life? It is even a vapor that appears for a little time and then vanishes away" (4:14). The image is of the morning mists or fog that hovers around the peak of a mountain and then dissolves as the sun rises and the winds blow.

Life is like that. Our purpose is to know, love, and glorify the Lord and become prepared to live with Him forever. In the brief span of this life He will guide our thinking and willingness to accomplish His plan for us. I've never known a person to have a nervous breakdown doing what the Lord wills. He never asks us to do more than He is willing to provide strength for us to do. He does not guide us into a burnout. The Spirit of the Lord in us is an eternal flame, and the promise made by John the Baptist is true for us: Christ baptizes with fire!

Ten words fan the fire of His Spirit in us. James tells us we are to say, "If the Lord wills, we shall live and do this or that" (4:15). There's the antidote to burnout, the motto of a beautiful life. Saying those words each hour of every day, in each decision, and in ordering our total life will bring peace and excellence. Success is doing what the Lord wants us to do. He will liberate our wills to implement our total nervous system to carry out what He guides in our thought processes. And He prepares us for decisions that are ahead of us. In consistent times of prayer with Him each day, He gets us ready to make guided choices. When we come up against a decision about which we do not feel sure, it is crucial to put off any choice until we have given Him time to build in us the clarity we need.

So then, my beloved brethren, let every man be swift to hear, slow to speak, slow to wrath; for the wrath of man does not produce the righteousness of God.

James 1:19–20

*P*rayer is the only way to get control of our angers and express them creatively. When we share with the Lord the things we've heard or seen that make us angry, we can then respond with His love and creative concern. Our task is to talk to Him about our angers before we tell others about them. People will not hear us unless they know that we love them. We can say, "This is how I'm feeling. Please hear me because what I am saying is a part of my love for you."

Being "slow to speak" follows naturally. We don't have to blurt out our angers immediately. Words can cut and hurt irreparably. A part of prayer is to get the Lord's perspective, then His timing, and then His attitude. Above all, our expression of anger need not multiply an endless cycle of mounting hostility.

Recently I heard a man say, "I really feel like getting good and angry." What he meant was that he felt like being really angry. I said, "If you are to be *good* and angry at the same time, you'll need the Lord's help."

We all do. Have you ever awakened in the early hours of the morning and thought back on your all-too-quick, angry retort to someone? I have! Those times make me all the more committed to waiting until I have the Lord's perspective, patience, and power for my reply. And those experiences have led to a commitment that has lowered my stress level. It is the commitment to ask people who say or do disturbing, anger-producing things to repeat what they've said, or to request that they explain to me why they did what they did. This gives me time not only to listen carefully, but to pray inside, "Lord, help me to respond with Your mind controlling mine and Your attitude guiding both the tone and intent of my words." These few moments keep me from blurting out a crippling response.

You ought to say, "If the Lord wills, we shall live and do this or that."
James 4:15

*P*eople burn out from lack of challenges as much as in trying to do too much. The Lord delights to press us into tasks crucial to the forward movement of His strategy for us and the kingdom goals where we live— in families, places of work, churches, and communities. The problem of some people is not burnout but never having a flame to worry about burning out. James deals with that in a decisive way: "Knowing what is right to do and then not doing it, is sin (TLB)."

There's stress caused by a dull, unadventurous life. It comes from the stifling of the strength the Lord gives us. It's holding Him off, saying no, not to life's demands, but to Him. We burn out because we do not flame the fire with obedience. We become dull, bland, unexciting people. Here again, the crucial thing is to ask the Lord what He wants for us in life's relationships and responsibilities. Our willingness provides the dry kindling for the Lord to set us ablaze.

Deo volente was the watchword of the early church. As a matter of fact, in many periods of history, the saints would end their letters with D.V., which means, "If God wills." Many of them would then follow it with another Latin phrase, *Carpe diem*—"Seize the day."

I like that. When we say *Deo volente*, we can also say *Carpe diem*. We will not burn out. Our constant prayer will be, "Whatever the Lord wills, I want to do with delight." Then we can live with freedom and joy in each day knowing that He will guide and direct each step of the way.

Therefore be patient, brethren, until the coming of the Lord. See how the farmer waits for the precious fruit of the earth, waiting patiently for it until it receives the early and latter rain.

James 5:7

I have a friend I've been worried about because of the way he has misused his immense talents and gifts. He has jumped from one job to another without settling down, and he has failed to complete his education.

In our conversations I always express my concern and hope for him, affirming my belief in his potential. But one day I became aware of how my impatience was causing stress. Each time I thought of my friend, my pulse quickened; I became judgmental and angry and felt agitated for hours afterward. That led me to pray more consistently for him.

As time passed, James's word about planting, watering, and waiting for the harvest thundered home to me that I had not planted a courageous seed of faith about this brilliant young man. I did that, claiming that the Lord, in His own timing and way, would break through to this young man about his future. Then I waited. Months went by. Whenever we visited, my temptation was to push or use guilt-producing tactics. By the Lord's grace I was able to withstand the urge.

After another long period of waiting, I received a phone call from him. Through circumstances I could never have arranged, the young man has been confronted with what he was doing with his life. Joy, not negative stress, surged within me when he told me about his decision to return to school and pursue his newly defined goals for his life. The Lord had used a person I would not have expected to enable the transition.

You also be patient. Establish your hearts, for the coming of the Lord is at hand.

James 5:8

The late Hans Selye, an authority on stress, divided people into two categories: some are racehorses who thrive on a fast-paced life, and others are turtles who move slowly. Racehorses tend to be very impatient with turtles. They find it difficult to get them to do what they want, when and how they want it. Their impatience is expressed in an attitude of frustration and judgment. They give the impression that there is something wrong with those who don't run at their pace, think as they do, and respond to their time schedule. Racehorses want everything yesterday. They are what is called Type A personalities.

James's words offer three gifts to us racehorses to help us maximize our personality type in a really creative way, and at the same time overcome the impatience that cripples our relationships. We can live on the Lord's timing, our energies can be multiplied by His supernatural power, and we can accomplish a greater purpose than our compulsive goals. The Lord is not against racehorses. But He wants us to bring our personalities and the attitudes we express under His control and be employed for His plan, our ultimate productivity, and the building up of others.

That sets us free of our tight grip on life and our worry over ourselves and other people's performance. The Lord is at hand; He is in charge. He controls not only when history will be culminated but everything that happens between now and then.

The only hope for the transformation of Type A racehorses is to surrender our lives, talents, and immense ambition to the Lord. We will be helpless victims of inordinate stress until we do. There is hope for us racehorses. The Lord has great plans for us in the work of communicating His love and power to others. Our personalities can be transformed so that our attitudes reflect the patient attitude of Christ. New patience will result. We will run with the Lord at His pace for us and toward His destination. And along the way we'll be far more patient with the turtles of our lives.

Jesus exemplified perfect unity of
mind, body, and spirit.
He said He came to give us both
abundant and eternal life
He promised that we would have
abundant life
here on earth if we would
abide in Him
and invite Him to abide in us.
And when He does abide in us,
I believe the reasoning brain
can be brought into unity with
our physiologic systems
which control the stress reactions
to external stimuli.
The indwelling Christ helps us
manage stress.

I am the vine, you are the branches. He who abides in Me, and I in him, bears much fruit; for without Me you can do nothing.

John 15:5

*W*hen Christ fulfilled His promise to abide in His disciples, a new breed of racehorses was released to live by His indwelling power and guidance. Type A personalities were harnessed, and they displayed the mind of Christ. His attitude was now in them. These early Christian leaders and, a few years later, Paul exemplify the patience that resulted. They loved people profoundly and trusted the Lord with the results. Living moment by moment with the conditioning of their attitudes by the mind of Christ, they overcame their racehorse impatience with the slowness and failures of others.

Listen to Peter: "And above all things have fervent love for one another, for 'love will cover a multitude of sins'" (1 Pet. 4:8); or to John, "In this is love, not that we loved God, but that He loved us and sent His Son to be the propitiation for our sins. Beloved, if God so loved us, we also ought to love one another" (1 John 4:10–11); and to Paul, "Let all bitterness, wrath, anger, clamor, and evil speaking be put away from you, with all malice. And be kind to one other, tenderhearted, forgiving one another, just as God in Christ also forgave you" (Eph. 4:31–32). There's solid evidence of the transformation of the previously misdirected personalities of racehorses! Perhaps we could call them "double-A" personalities, A types who superseded their category by the inspiration of the mind of Christ.

You and I are meant to be among them. It can happen today. I know. Since Christ took charge of my life, my racehorse personality has been channeled into His purposes. His indwelling love constantly frees me from judgmental impatience with others. I'm still a racehorse, but Christ's racehorse, seeking to be responsive to His reins to do what He wants by His enabling power and not my own.

Confess your trespasses to one another, and pray for one another, that you may be healed.

James 5:16

A woman who is a racehorse personality confessed to her Bible study and prayer group the stress she was living with because of her recurring impatience with almost everyone in her life. At the end of her explanation, she said, "I really want to be different. Talking this out has made me realize how little of Christ's attitude controls either my reactions to people or the inner stress that results. I want the group to pray for me in the next week, so that I might become more sensitive and understanding of the people in my life."

With that she began to cry. She had turned off most of the people in her life by her impatience and was feeling the loneliness caused by her "righteous" indignation. The group gathered around her and prayed for her.

In the week that followed, she kept a log of her feelings and reactions. She consciously yielded her attitudes to Christ's guidance at the beginning of each day and in her encounters with people. A few startling evidences of a change of attitude convinced her that she was on the move and built up her confidence. She prayed her way through encounters and meetings that previously had tied her in knots. That relaxed her and opened her up to Christ's conditioning. She was amazed at how peaceful she felt inside.

Each time this woman meets with her group she reports on what's happened. She's on the way—still a racehorse in all she enjoys doing, but different in that the purpose of the race has changed. She now has the goal of being to others the patient person Christ has been to her.

I have shared this woman's story because it shows that no one need remain as he or she is. If we really want to change, we can ask the Lord for help and ask others to pray for us. We can be different!

Now to Him who is able to establish you according to my gospel.
Romans 16:25

*T*he word translated above as "establish" means to fix, make fast, stabilize, or strengthen. Christ is able to create stability in our lives. He makes us secure.

So often I find that stress in people is blamed on the pressures of life, when the real cause is something that is gnawing at their vitals.

I visited with a man who complained about the stress caused by overwhelming schedules and responsibilities. The more we talked, the more the man realized that he was running from the person inside him. A few years ago he did something that has remained in his memory as a source of self-condemnation. Because he did not deal with it at the time, he has tried to atone for an inner feeling of guilt by busyness. It astonished him to realize that he was running off in all directions away from the conscience-stricken person in his own skin.

That day he stopped running, faced himself, and met the Savior. He accepted the forgiveness offered him and decided to stop hiding from himself and others behind an impossible schedule that gave him a false sense of worth.

Imagine yourself stabilized by the gospel. How would you look and act? What would your schedule, involvements, and priorities be? Get in touch with yourself. Are you under uncreative stress? What is it doing to your peace of mind and health of body? What are the causes of stress in your life? What is bending you out of shape, boxing you in, stretching you beyond what Christ has ordained? Most of all, what is Christ stressing in the stress?

Christ will give us stability and strength to accomplish His work by His power. We will be given resiliency to follow through on the seemingly impossible tasks He guides. He will help us reorder our lives around Him and the gospel so that the self-induced causes of stress can be eliminated.

But if we walk in the light as He is in the light, we have fellowship with one another, and the blood of Jesus Christ His Son cleanses us from all sin.

1 John 1:7

One afternoon I watched a Japanese freighter being unloaded in the harbor. Each container had instructions stamped on the side in bold letters, both in Japanese and English. I suspected that something had been lost in the translation. "If this side is up, this container is upside down!"

I laughed, then I began to think about what the words meant for my life and the people I love. "If this side is up, this life is upside down!" How could I tell if my life was right side up? What are the identifiable signs that we are accomplishing the purpose for which we were born? Or what would be the undeniable marks of missing the reason we're alive?

We were created for an intimate relationship with God and one another. Few words are as misunderstood as *intimacy*. It implies more than just romance or sex. An intimate relationship is one that is distinguished by close association, contact, familiarity. Personal. Innermost. Intimacy implies an encounter that reveals the essential nature of two persons. The intricate *I* meets the real *you*.

John wrote his letter to help his friends recapture intimacy with God. In the opening of his letter, he declared that, in Christ, God had opened and revealed His intrinsic, essential, innermost heart. God had dwelt bodily in Jesus. The eternal life of God was revealed in time and space for all time and for all people. Nothing had been left out or held back. He had made the first move toward His people. Out of unreserved love He had offered Himself. "In Him was life, and the life was the light of men" (John 1:4). The light of the world revealed both God and His love. In that illumination, people saw God as He is and themselves in their need of Him. The purpose of it all was fellowship with God and a new quality of fellowship between those in whom the light had shown.

He who says he abides in Him ought himself also to walk just as He walked.

1 John 2:6

*T*he bottom line is always red for a Christian. Outgo must exceed income. When it comes to giving ourselves away to others in creative, healing, forgiving love, our relational books will never be balanced. Love is a careless spendthrift when it comes to the needs of people—regardless of what they do in return! We are called to give more of ourselves to others than we either expect or demand to receive from them. If we take Jesus seriously, we will be in the red.

Look at the unpolished directness of John. He exposes our carefully balanced ledgers of giving as much as we get, of loving those who love us, of parceling out affection in cautious proportion to what we have received from others. Our black, balanced line of neat quid pro quos suddenly embarrasses us.

"Anyone who says he is a Christian should live as Christ lived." There's the motive and method of living in the red. Verse 6 of chapter 2 is the distilled result of John's years of fellowship and experience with Christ. It was the message of his life.

Our audit of Christ's balance sheet is alarming. The bottom line is red! He came as God's gift; He gave Himself away; He recklessly invested His whole life for you and me. The cross is the plus mark against the debits of our deliberate sins. All we have to offer Him is our failures and rebellion. He did not love in proportion to the love offered Him. No bartering lover, this Jesus! He was misunderstood, misused, and mistaken. Neglected by some; negated by others. Betrayed by those who followed Him; beleaguered by those who feared Him. Love was His only response.

This is the way Christ walked, lived, and lives! Nothing we have done or do qualifies us for His comforting presence. He comes to us, stands with us, absolves us, and cleanses us. His love enables us to keep on giving. He more than makes up for the deficit.

Give, and it will be given to you: good measure, pressed down, shaken together, and running over will be put into your bosom. For with the same measure that you use, it will be measured back to you.

Luke 6:38

*I*n the eighteenth century, an economist by the name of Turgot established what he called the law of diminishing returns. Stated simply, he reasoned that an overinvestment of capital or labor results in a diminished profit.

For example, in a business, a certain amount of capital is needed for raw materials, facilities, and labor to produce, package, and distribute a product. Once a selling price is established in the competitive market, any unnecessary or excessive investment for production eventually lessens the profit. The overinvestment really becomes counterproductive to the ultimate purpose of making a profit.

Seventeen centuries before Turgot, Jesus proclaimed a spiritual law that is just the opposite. It is the law of multiplying returns. We find the basis for that law in Luke's telling of the Sermon on the Mount, where Christ says: "Give, and it will be given to you: good measure, pressed down, shaken together, and running over will be put into your bosom. For with the same measure that you use, it will be measured back to you" (Luke 6:38).

From this we see that we are called into partnership with the Lord to live a merciful, nonjudgmental and noncondemnatory, giving and forgiving, generous life. That's the product. To produce that through us, the Lord lavishes us with an overabundance of His grace because He wants us to emulate His own generous heart. We can't outgive the Lord. The more we give away of what He has entrusted to us, the more He invests in us. He's willing to overinvest in us because we are His strategy for communicating His generosity to the world.

> *Again, a new commandment I write to you, which thing is true in Him and in you, because the darkness is passing away, and the true light is already shining.*
>
> *1 John 2:8*

*A*re there people in your life who have pulled you down to their level of darkness? Light and darkness are both contagious. Can you think of anyone whom you would rather not see again?

In each relationship where love has been distorted, I find the Lord is giving me something to do. A letter, a phone call, an act of involved love—each perfectly suited for the person—becomes clear. It would be so easy to evade the challenge, to straighten out the Lord about the fact that I am a victim of the other person's confused thinking or immaturity. He's not impressed.

Hatred for fellow Christians is a stumbling block. Those people become a cause for our tripping in our strides to grow as Christ's disciples. But the Lord told us that He would meet us in the lost, the lonely, and the imprisoned. The people who disturb and distress us are placed in our path by Christ Himself for us to love in the power of His love. If we refuse, we trip on the Lord Himself.

The darkness of animosity makes the path treacherous, but Christ's light makes stumbling stones into steppingstones. When we ask the Lord for the specific strategy for doing love in each troublesome relationship, He illuminates the person so we can see not an enemy but a person desperately in need of healing and hope. He shows us the inner cause of the problem. The particular thing He tells us to do will touch the deeper level.

I find it's good to set a time line on our reconciling action. When will we be able to do the loving act? Set it carefully. At the end of tomorrow or next week the Lord will be waiting with that same disturbing question. "Have you done what I asked you to do?"

Do not love the world or the things in the world. If anyone loves the world, the love of the Father is not in him.

1 John 2:15

I have discovered that praise is the only antidote to pride. The new freedom I'm experiencing is to relish the delight of the gifts and opportunities God has given me. I could not breathe a breath, think a thought, write or speak a sentence, or be an enabling leader without God's presence and power. All that I have and am is a result of His blessing. If He is the author of it all, I am free to enjoy being me and being used as a part of the Lord's strategy. Everything He entrusts to us is to be used for His glory. That realization can heal the pride of life. Jesus offers us an abundant life filled with love, forgiveness, and joy. When we belong to Him, pride is replaced with gratitude and unrestrained celebration of the capacities, talents, and gifts He has entrusted to us. We do not need the booster of pride; that usually leaves us depressed when the upper wears off and we are alone with reality. We will not be like the man described by Billy Sunday. He said the proud person was all front door: When you go in, you're immediately in the backyard!

Personal checkup time: Are there any evidences of pride that indicate that a false love for the world has gotten to us? Love for God more than the world frees us to live in the world in the security of the imputed, personal resources He has given us. Our need for approval will be satisfied by the approbation of God's delight in us. Praise, not pride, is our response.

Finally, John tells us that the world is not worthy of our ultimate love because it is transitory: "And the world is passing away, and the lust of it; but he who does the will of God abides forever" (1 John 2:17).

We shall be like Him, for we shall see Him as He is. And everyone who has this hope in Him purifies himself, just as He is pure.

1 John 3:2–3

One of our most crucial faculties is the God-given gift of imagination. Our imagination is transformed when we are converted and become new creatures in Christ. Previously our imagination was distorted and misused as the picture screen of our fantasies and fears. After conversion, however, our imagination can become a powerful faculty for enabling us to picture the person we can become in Christ.

The imagination is the capacity to form, hold, and achieve images. We are all in the process of becoming what we dare to imagine. The more we focus on Christ the more we become like Him. He is the image of the invisible God; He is no less the image of what we were meant to be.

This is the incredible promise John gives us in today's verse. "We know that when He is revealed, we shall be like Him, for we will see Him as He is" (1 John 3:2). When we get to heaven, or Christ returns, whichever comes first, we will discover that a lifetime of focusing our attention on Christ has made us like Him. When we invite Christ to live in us, He uses our imagination to help us envision our lives transformed into His likeness. The power of a Christ-captivated imagination is suggested in John's further words, "And everyone who has this hope in Him purifies himself, just as He is pure" (1 John 3:3). When our imagination is focused on the hope that we shall be like Him, all lesser goals are purged. Sören Kierkegaard said that purity of heart is to will one thing. A Christian, according to John, purifies himself or herself in a progressive movement toward Christ and Christlikeness. Impurities and conflicting goals are drained off like dross when we center our imaginations on Jesus. The unique capacity of the imagination is to make us like Christ in thought, action, and reaction.

Trust in the LORD with all your heart, and lean not on your own understanding; in all your ways acknowledge Him, and He shall direct your paths.

Proverbs 3:5–6

*L*et's continue our thoughts about the power of a Christ-captivated imagination. The gift of imagination is the bridge over the interface between our presuppositions and our potential. In Christ we hold magnificent convictions. The practical application of these strong convictions is the function of the imagination. This is not self-generated wishing but Christ-motivated hope. The imagination, when committed to Christ, becomes the servant of the intellect and the instigator of the will. Our discipleship is giving the truths we hold a local habitation and a name.

For example, we know that we have been called to be servants of Christ. We ask, Now that I believe that, what am I to be and do for the glory of Christ? His Spirit invades our imaginations to etch the guidelines of our obedience. He forms an image in our brains of what we would be to others and what we would do in society if we trusted Him completely.

Charles Kettering said, "I expect to spend the rest of my life in the future, so I want to be reasonably sure of what kind of future it's going to be. That's my reason for planning." I agree, but I would add the word *prayer*. It is in prayer that the Lord gives the vision of the future. He is the draftsman of our planning and uses our imagination to help us see His long- and short-range goals of building a magnificent life.

Roger Bagson was right: "The future has a way of becoming the present." We become what we imagine. That's why it's so crucial to take time for silence in our daily prayer so that the Lord can give us the picture of what we are to be and do in that day as part of our forward progress in claiming His maximum plan for our lives. Specifically, this is how the Lord turns our struggles into steppingstones.

*Whoever has been born of God does not sin, for His seed remains in him;
and he cannot sin, because he has been born of God.*

1 John 3:9

I meet defeated Christians everywhere. They are living on self-effort,
trying to be adequate and perfect on their own strength. The great need
is to abide in Christ and for Him to abide in them. The first is the best
we can do, and the second is the best He can offer. Abiding in Christ is
concentrating our total experience on Him. We all need to think a great
deal more about Christ. That releases emotions of love and praise. Willingness to do His will follows naturally. We all become what we think
about during the waking hours of our day.

But focusing on Christ is only the beginning. Liberating power
comes from the indwelling Christ abiding in us. From within He enables
us to think His thoughts, express His love, and be willing to follow His
guidance. Extraordinary wisdom, strength, sensitivity, courage, and vision are given to multiply our human capacities. The same passionate
obedience to God that we observe in Jesus during His ministry is engendered in us as the urgent desire of our lives. What the Lord requires He
releases within us as a gift.

We can supersede the syndrome. The Lord breaks the bind of the
cycle of repeated failures. We don't have to stay the way we are. The
Lord's nature is growing in us. Ours is to choose to give Him complete
freedom to dominate our desires. We are to be the Lord's miracle in the
midst of a world longing for power to live life to the fullest.

John's focus of sin in this passage deals with relationships. Sin is refusal to love. Specific acts of sin are what we do to hurt or debilitate
people. But each time we fail, we are called back to our essential purpose
of becoming lovers, and the Lord is always more ready to help than we
are to ask.

But whoever has this world's goods, and sees his brother in need, and shuts up his heart from him, how does the love of God abide in him?

1 John 3:17

*H*ow can we lay down our lives for fellow Christians? It means involvement, caring, and openness. Loving means listening. People need to articulate their struggles. They long to be drawn out by someone who can understand and probe with identifying tenderness. We lay down our lives by sharing what we've been through or are facing right now. That means sacrificing our personal privacy and images of adequacy. We lock people in a prison of self-doubt if we create the impression we have it all together. No one has! When we dare to be vulnerable, we earn the right to share the answers we have found and to witness to what the Lord has done in our lives.

Caring for people takes time, surrender of our schedules, and relinquishment of aloof judgmentalism. We will communicate on our faces and in our attitudes whether we are available to care. We all need positive, supportive brothers and sisters in the family of faith to reverse the negative influence of people who have stifled our capacity to give and receive love. There is no more exciting vocation for a Christian than to be a liberator of people through divinely inspired human expressions of love.

Loving may demand very specific expressions of material help. John presses on to that. The point is that some people cannot hear our words of love until that love is expressed in a way that convinces them we understand what they are going through. An act of love opens people's hearts to hear our words of love. What is the unique and personalized thing you could do to help them in their situations? The Lord is motivating us to act. To refuse the opportunity will debilitate future communication with Him. I know what I must do. How about you?

And by this we know that we are of the truth, and shall assure our hearts before Him. For if our heart condemns us, God is greater than our heart, and knows all things.

1 John 3:19–20

*H*ave a heart!" is a familiar expression when we need a person's understanding, sympathy, or compassion. That's based on a grand assumption. How can we be sure that a person's heart is filled with those qualities?

We think of the heart as the center of feelings. But what's in our hearts depends on what's in our minds. The values, beliefs, and convictions of a person's mind control what's expressed by the heart. It would be well to find out what a person thinks before we plead for him or her to "have a heart." The mind is the control center for what's sent to the nervous system and emotions. The Hebrew understanding of the heart included intellect, emotion, and will. The attitude of the heart is rooted in our beliefs. We'd better check that out when we want someone to "have a heart" for us.

Many of us suffer from a lack of self-affirmation. Life has conditioned us to be very hard on ourselves. We are more aware of our liabilities than our assets. Past failures haunt us and rob us of the delight of the present or excitement for the future. It's difficult to be up for life when we are down on ourselves.

We need a new heart of love and acceptance, affirmation and encouragement for ourselves. But that will not be possible without a new way of thinking about ourselves. Our hearts need different signals from our brains—a new objectivity based on something ultimately reliable. Only God can do that. We need to exchange our thinking about ourselves for His. "A new heart I will give you!" is an ancient promise from God that we desperately need to hear and receive. To "have a heart" for ourselves is to relate to our inner person with the same love and forgiveness that God has shown us in Christ.

You are of God, little children, and have overcome them, because He who is in you is greater than he who is in the world.

1 John 4:4

*T*he other day a friend gave me a new definition of a pessimist. Jokingly, he said that a pessimist is a highly experienced optimist.

I thought about that after the laughter died down. My experience is just the opposite. An optimist is a highly experienced pessimist. True optimism is born out of experiences of Christ's power in the midst of what would make a person pessimistic.

What's it all about, Alfie? Don't ask Alfie, Alice, or Albert. They don't know! But who does? Where can we find the purpose of it all in a world like this? What makes Sammy run? Sammy's the last person to ask!

We look around us. The aspirations we experienced in the asphalt jungle leave us no clearly marked path. We try, with Franz Kafka, to "see through the thickness of things." We are tempted to give in to what Albert Camus called "that hopeless encounter between human questioning and the silence of the universe."

When we allow ourselves to get in touch with life, we feel the pain, disappointment, and anguish around us. People are irresponsible and society is careless. Evil people enrage us, neutral people upset us, and good people who do little alarm us. The natural world has more than enough catastrophes to balance off its resources and beauty. The institutions of our culture are painfully slow to respond to human need. The church is often anachronistic, communicating more defensiveness than decisiveness. People we love trouble us, and some we depend on to lead us let us down. It's not easy to be optimistic about life or the future.

Unless—! We will be pessimistic until we have power within us that is greater than the evil in the world. Christ in us is the source of true optimism.

Beloved, let us love one another, for love is of God; and everyone who loves is born of God and knows God.

1 John 4:7

Over the years I have observed that the people who are able to infuse the precious, liberating experience of self-esteem in others are people who feel good about themselves. They feel special and help others to know they are special.

But that's not easy for most people. They are more aware of their shortcomings and inadequacies than their strengths and abilities. The ledger of self-evaluation lists more liabilities than assets. Creative self-love is difficult for many of us, knowing all we do about ourselves.

Many of us were conditioned in childhood to feel that self-appreciation was arrogance. Enjoying ourselves was considered a sure sign of pride. So few people reach maturity being able to say, "I'm glad I'm me!" The theme woven throughout this book is that the antidote to pride is praise. A deep sense of gratitude for our abilities and talents is the true source of creative self-affirmation. The freedom to love ourselves is the result of the realization that all that we have and are is a gift. The people who make others feel special have this authentic humility. The question is: How can we discover that?

It's a gift of God. He alone can break the bind of self-depreciation and free us to enjoy being ourselves. It begins with a personal relationship with Him, grows with a realization that He is the source of our life, and is expressed in thankfulness for the person He has enabled us to be. The challenge is to accept His attitude toward us as our own attitude toward ourselves. His personal word to each of us is, "I know all about you. The needs and failures. I love you just as you are! You belong to me. I created you. Have cared for you through the years. Blessed you with abilities and talents. Made the future your friend. All is possible. You are very special to Me!"

*Prayer does not enable
us to do a greater work for God.
Prayer is a greater work
for God.*

Thomas Chalmers

> For whatever is born of God overcomes the world. And this is the victory
> that has overcome the world—our faith.
>
> *1 John 5:4*

*T*he Duke of Wellington, who defeated Napoleon at Waterloo, recorded in his journal the need for "three o'clock in the morning courage."

We would agree. Before and in the midst of the battles of life, we need courage. Courage is fear that has been on its knees in prayer. Whenever we start thanking God in tight situations, courage begins to flow. It is a quality of spirit that meets danger or opposition with intrepidity, calmness, resoluteness, and determination.

The early Christians to whom John wrote needed to know that they had been born into Christ for a time like that they were facing. The apostle wanted them to know that their faith could overcome the world. The word *kosmon* ("world") is used here for the composite of all the forces antagonistic to the new life in Christ. Satan was the divisive general of those forces. The company commanders were the leaders of the Gnostic movement that denied the incarnation. The foot soldiers were the antichrist troops who constantly unsettled the Christians' security in Christ. It was not easy to be a Christian in Roman Asia. Ridicule, conflict, denial of employment, harassment, and loss of personal dignity confronted the followers of Christ. Political punishment was always a danger. The church was often forced underground.

John did not offer glib advice. He simply told the Christians they would overcome. "Whatever is born of God overcomes the world. And this is the victory that has overcome the world, our faith." Born of God means begotten of God—called, chosen, given birth as a son or daughter of God. John wanted his people to remember that they were the cherished children of God. As such, they would overcome the world by His power. And so can we—today!

And this is the testimony: that God has given us eternal life, and this life is in His Son. He who has the Son has life; he who does not have the Son of God does not have life.

1 John 5:11–12

*T*he key that unlocks heaven, now and forever, is belief in the inner heart and unashamed confession in word. We can be sure that we are alive in a quality of life that death cannot end. Then we can be absolutely sure about the future. "And if Christ is in you, the body is dead because of sin, but the Spirit is life because of righteousness [rightness with God]. But if the Spirit of Him who raised Jesus from the dead dwells in you, He who raised Christ from the dead will also give life to your mortal bodies through His Spirit who dwells in you" (Rom. 8:10–11).

A young man sat across from my desk. He said, "Why all this talk about eternal life? I want one life at a time. Let me live this one now. I'll worry about the other one later." My response was, "But think of all that you're going to miss between now and then." I tried to tell him about the reality of eternal life now. How I wish I could tell you a success story that ended with the brilliant, handsome athlete accepting Christ. This story doesn't end that way. The young man died in a tragic auto crash two weeks later. He had refused the gift of life eternal, thinking he had all the time in the world. Now he has all the time of infinity without the joy he refused during his twenty-two years. He has immortality without eternal life.

Christ's great declaration of His gift to us ends with a question. "I am the resurrection and the life. He who believes in Me, though he may die, he shall live. And whoever lives and believes in Me shall never die. Do you believe this?" (John 11:25–26). How we answer determines whether or not eternal life will pervade our immortality.

Now this is the confidence that we have in Him, that if we ask anything according to His will, He hears us.

1 John 5:14

*P*rayer is not a device to get God to do our will, but a means by which our petitions may be redirected according to the will of God. One of the most demanding things Jesus said about prayer was that it requires time to know the will of God. "Therefore I say to you, whatever things you ask when you pray, believe that you receive them, and you will have them" (Mark 11:24). With a power like that available, we need to be sure of what we ask.

Some time ago our church sponsored a Saturday each month called a "Day of Discovery." In addition to Bible study about intimate prayer, we set aside long periods for silent meditation. We helped each person focus the hurts and hopes he or she wanted to take into the time of creative listening. The people's evaluation of the day indicates that those hours of silence gave them insights and discernment that had not occurred to them before they were quiet. Many of the people found it difficult to center on God and block out the noise of their overinvolved and busy lives. Some found that only after a long period of concentration on God and His love could they open themselves to hear what He was trying to say to them. What alarms me is that, in most cases, people were given wisdom which has subsequently unraveled the personal, interpersonal, and social needs they had finally been enable to pray about creatively. The question I keep asking myself is: What if they had not learned to meditate until they had a breakthrough to awareness?

I am very aware that most of us miss the power of prayer and many of the blessings God is ready to give simply because we will not take the time for God to tell us what He is more ready to unleash than what we are ready to ask. It's part of the mystery that God waits to bless us until we ask for what blessings we really need.

Grace, mercy, and peace will be with you from God the Father and from the Lord, Jesus Christ, the Son of the Father, in truth and love.

2 John 3

I awoke with a feeling of anxiety. There was no apparent cause that I could readily identify. It did not go away as I showered, dressed, and ate breakfast. The uneasy mood increased by the time I reached my study for the day's work. I sat at my desk wondering what was wrong, trying to get in touch with the panic inside me.

In my morning prayer, I asked God to help me. The quiet time finally revealed the cause of the alarm signal ringing in my soul.

Suddenly I realized that I was anxious about the future. How would things work out? What would I do if the dreams didn't come to fruition?

There are times when we all get hit with a mixed blast of anticipation and worry about the future, often when we least expect it. Our personal or professional future seems to be up for grabs. There may be little concrete evidence that this could be true, but the uneasiness persists. The problem is not in the unknown future circumstances, but inside us.

John's greeting had been written to a church in Roman Asia, but the Holy Spirit made it a very personal word for me that morning. It broke the bind and released me to trust all of my "future jitters" to God.

"Grace, mercy, and peace *will* be with you." The future tense leaped off the page. Most of the New Testament letters have a salutation delineating several of the blessings of God. This is the only one in the future tense. I believe John wanted his beloved friends to know that the essential gifts of God offered through Jesus Christ's life, death, and resurrection would be more than adequate for the unexpected eventualities of the future. Regardless of what happened to them, grace, mercy and peace would be their experience.

Peace be with you. All your friends send greeting. Greet all our friends personally.

3 John 15 (TEV)

*P*eace cannot be kept unless it is shared. We are not to keep the peace but give it away. Peace is the result of peacemaking. The climax of the Beatitudes is "Blessed are the peacemakers, For they shall be called sons of God" (Matt. 5:9).

Anything that keeps people apart is the concern and responsibility of a peacemaker. If we want peace in our own hearts, negative criticism, gossip, and innuendoes no longer can be part of our conversation. Our constant concern is what will help people understand, forgive, and accept each other.

A friend underlined this for me the other day. He said, "I've searched for peace all during my Christian life. I tried to find peace in confession and in keeping a clear conscience. Then the Lord put on my conscience a greater sin than any of the little sins I kept fussing about. He told me that I was responsible to help bring peace into all the misunderstanding and angry hostility among people around me. I've learned that being a reconciler is essential for a continued, sustained experience of peace." The man was on target!

Peace is the result of the indwelling of the Holy Spirit. It is a manifestation of the living Christ, the Holy Spirit, working through us. Peace is the presence of the Lord in our hearts and minds. John's oft-repeated plea for us to abide in Christ and allow Christ to abide in us is the secret of prolonged, lasting peace.

There's a lovely story about the elder John in the last year of his life. He was carried into the fellowship of the church, and his message was predictable. Though he was frail in body, his spirit was indomitable. With a strong, unwavering voice he said, "Little children, love one another."

A bright but impetuous young deacon asked, "Why do you always repeat the same message?" John's response was, "That's all you need to know!"

I am convinced he was right. Peace be with you!

May the Lord go with you:
before you to show the way
beside you to befriend you,
behind you to encourage you,
above you to watch over you
and within you to give you power
to turn your struggles into
steppingstones.